Mare.
663

BLACK EDUCATION IN NEW YORK STATE

A New York State Study

BLACK EDUCATION

"Kept In," painting by Edward L. Henry, 1888.

IN NEW YORK STATE

From Colonial to Modern Times

CARLETON MABEE

SYRACUSE UNIVERSITY PRESS • 1979

This book is published with the assistance of a grant from the John Ben Snow Foundation.

Winner of the 1979 John Ben Snow Manuscript Prize

Library of Congress Cataloging in Publication Data

Mabee, Carleton, 1914–
  Black education in New York State.

  (A New York State study)
  Includes bibliographical references and index.
  1. Afro-American—Education—New York (State)
I. Title.
LC2802.N7M32   370′.9747   79-21262
ISBN O-8156-2209-0

Manufactured in the United States of America

To my Mother

MIRIAM BENTLEY MABEE

(1887–1971)

who was equally earnest in teaching blacks in the South,
whites in the North, and Chinese in China.

Carleton Mabee is Professor of History at State University of New York, College at New Paltz, and the author of *American Leonardo: A Life of Samuel F. B. Morse,* for which he won the Pulitzer Prize in Biography, and *Black Freedom: The Nonviolent Abolitionists from 1830 through the Civil War,* for which he received the Anisfield-Wolf Award.

CONTENTS

Text Table

Appendix Tables

Illustrations

PREFACE

IN OUR TIME AMERICANS KNOW LITTLE about the long story of black separate schools in the North. Many Northerners prefer to think that legally separate black schools existed only in the South and were abolished largely by Northern righteousness.

Even black leaders often know little of the Northern experience with black schools. Not long ago the black novelist James Baldwin, in recalling his childhood in New York City, said his own school principal was the only black principal as far as he knew in the entire history of New York. Evidently he did not know that before his time there had been dozens of black principals in the New York metropolitan region when legally separate black schools were common in New York State.

In recent years, the spread of *de facto* segregation in the schools of the urban North has made the history of the North's black schools especially relevant—the *de facto* segregated schools are in a sense merely the latest phase in the long history of Northern separate black schools. Exploring this subject, I was surprised to learn that, although there are useful studies of black education in certain places and periods in New York State, there is no comprehensive study of the history of black education in the state. I decided to try to write one, concentrating on the theme of black schools in the period from the early 1700s to 1945.

Believing that the kind of educational history which is especially worth writing in our time is that kind which places education in a broad social context, I wanted to relate black education to the whole history of the black-white relations in New York State, and in particular to the history of the state's blacks. However, I gradually came to realize that much of the history of the state's blacks has not yet been written. I found that I had to construct painfully, piece by piece, a black history framework on which to hang the history of black education.

Early in my investigations, I hunted through such sources as biographies, city directories, and state education reports to develop a list of cities and towns which once had black schools. When I enquired in those places if school officials—whether public or not—had preserved records about their black schools, I found that a few of them had. I began to believe that, while there would be disturbing gaps, enough of the records of the black schools were available to provide revealing detail.

In the cities and towns where there had been black schools, I examined local histories and newspapers. In time I learned that by struggling through large numbers of local histories, I might discover how a black school was created. I also found that by turning page after page of local newspapers, year after year, I might come across a report of a controversy about a black school, as on whether its teachers should be black or white.

Blacks themselves, having often been preoccupied with survival, have preserved relatively little about black education, and yet I found that what they have preserved could be worth ferreting out. Some black autobiographies poignantly reveal the feelings of black pupils or black teachers. While, unfortunately, most of the black newspapers which were once published in the state appear to have been entirely lost, enough issues of some papers have been preserved to provide a treasure house for black history in the state, including black education.

In the nine years I have worked on this project, I have pored over scrapbooks, legislative reports, college records, and manuscript collections. I have interviewed town historians and school superintendents. I have corresponded with curators, librarians, and alumni secretaries both in and out of the state. With the generous help of many people, I have gathered scraps of information about the teachers who taught in the black schools, information which proved to be of increasing value as my list of teachers lengthened.

As I gradually acquired perspective on the long story of blacks in New York State, some of my preconceptions about it gradually dropped away. I was surprised to learn that the proportion of blacks in the state by no means steadily increased through the years; it rose to about 14 percent in the eighteenth century, dropped to 1 percent about the time of the Civil War, and did not climb significantly again until the twentieth century. I came to realize that consciousness of racial differences was deeper and more persistent in the state than I had supposed. I found that separate schools for blacks were established even in colonial times. I found that beginning as early as the 1830s some blacks waged a long, intermittent struggle to abolish black schools, and that in the period from the 1870s through the 1910s the struggle was often successful. Although the few historians interested in the subject have long repeated that Governor Theodore Roosevelt led in outlawing all separate black public schools in the state in 1900, I learned that black public schools continued to exist legally in rural areas into the 1930s, and in fact illegally thereafter. Moreover, I discovered that beginning early in the twentieth century, the waves of blacks arriving from the South renewed the impulse to segregate blacks, putting the long struggle against school segregation in jeopardy. I found that the New Deal relief programs in the 1930s furthered the educational separation of blacks, and that by the 1930s and 1940s more blacks in the state were in separate black schools—including *de facto* segregated schools —than ever before.

I expected that public school officials would spend less per pupil in black than white schools but found that this was often not the case. I expected that the black schools might be overwhelmingly concentrated in the New York metropolitan region but found that at various times in the eighteenth, nineteenth, and twentieth centuries they were well scattered over the state. I found that black schools were of many varieties: they were not only legally segregated but also *de facto* segregated; they were public, church, and private schools; for children and for adults; on the elementary, secondary, and post-secondary levels; and intended to educate not only in religion or academics but also in practical arts such as commerce, navigation, nursing, or trades.

As I continued to pursue the sources, I found that pre-1950 blacks were often not the "Uncle Toms" which legend has made them out to be; in fact, black teachers were often surprisingly militant about black rights. In the nineteenth century, black schools provided jobs for many black protest leaders and thus were an important base for blacks in their struggle for equal rights. Why the whites who usually controlled the black schools would permit the black teachers to be so militant became a tantalizing question to explore.

In both the nineteenth and twentieth centuries a recurring theme proved to be black ambivalence about the issue of separatism. Thus I found that blacks as well as whites often participated in both establishing and abolishing black schools. I began to wonder who among blacks usually led in such activities. Were they usually from the small black upper class of professionals and businessmen? The story of the "war" against the black school in Jamaica, Long Island, in the 1890s is a dramatic reminder that considerable numbers of lower class blacks were willing to take drastic measures to open white schools to blacks.

As my study continued, I found myself asking more and more questions of the sources. Were black schools wise for some places and times but not for others? Why did some of the most prominent blacks in the nation teach in the black schools of New York State? How much control did black parents have over the education of their children? Why were black public schools abolished in some parts of the state sooner than in others?

Many such questions proved to be too complex to answer adequately, especially given the long period I had chosen to study and the great variety of types of schools, their locations, and their social contexts. Some of the questions for the time being remained unanswerable, others dropped away as less significant. Still others, however, seemed so essential that I struggled to suggest possible answers as well as I could.

Altogether the gaps in the evidence available, the dearth of local research completed, and the lack of an already coherent statewide historical framework have meant that the resulting work must be regarded as more tentative than I would wish. However, this work, as a thrust into a neglected field, suggests, I hope, not only the need for further study, but also a fresh perspective on one of the most troubled areas of American democracy in our time.

In the preparation of this book I have had assistance without which the project would have been impossible. The American Philosophical Society gave me a grant which helped to start me toward this project, and later the National Institute of Education gave me funds for the necessary travel. My own institution, the State University College, New Paltz, has generously given me leaves as well as library and photographic services. I have had help from several research assistants, among them Paul Royer and Robert Moson; loyal typing from Elisabeth T. Blair; computer assistance from my colleague Paul Zuckerman; indispensable criticism of my writing from my daughter Susan M. Newhouse. Innumerable people of good will have given me information or advice, including Professor and Mrs. Clyde Griffin of Vassar College, James P. Hurley of the Long Island Historical Society, Gail Schneider of the Staten Island Institute of History and Art, President Lawrence Cremin of Teachers College, Professor David E. Swift of Wesleyan University, and Ernest Kaiser of the

Schomburg Center of the New York Public Library. Officers of various colleges, especially Thomas J. Jennings of Teachers College and Howard D. Williams of Colgate, have dug for records of early black students. Several persons have shared with me their own recollections about the education of blacks earlier in this century including the black Quaker, the late Barrington Dunbar of New York, and Emeritus Professor Roland Will of New Paltz. Scholars writing on various related subjects have offered suggestions, including Carl Nordstrom on blacks in Rockland County, Harold Connoly on blacks in Brooklyn, and Professor Barret Potter of Alfred University on CCC camps in New York State. I thank them and many other scholars, librarians, schoolmen, and archivists across the state.

I acknowledge permission from the following to quote manuscripts in their possession: Amistad Research Center, Dillard University, New Orleans, Louisiana; Arents Library, Syracuse University, Syracuse, New York; Beinecke Library, Yale University, New Haven, Connecticut; Columbia University Library, New York City; Cortland County Historical Society, Cortland, New York; New-York Historical Society, New York City; New York State Library, Albany, New York; and Schomburg Center for Research in Black Culture, New York Public Library, New York City.

I also thank the following for permission to republish here, in revised form, portions of articles of mine: *Long Island Forum* (November and December 1973); *Bates College Bulletin* (April 1976); *Afro-Americans in New York Life and History* (January 1977); *New York History* (October 1977); and *Phylon: The Atlanta University Review* (March 1979).

New Paltz, New York   Carleton Mabee
Spring 1979

BLACK EDUCATION IN NEW YORK STATE

SCHOOLS FOR SLAVES

THE DUTCH OF NEW NETHERLAND were easy-going about their black slaves. Regarding themselves as only temporary settlers in the New World, the Dutch were more concerned about their slaves as a means of making money than about fitting them into a permanent social system. Slavery in their feeble colony on the Hudson was on a small scale; it scarcely had time in the mere forty years of Dutch rule to develop into a rigid system.

In the Dutch colony there were few laws to restrict blacks, whether slave or free. Blacks could testify in court the same as whites; they could marry whites. What discrimination there was in New Netherland was more religious than racial. While Jews for a time could not hold real estate, blacks could. The Dutch Reformed Church, the established church of the little Dutch outpost in America, welcomed blacks. It tried—if not zealously—to Christianize blacks, and if they became Christians, accepted them in theory as equals before God. It married blacks in church. The Dutch pastor, Henry Selyns, wrote his superiors in Holland that he had "taken much trouble in private and public catechizing" of blacks. "This has born little fruit among the elder people who have no faculty of comprehension; but there is some hope for the youth who have improved reasonably well."[1]

The Dutch church and government together controlled the schools of New Netherland. Following a tradition brought from Holland, the Dutch provided public education for all children in the same school. In 1636, in what has been called the first known reference to education in surviving New Amsterdam records, the officials of the settlement reported with approval to their superiors in Holland that a local Dutch pastor "has very earnestly requested us [to secure] a school master to teach

1

and train the youth of both Dutch and blacks, in the knowledge of Jesus Christ." Within two years the first school teacher had arrived from Holland and was teaching a school—evidently for both blacks and whites—in the settlement on the southern tip of Manhattan.[2] Like others of the early settlers of New Amsterdam, this teacher was quarrelsome and given to brawling in the streets, and the education he put across to his pupils, whether black or white, was doubtless limited.

There is no available evidence that there were any separate schools for blacks in Dutch New Netherland. The Dutch tradition of public education for all in the same school was against it; the number of slaves was not large enough; the slave system has not hardened enough; and there was not yet discomfort enough between blacks and whites to require separate education.

After the English seizure of New Netherland in 1664, the English encouraged the importation of more slaves into New York. By about 1750, the proportion of slaves in the colony had risen to about 14 percent of the population (see Table 1 in Appendix), higher than in any other Northern English colony. Unlike the Dutch, the English—regarding themselves as permanent settlers—were inclined to systematize the relation between masters and slaves. The English restricted slaves more by law. Slaves could no longer testify in courts against whites, and even freed blacks could no longer hold real estate.

In keeping with these trends, blacks under English rule were more separated from whites than they had been under the Dutch, though still not rigidly separated. In 1697 blacks were forbidden to bury their dead in the Anglican Trinity Church yard in New York City. In 1713 a military chaplain reported that in the colony's churches slaves were seated, "if so much care is taken," at such a "great distance" from the pulpit that it was "inconvenient for hearing."[3] Moreover, the English did not bring from Europe a tradition of public education for all in common schools, as the Dutch had. It is not surprising, then, that a significant part of the little education offered to blacks in the English colony of New York was in separate schools.

As with the Dutch, when the English tried to educate slaves, their purpose usually was to Christianize them. Officials of both the English state and the English church not only recognized the Christian mission to evangelize the heathen everywhere but also equated Christianity with civil order and the safety of the state.

In the colony of New York, as in most of the English colonies, formal education was usually available only through private tutors or church schools, and it could be costly. While at best the colony offered the privileged some quality education, probably most of the children of this predominantly poor and rural colony never attended school, even for elementary education. Under the circumstances, of course, most blacks, being at the bottom of the social scale, never attended school.

As far as available evidence indicates, the Anglican Church was the only agency in the colony of New York which organized a long-term campaign for the education of blacks. The Anglican church, while it had considerable upper class membership, represented only a small minority of the people of the already cosmopolitan colony. It claimed to be the established church in only four counties (Queens, New York, Richmond, and Westchester), and even that claim was disputed. It had limited funds. However, the Anglican Church operated its campaign particularly through its missionary organization, the Society for the Propagation of the Gospel in Foreign Parts. This society, founded in 1701, was probably the most powerful organized philanthropy in the British world in the eighteenth century. Having its seat in distant England, it was somewhat insulated from pressure by American slaveholders against the education of slaves.

The Society for the Propagation of the Gospel never advocated the abolition of slavery. It even permitted its missionaries in the colony of New York, as elsewhere, to own slaves. But it repeatedly instructed its missionaries, both clergy and teachers, that evangelizing the blacks was one of their primary functions. According to its secretary in 1730, the society regarded "the instruction and conversion of the Negroes as a principal branch of their care." It was "a great reproach" to Christians, he explained, that Negroes in a Christian land should continue as pagan as they had been in Africa.[4] The society also argued that Christianizing the slaves would not injure the slavemasters; in fact, it would teach the slaves to serve their masters more loyally.

The most effective work of the Society for the Propagation of the Gospel among blacks, according to a recent historian of the society, was done in the colony of New York.[5] In this colony alone at various times in the eighteenth century the society gave at least partial support to a total of twenty-eight teachers whose names are known, as well as others whose names are not known, who taught blacks either in separate schools for blacks or in racially-mixed schools. All the known teachers were white.

In 1704 in New York City, the society opened its first separate school for slaves anywhere in the colonies. It was a "catechizing school" as the society called it; that is, essentially a school to teach church catechism and thus prepare the pupils for baptism. The society hoped, it explained later, that this school "might kindle a zeal in some other good people" to establish similar schools everywhere in the colonies, and that eventually the colonial legislatures would, by law, "oblige all slaves to attend for their instruction."[6] However, the New York colonial legislature never passed such a law, and the blacks who attended the Anglican schools usually did so voluntarily.

In creating its first school for blacks, the society faced formidable obstacles. Some whites believed that blacks had no souls and hence were incapable of being converted. Other whites believed that education and conversion would make slaves grow insolent, or more insolent than they already were. Still other whites feared that if slaves became Christian they could claim, with some support from ambiguous English laws, the right to be free.

The first teacher the society selected to face these obstacles in New York was a Frenchman, Elias Neau, who knew something of what it was like to be a slave from his own experience. In France, Neau had been persecuted for his Protestant faith. The French government had confined him as a galley slave, chained to his oar. Repeatedly offered his freedom if he became a Catholic, he had as repeatedly refused. After a total of six years in prison or galleys, he had finally been freed as a result of English negotiations with France, and he had settled in New York. The Society for the Propagation of the Gospel said, "His former sufferings on the account of his religion did, with great advantage, recommend him to be a teacher of the Christian faith; and his humility enabled him to bear with the many inconveniences in teaching those poor people."[7]

At first Neau went from house to house to instruct blacks, but this proved time-consuming. Then adopting a practice already common for teachers in the city, he arranged for his pupils to come to his house, and they did so several evenings a week.

Neau found his pupils to be sleepy and dull in the evenings. Slaves were likely to be tired because masters worked them long hours. Moreover, when slaves had free time, they had much to do besides study. They visited members of their families scattered in the households of different masters. They gardened, fished, or hunted to supplement the limited food their masters supplied. They played or drank hard as relief from drudgery and oppression. On Sundays in New York City, teacher Neau wrote unhappily, "while we are at our devotions, the streets are full of Negroes who dance and divert themselves."[8] If slaves got to school at all, they might be sluggish in learning to read, both because their native African languages were not written and because they could speak little English, many of them having recently been brought from Africa or from the Spanish, French, or Dutch West Indies.

At first there came to Neau's school not more than thirty pupils, representing both sexes, and both adults and children. Not being satisfied with the number of pupils, in 1706 Neau and the rector of Trinity Church, the local sponsor of the school, urged the colony's Assembly to make clear that masters did not need to fear that their slaves would become free if converted. In response, after some delay, the Assembly decreed that the legal status of slaves would in no way be altered by baptism. After that, although the law continued to be somewhat ambiguous on this point and public opinion changed only slowly, the number of pupils in Neau's school went up. In 1707 he had as many as one hundred pupils, and by 1710, two hundred.

Neau read to his pupils. He taught them prayers and scripture. He taught them the alphabet—Neau, in fact, insisted on securing catechism books which included the alphabet so he could use it to help beginners to learn to read. He encouraged those who could read the catechism to do so. He drilled them all in memorizing catechism.

Suddenly in 1712 his work was stopped by a slave revolt. A few slaves in the city set fire to a building, and when whites came to put out the fire, deliberately killed nine of them, wounding others. Many whites, being deeply distrustful of the education of slaves, jumped to the conclusion that the revolt had been planned at Neau's school. In the popular hysteria, for some days Neau hardly dared to appear outside of his house, and his school was closed.

However, at the trial of the slaves accused of taking part in the uprising, only two of Neau's pupils were even charged with taking part. One, a baptized man, was, on slender evidence, condemned and executed but later found to be innocent of any involvement in the plot at all.

When at last the slaveowners became convinced that Neau's school was not responsible for the revolt after all, the school was able to open again. To help it recover, the provincial governor, Robert Hunter, himself a member of the Society for the Propagation of the Gospel, visited the school accompanied by several prominent persons and publicly endorsed it.

At about the same time, the chaplain to the British forces in the province wrote to the Society for the Propagation of the Gospel a moving tribute to Neau as a teacher. Neau can talk "familiarly . . . with those poor slaves who are put to the vilest drudgeries and [are] consequently esteemed the scum . . . of men," the chaplain wrote. "He can take pains to accommodate his discourse to their capacities whilst he inculcates the great truths of the Gospel." He creeps "into garrets, cellars, and other nauseous places, to exhort and pray by the poor slaves when they are sick." He has won the confidence of the slaves, the chaplain explained,

New York City in the 1730s when blacks were about 16 percent of the population. Trinity Church (at far left) sponsored classes in reading and religion for blacks. *Courtesy of The New-York Historical Society, New York City.* Engraving by Carwitham.

because they know that he himself had been a galley slave, and because they see that whites hate him for teaching slaves.[9]

Neau continued to teach his unpopular catechetical school till his death in 1722. Thereafter, the school was continued by various appointees of the Society for the Propagation of the Gospel, with varying enthusiasm and success, but always under the local care of Trinity Church. Sometimes the school was taught several times a week, at other times only on Sundays. Sometimes it was taught in the teacher's house, at other times in the steeple of Trinity Church, at still other times in the building of the church's charity school for whites. This part-time catechetical school for blacks existed virtually continuously from its founding by Neau in 1704 through much of the confusion of the American Revolution to 1783.

In addition, in 1760 the Anglicans created a full-time day school for black children in New York City with a somewhat more academic curriculum. This was the only known full-time separate school for blacks in colonial New York. It was taught by a white woman, Mrs. Lowner, and like many colonial schools, it was held at the teacher's house.

An advertisement in the *New York Mercury* of September 15, 1760, announced the opening of the school. It was to be for children five years of age and up. Instruction was to be "in reading and in the principles of Christianity, and likewise sewing and knitting." Those masters having "the present usefulness and future welfare of their young slaves at heart (especially those born in their houses)," are invited to apply to any of the Anglican clergy "who will immediately send them to the aforesaid school. . . . All that is required of their masters or mistresses is that they find them in wood for the winter. Proper books will be provided for them gratis."

Within four months, Mrs. Lowner had the full number of thirty pupils planned for her school. Nine were boys and twenty-one girls, most of them slaves.

This full-time day school survived at least fourteen years. That it did so, and without as far as is known any serious public criticism, suggests a more favorable attitude toward the education of blacks as the American Revolution approached than in Neau's time.

In 1763 the Reverend Samuel Auchmuty, the assistant rector of Trinity Church who supervised this school, reported that the scholars improved every day in reading and spelling. In 1774 the Reverend Auchmuty, who by this time had become the rector of the church, reported that "several of the children read very well and know the whole of their catechism. They attend church constantly on Sundays and often on week days."[10]

Despite his giving such favorable reports, the Reverend Auchmuty questioned whether the full-time academic school should be continued. Many of the black parents, he claimed, were now ready to instruct their own children, and some slave owners would, if there were no free school, pay for the education of their slave children, he said, implying that there were other schools where slaves could go if their masters paid for them. Significantly, however, his church superiors in England were more insistent on keeping the black school open than he was. They tried to persuade him to continue the school but probably did not succeed. The teacher died in 1774, and the American Revolution soon made the continuation of any schools in New York City difficult, whether for whites or blacks.

In the meantime, however, the Anglicans spread their separate black schools from New York City to other places in the province of New York. As far as available evidence indicates, Anglican black schools, primarily part-time catechetical schools, were in operation by the 1710s to

1730s in Staten Island; in Southampton, Long Island; in Rye, West-chester County; and in Albany; and by at least the 1760s or 1770s, also in Yonkers (Philipsburg) and Schenectady. While some of these schools probably lasted only briefly, the one in Albany, despite interruptions, survived over a period of at least fifty-nine years.

The number of pupils in these black schools was not large. In Southampton, Staten Island, and Schenectady there were perhaps ten to twenty in each school. In Albany in 1714 there were thirty, all adults. In New York City the highest known in the catechetical school was two hundred. Adding together the largest number of pupils known in each of the schools at any time, we find that a total of perhaps 325 black pupils at the most were in the separate schools for blacks.

Of the teachers in these black schools, nineteen are known by name. That their educational preparation was at least adequate by the white standards of the day is suggested by the fact that either before, or at the same time that they taught blacks separately, several of the teachers also taught schools for whites. Moreover, the education of seven of the teachers, all clergymen, was known to be excellent for the times. Of these seven, one had studied at St. Andrews and Edinburgh Universities, in Scotland; one at Trinity College, Dublin; one at Harvard College; one at King's College (later Columbia); and two at Yale. The seventh one had received a private education in the British Isles, had become a scholar in Hebrew, and had been acting president of the King's College before he taught blacks in New York City.

From the twentieth century point of view, it is natural to ask whether it was wise at this time to select, as teachers of separate schools for blacks, considerable numbers of persons whose high academic quali-fications removed them far from the life and thought of their black pu-pils, but this is a question which did not arise at the time. At any rate, white Anglicans were certainly not selecting poorly-educated teachers to instruct blacks or allowing prejudice against blacks to prevent persons of status from teaching them.

At the same time that Anglicans were educating blacks separately, in a number of places in the province they were also educating blacks in the same classes with whites. In Staten Island in 1721, the teacher of the Anglicans' full-time school for whites reported, "I keep night school, for teaching of Negroes and of such as cannot be spared from their work in the day time."[11] In Hempstead, Long Island, in 1741, a teacher reported keeping a day school of pupils including four blacks, and the next year teaching a night school of perhaps ten pupils including four blacks and one Indian. In Rye in 1738 a teacher reported having forty-one pupils in

The Reverend John Ogilvie, of St. Peter's Church, Albany, taught a class of blacks on Sunday afternoons. He was typical of many of the Anglican teachers of blacks in the 1700s in that he was white, well educated (Yale), closely tied to Britain (he had been ordained there), and that he was primarily devoted to other duties (he was both pastor of a predominantly white church and a missionary to the Mohawk Indians). *Courtesy of The New-York Historical Society, New York City.* Painting by J. S. Copley.

his day school of which fourteen were dissenters, two Dutch, two Jews, and one black. In Oyster Bay, Long Island, in the 1730s, after the teacher gave public notice that he would teach free blacks and poor whites without charge, four free blacks attended his day school.[12]

That Anglicans often took a few blacks into their schools intended primarily for whites suggests that when Anglicans taught blacks separately they did so more as a practical means of reaching them than as a matter of rigid compulsion to separate the races. Slaves were often available for schooling at different hours than whites, and their needs in language, reading, and religious indoctrination could be considered somewhat different than those of whites. While there was more separation in both churches and schools under the English colonial control than under the Dutch, the need for separation was still not as greatly felt as it would be later when slavery was on the way out or already abolished.

Why denominations other than the Anglican scarcely undertook any organized education for blacks in the English colonial period is an intriguing question.

As the American Revolution approached, Quakers, unlike any major American denomination, were going through the searing process of requiring their own members to free their slaves or be rejected from membership. In this process, Quakers felt a concern for the education of slaves, particularly those owned by Quakers, as a means of preparing them for freedom. However, while in Pennsylvania and New Jersey, where Quakers were more numerous, they had already established schools for blacks by the 1750s, there is no available evidence that Quakers created schools for blacks in New York in the colonial period. Quaker education for blacks in New York was especially informal, as in the household, or indirect, as in the form of financial aid to encourage blacks to attend existing schools.[13] More direct involvement of New York Quakers in organized education for blacks came in a later period, after the American Revolution.

A larger denomination than the Quakers in the eighteenth century colony of New York was the Reformed, the church which especially served the Dutch who remained in the colony. In 1747 the Dutch Reformed council in Holland, continuing its earlier interest in the conversion of slaves in America, adopted a revealing plan for the instruction of slaves. Catechists under the direction of local pastors would provide the slaves with books in simple language, including prayers and selections from the

Bible. They would teach slaves that their becoming Christians would not make them free; in fact, it would lay upon them the duty of serving their masters more faithfully. When the slaves were judged ready, they would be baptized in the Dutch church, but they were to approach the communion table only after the whites had been served. However, this plan was intended for the Dutch colony of Surinam in South America.[14] It is uncertain if the Dutch Reformed Church in the colony of New York would have accepted such a plan if it had been urged on them from Holland, not only because of the usual white distrust of the education of slaves, but also because at this time the Dutch Reformed of New York were struggling to limit interference from Holland in their affairs. At any rate, while the Dutch Reformed probably admitted a few blacks into their parish schools, a study of the Dutch effort to convert blacks in colonial America —although mentioning the Dutch Church plan for catechizing slaves in Surinam—reports no similar Dutch plan for the English colonies in America and gives no specific evidence of organized education of blacks —catechetical or otherwise—actually provided by the Dutch Reformed in New York or anywhere else in the English colonies.[15]

The Baptists and Methodists, the two denominations which were later to capture the loyalty of most black churchmen in New York State, as elsewhere in the United States, relied more on emotion in their worship than the Anglicans or Dutch Reformed did, a trait which probably contributed to their ability to communicate to the poorly-educated backs. The Baptists and Methodists also developed more antislavery sentiment than either the Anglicans or Dutch Reformed, which might be expected to have encouraged them to educate blacks. But until after the American Revolution, the Methodists in New York, as elsewhere, were scarcely more than a small lay movement within the Anglican Church, and Baptists, having a poorly educated ministry themselves, were only slowly developing an interest in education in this period even for whites.

Though only Anglicans are known to have provided formal separate education for the New York colony's blacks, many New Yorkers— religious and non-religious, black and white—helped provide them with informal education.

Considerable education of blacks, as of whites, proceeded on the job. Because ownership of slaves was widely diffused in New York Colony —the average owner held only one to three slaves—slave boys often worked beside their masters, learning directly from them a wide variety of occupations, such as farming, milling, coopering, or baking. They learned well. Probably because of the relative importance of the trades in New York, according to a recent historian of slavery, New York slaves mastered technical skills more than the slaves in any other colony.[16]

Many slave girls were trained in their masters' households, often by their own mothers. According to a contemporary observer, Mrs. Anne Grant, in Albany before the American Revolution slave women were all domestics, and if they were good workers and sagacious, they often exerted as much authority over the white children of the household as the white parents did. These slave mothers prided themselves "on teaching their [own] children to be excellent servants, well knowing servitude to be their lot for life, and that it could only be sweetened by making themselves particularly useful."

Religious education could also proceed informally in the master's home. In 1717 the Anglican rector in New Rochelle reported that a number of slaves in his town had learned the principles of Christianity by listening to their masters' family devotions; he encouraged them by assigning them seats in his church. In the heavily-Dutch Albany region, just before the American Revolution when masters had become less fearful of the Christianization of slaves, Mrs. Grant said that slave children were often born in their master's house along with the master's children, were rocked in the same cradle, shared almost the same food and clothing in their first years, and shared the same religious instruction.[17]

An example of a black who received education in his master's household is Jupiter Hammon, who has been called the first American black to publish poetry. From his writing we have the rare experience of knowing directly how one New York slave felt about the education of slaves.

Hammon was the slave of the wealthy Anglican Lloyd family of Queens Village near Huntington, Long Island. He may have had a formal, as well as informal, Anglican education. The Lloyd family built a school building on their manor when Jupiter was about twelve or thirteen years old; it is possible that he was educated there. At any rate, Hammon's style of writing indicates that he had secured an adequate elementary education by the standards of the time. Moreover, in one of his publications, Hammon tells slave masters that it is their duty to give the slave children born in their households a Christian education. "Have they been baptized, taught to read, and learnt their catechism?" he asked. "Surely this is a duty incumbent on masters or heads of families."[18] As a slave, Hammon would not have been likely to publish such a statement unless his own master had given him such an education.

The Lloyds allowed Hammon to earn and spend money. When he was about twenty-two years old in 1733 he bought a Bible from the Lloyds. The Lloyds possessed a library of their own, which they lent to friends. They also dealt in books, importing them from Europe. Hammon refers in his writings to two Anglican authors whose books were known to be in the Lloyds' library. The Lloyds probably lent or sold such books to Hammon.

The Lloyds, seeing Hammon's unusual abilities, allowed him time to read, time to attend church, time to preach, write, and publish. Slave Hammon, with the encouragement of both blacks and whites as he acknowledged, published, between 1760 and 1787, six known works, three primarily poetry and three primarily prose.

In his writing this talented slave made clear that he valued education. He insisted—as few New Yorkers did at the time and as even the Society for the Propagation of the Gospel did not clearly do—that every slave should be educated to read. He begged his fellow blacks "to spare no pains in trying to learn to read," and he gave a hint that much slave education was informal when he added: "Get those who can read, to learn you." His argument was the traditional Protestant one that everyone should learn to read in order to be able to read the Bible for himself. But he indicated the limits of his own education when he also wrote: "Remember that what you learn for, is to read the Bible. If there was no Bible it would be no matter whether you could read or not."

Hammon deplored the wickedness of many of his fellow blacks, including their drunkenness, stealing, and idleness. But God is no respecter of race, he assured them. "If we love God, black as we be, and despised as we are, God will love us."[19]

In his last two works, published in the 1780s, slave Hammon advocated emancipation for blacks at large—not for himself because he considered himself too old. He argued for emancipation clearly but gently, as might be expected because, as a slave, everything he publicly did was with his master's knowledge; his master's name even appeared on the title page of his publications.

The better-known Negro poet, Phillis Wheatley of Boston, began to publish her poetry a few years later than Hammon. The Boston merchant who owned her had given her a Puritan education in his own family—an education that surpassed Hammon's including as it did Latin, the English poets Milton and Pope, and a visit among admiring high society in England. Both Hammon and Phillis Wheatley were deeply religious, and both were concerned for the unhappy lot of their own African people in America. But the later life of these two poets provides an ironical contrast. Wheatley, after she was freed from slavery, lived in poverty and un-happiness, unable to publish her second volume of poems, and died in Massachusetts in her early thirties. Hammon, who was content to remain a slave all his life, lived in comfort, continued to publish his writings, and died in New York State in the ripeness of his years.

As the Anglicans taught blacks—whether formally or informally—they faced seemingly staggering obstacles. The Anglicans had only lim-ited funds and time, and the demands on them to strengthen and extend their churches among the often unchurched people of the colony were heavy. As one of the Anglican pastors in Hempstead wrote, he had insuf-ficient time to work with black infidels partly because he had in his parish too many white infidels. Denominational rivalries interfered too. Quak-ers avoided allowing Anglicans to educate their slaves; Presbyterians, while they did not forbid instruction by Anglicans, sometimes would not allow them to baptize their slaves. The distrust by many colonists of the Anglican Church as an instrument of an oppressive overseas government, if not of Satan, made it difficult for Anglican agents to get the coopera-tion of either masters or slaves or secure the local financial support they hoped for.

Whites at large often showed little concern for blacks, whether Christian or not, a fact which must have discouraged blacks from trying to improve themselves by Christian education. Teacher Neau charged bit-terly that slaves "are kept after the same manner as horses, to get from them all the work one can without any concern for their salvation." Even if slaves became Christians, they were still usually called by the same epi-thets and treated with the same severity; they were still not allowed to tes-tify in court against whites; they were still much restricted by law while scarcely being protected by law at all. Even if slaves became Christians, their marriages were not generally recognized by church or state, and might be broken up at any time by the sale of husband or wife. Under these circumstances it must have been difficult for the slaves to practice the strict sexual code demanded by the missionaries. The slaves are "natu-rally libertines," Neau wrote, but, he explained compassionately, in their vice "these wretches are in some sort more excusable" than whites are in theirs.[20]

In view of the enormity of the obstacles to education for blacks, it is not surprising that the Anglican missionaries were sometimes disap-pointed with their progress in teaching them. A missionary in Brookhaven, Long Island, who was trying to teach a Negro girl of about nine years to read, mourned that he could not "yet make her to know her alphabet, nor have all the endeavors hitherto used with her, which have not been inconsiderable, been sufficient to make her to number ten, though she was born this country." A teacher wrote of his night school for blacks at Southampton, Long Island, that while he had some hope for the future, last year few of them learned anything. An English bishop, reviewing the black work of the Society for the Propagation of the Gospel in the colonies, said in 1783 that it had not met with the "desired success." In the colony of New York, as in all the colonies, by the end of the colonial period the proportion of blacks who could be called Christians was still small.

Yet many Anglican missionaries—no doubt impelled in part by a natural desire to think of their work as useful—gave favorable reports of their black pupils. A clergyman wrote from Yonkers that his pupils had a great desire to learn. The Reverend Charlton wrote from New York City that the spiritual knowledge which some of his pupils showed at examinations was such "as might make many white people (who have had more happy opportunities of instruction) blush, were they present." A rector in Huntington reported that some of the Negroes in his congregation could read well and accurately performed the responses in church, and that many of them were "patterns of goodness."[21]

It is possible that a typical product of the Anglican education for blacks was, like Jupiter Hammon, an honest and obedient slave, who nevertheless—contrary to the direct teaching of the Anglicans—believed slavery morally wrong. There is no evidence that Anglican education caused the slaves to be rebellious. Aside from the case of Jupiter Hammon, there is little evidence that Anglican education produced black leaders of any kind. Though the Bishop of London had recommended it, Anglicans in New York in the colonial period did not deliberately try to educate blacks as teachers of their own people, as they did in South Carolina in the case of a few blacks, and as they did in New York in the case of a few Indians educated to become teachers of Indians.[22] Nor did the Anglicans train any New York blacks to be clergymen, though by the end of the colonial period, Congregationalists in New England and Baptists in the South were beginning to do so.

However, in the long run, slave masters were right to suspect that Christian education for slaves would help to undermine slavery. The blacks and whites who attended church together, reading and singing the same responses, being examined in the same catechism, and receiving the same communion, were likely to feel the implication, as Hammon did, that in the sight of God blacks were the equals of whites. If blacks were considered equals in the most fundamental sense in which men could be viewed —in their ultimate meaning—then in the long run the ideological basis of slavery, the belief that blacks could be enslaved because they were inferior, was likely to be destroyed.

A recent historian, Edgar J. McManus, in presenting this view, overstated it when he claimed that: "In all meetings sponsored by the Society for the Propagation of the Gospel, whites and Negroes came together on terms of complete equality."[23] As long as Anglicans ran separate schools for blacks over many years in different places in the colony, as long as they often seated blacks separately in church, as long as there were no Anglican black teachers or black clergy, blacks and whites scarcely met "on terms of complete equality" in the Anglican Church. Discrimination in the Anglican Church, like that in other churches, if it did not directly deny the spiritual equality of blacks and whites, at least blunted it.

The American Revolution interfered with the Anglican education of blacks. The Anglican teachers—loyal to the king as they almost all were—were often ridiculed by the American rebels or jailed or driven out, their churches and schools closed or sacked, their work discredited. With the British recognition of the independence of the American colonies, the Church of England stopped its American missionary work, including its schools for blacks.

It was left especially to later benevolent societies to organize black education on a large scale, to push black education above the elementary level, and for the first time, to educate black teachers, black pastors, and black protest leaders.

WHITE BENEVOLENCE

$\mathbb{T}$HE AMERICAN REVOLUTION, besides bringing the Anglican church schools for blacks to an end, helped to move Northern blacks toward freedom. The Revolution encouraged some Americans to ask, as slave Jupiter Hammon did, whether it was not inconsistent to struggle for liberty for whites but leave blacks in slavery. Moreover, both parties in the Revolution, the Loyalists and the Rebels, courted slaves as soldiers (Alexander Hamilton said they were stupid and obedient enough to make good soldiers)[1] and gave them their freedom for fighting on the "right" side.

In 1785 almost half of all the slaves left in the North lived in New York State, and especially in the New York City region. It was in that year that a few whites organized the New York Manumission Society to work for the gradual abolition of slavery. This society, which was soon to operate schools for blacks, was composed of middle and upper class citizens like merchants, landowners, and lawyers. The first president of the society was John Jay; other early officers included Alexander Hamilton and New York City mayor Cadwallader D. Colden. Many officers were Episcopalians, suggesting some continuity from the colonial period of the Anglican concern for blacks, but those who did most of the consistent, plodding work for the society were Quakers. A weakness of the society was that it was concentrated in the New York City region and failed to extend itself into the rest of the state. But the society, if geographically limited, included prestigious members and was well organized.

Under the prodding of the Manumission Society, New York State adopted a policy of gradual emancipation which culminated in the requirement that all slaves be freed by 1827. New York, with its relatively large proportion of slaves, was one of the slowest Northern states to move significantly to emancipation, New Jersey being the slowest.

But abolishing slavery in New York State—and elsewhere in the North—by no means settled the question of the relation of whites and blacks. In fact, blacks, whose position under slavery was clearly defined as subordinate, after the abolition of slavery seemed to pose more threat to whites because their position was no longer so clearly defined.

In addition, the Haitian Revolution, beginning in the 1790s and extending into the early 1800s, helped to polarize the races in New York State. Blacks gloried in a successful black revolution and in the existence of an independent black nation in the Western Hemisphere. Whites— alarmed by the tales which white slaveowners, fleeing Haiti, brought with them to New York—dwelt on the violence of blacks. Prejudice against blacks was growing.

According to a British traveller in about 1817, a common topic of conversation among New Yorkers was the "bad conduct and inferior nature of niggars."[2] Whites did not want the blacks' low style of life, their speech, manners, and morals, to corrupt their own. In 1830 lawyer John A. Dix of Cooperstown, who was soon to become state Superintendent of Schools, said that slavery in the South effectively restrained blacks, but in the North there was no restraint upon blacks except the general law. He charged that the crimes committed by Africans were greater in proportion to their numbers in the free states than in the slave states.[3]

Having such attitudes, New York State whites increasingly found ways to separate themselves from blacks, which they had not found necessary while slavery still continued strong in the state. Although free blacks for a time had been allowed to vote equally with whites, in 1821 the state constitution was revised so that for whites to vote, they were no longer required to possess property, but for blacks to vote, they still were required to hold a substantial amount of property. Moreover, as slavery declined, the custom of segregation grew. In New York City by the 1810s, many whites would not walk or eat with blacks, and it was already customary for black barbers who wanted white trade to refuse to serve blacks. In the 1820s President Eliphalet Nott of Union College in Schenectady said that blacks "may be met as menials in stables and kitchens, but [they are] excluded from the parlor of fashion and the hall of science; they are nowhere met, not even in the temple of grace, as equals and companions. . . . All the avenues to wealth and honor are barred against them."[4] By this time segregation was already well developed in the state— in schools as well as elsewhere—as a substitute for slavery to keep blacks subordinate.

In the first generation after the American Revolution, there was still very little education available for blacks in New York State, especially in rural areas. As in the colonial period, most blacks still did not learn to read or write, and many were not even given religious instruction. When a French duke visited the mid-Hudson valley in the 1790s, he reported that farmers treated their slaves more mildly than farmers in the South because they had fewer slaves. Nevertheless, the slaves "were not baptized or instructed in religion," he said, "but are in that respect kept in the lowest state of degradation."

As part of the process of preparing slaves for freedom, a state law was enacted in 1810 requiring slave masters to have their slave children taught to read the scriptures—something similar to what Elias Neau and the Anglicans had hoped for a hundred years earlier. However, it is probable that the law was widely disregarded. Sojourner Truth, who later became a preacher and abolitionist crusader, remained a slave in the mid-Hudson region until she became a young adult in the 1820s, and yet she never learned to read or write; in fact she said that her pious Dutch slave owners would not even allow her to hear a Bible read. Further upstate in the Mohawk Valley, Thomas James, the slave of wealthy farmers, reached his seventeenth year in about 1821 without knowing how to read, and without ever having been inside a school or church. About the same time in western New York at Bath, the young slave Austin Steward purchased a spelling book and tried to teach himself to read. Once when Steward was out in the sugar bush, one of his master's family caught him reading his speller, flogged him, and burned the book.[5]

In the South by the second generation after the Revolution, education for blacks was increasingly prohibited by law out of fear that it would lead slaves to be more discontented. In New York State, education for blacks was never legally prohibited, but whites sometimes tolerated it reluctantly, only a little less reluctantly than in the colonial period.

It was benevolent whites who were primarily responsible for what education blacks were offered in New York State in the period from the American Revolution into at least the 1830s. It was the fashion in these years for benevolent whites to organize themselves into benevolent societies. They organized themselves into four types of benevolent societies in New York State which were related to black education: societies for the abolition of slavery, for the education of the poor, for the colonization of American blacks in Africa, and for Sunday schools. We will consider the first three of them here.

It was a society for the gradual abolition of slavery, the New York Manumission Society, which established the earliest benevolent so-

Sojourner Truth, the crusader for equal rights for women and blacks, commanded respect by her intuitive eloquence without the aid of formal education. *State University College, New Paltz.*

ciety school for blacks in the state, in New York City in 1787. This school, known as the African Free School, was to multiply into several schools while still under the control of the Manumission Society and eventually was to evolve into the city's black public school system. While the gradual abolitionists later created other black schools—including part-time schools for adults in New York City and elementary schools on Long Island[6]—this African Free School was the earliest and most significant. In its early years it was the only known black separate school in the state.

The Manumission Society believed that educating blacks would reduce white prejudice against blacks, and thus was the best way to work against slavery.[7] There is no hint in available evidence that blacks shared in initiating the society's African Free School, or were even consulted about it; nor is there evidence that the issue of separate as opposed to racially mixed education even arose. In an age when there were still virtually no public schools in the state, it seemed to the society that where there were enough blacks to make it practicable, the obvious way to bring education to blacks was to establish a separate school for them.

In their African Free School, the gradual abolitionists of the Manumission Society, like the Anglicans before them, taught blacks such conventional virtues as piety, frugality, and work. They knew that many of their pupils would attend school only in the lower grades and would drop out early to become domestics, laborers, waiters, and the like. However, going beyond the Anglicans, the gradual abolitionists retained into their upper elementary grades a few of their brighter pupils, including James McCune Smith who was to become a prominent black physician.

As Smith recalled his school afterward, the pupils "were equal if not superior" to pupils in white schools in the city in such subjects as spelling, penmanship, grammar, and astronomy. The white principal, Charles Andrews, made his pupils feel that they "had as much capacity to acquire knowledge as any other children, . ." according to Smith, "and it was thought by some, that he even regarded his black boys as a little smarter than whites. He taught his boys and girls to look upward: to believe themselves capable of accomplishing as much as any others could, and to regard the higher walks of life as within their reach."[8]

It is instructive to compare Smith as a product of the abolitionist education of blacks in the 1820s with Jupiter Hammon as a product of the Anglican education of blacks in the colonial period. Smith's education in the Manumission Society schools was more advanced than Hammon's, and encouraged him to expect more of himself. It prepared Smith, as Hammon's education did not prepare him, for higher education—because of discrimination Smith could not enter a medical school in America, but he did in Scotland. The Manumission Society prepared a few of its pupils, as the Anglicans did not, to be active leaders for blacks. Smith's abolitionism, like that of many of the black leaders who came out of the Manumission Society's schools, was more vigorous than that of Hammon or even of the Manumission Society itself. Smith became, as Hammon did not, a militant leader for equal rights.

In the Manumission Society's early years, most of the teachers in its African schools were white, like Principal Andrews. About 1830, however, black parents came to lack confidence in Andrews. Enrollment dropped, and some of the parents demanded that a black replace him.

There seem to be two reasons for black parents losing confidence in Andrews. One is suggested by a story for which there is probably some foundation. One day when a knock came to Andrews' schoolroom door, Andrews asked a pupil to go to the door. The boy went, and returning, reported to Andrews that a "colored gentleman" desired to speak with him. Andrews bristled at the boy's language, and after the visitor left, Andrews severely caned the boy for calling any colored man a "gentleman." Black parents were outraged with Andrews.[9]

The other reason was that Andrews, who grieved that discrimination often prevented blacks from finding employment that was suitable to their education, was charged with supporting the movement to send blacks back to Africa. Andrews took two blacks into his school to prepare them to become teachers in Liberia, the new African colony established by the American Colonization Society for American blacks. Also when the prominent black editor John B. Russwurm was preparing to go to Liberia in the summer of 1829 as a school principal, Andrews advised him on how to administer a school.[10] Naturally, black abolitionists, who were known for their virulent opposition to white plans to send blacks back to Africa, were upset.

Several black abolitionist leaders—especially carpenter William Hamilton, porter Henry Sipkins, and restaurateur Thomas Downing—demanded that Andrews be let go. However, some of Andrews' former pupils fought to keep him because he was admittedly a thorough teacher, a good disciplinarian, and had faith in the capacity of blacks to learn. The Manumission Society had long been satisfied with his performance; over many years under his leadership the number of the society's teachers had grown from one or two to more than twelve. But now black parents, in a significant sign of their rising expectations, held mass meetings and threatened to withdraw their remaining children from the black schools unless they were taught by blacks. Finally, in 1832, Andrews and the Manumission Society bowed to black pressure. Andrews resigned and so did his daughter who taught in another of the society's black schools. The Manumission Society appointed black teachers to take their places as well as additional black teachers, many of them graduates of its own black schools. From soon after this, most of the society's teachers were black.

With the change to predominantly black teachers, attendance in the Manumission Society's black schools went up sharply. Partly because this growth made their schools a heavy burden, in mid-1834 the Manumission Society turned them over to a larger benevolent society, the non-abolitionist New York Public School Society, a white charity society which we will soon describe. After forty-seven years of patient, unglamorous, unpopular effort, the gradual abolitionists of the New York Manumission Society ceased to operate black schools.

In the early 1830s a new movement for the "immediate" abolition of slavery arose in the North. Its major leaders included William Lloyd Garrison, who was the editor of the Boston *Liberator,* and the Tappan brothers, Lewis and Arthur, who were merchants in New York City. The new movement arose in part in reaction to the slow, quiet style of the gradual abolitionists like those of the Manumission Society, who, after having sucessfully abolished slavery in the North, seemed to be making no progress in doing so in the South. It also arose in reaction to the colonizationist drive to send blacks back to Africa.

Unlike the gradual abolitionists, the immediate abolitionists claimed to believe in equal rights for blacks. They exemplified their claim by including blacks among their members and officers, as gradual abolitionists did not. Virtually all the major black activists in the state became immediate abolitionists, and they kept prodding white abolitionists to treat blacks more equally in all aspects of life, including education. Black abolitionist editor Sam Cornish charged in his *New York Colored American,* of November 4, 1837, that "our white friends are deceived when they imagine they are free from prejudice against color, and yet are content with a lower standard of attainments for colored youth. . . . This is, in our view, the worst feature in abolitionism—the one which grieves us most."

In response to such black criticism, in 1839 a committee of an immediate abolitionist convention in New York City declared it believed in increasingly higher standards of education for blacks. During earlier times, the committee said, "when but little was expected of colored persons as ministers and teachers, and in other professions, the standard of education might be comparatively low." At that time blacks so educated

African Free School No. 2, Mulberry Street, New York City, built by the Manumission Society in 1820. *Andrews,* History of the New York African Free Schools, *1830.* Engraved from a drawing made about 1830 by Patrick Reason, a 13-year-old pupil in the school.

Gerrit Smith, a wealthy upstate landowner and congressman, promoted education for blacks in both separate and mixed institutions. *New York Public Library Picture Collection.*

might still be highly useful. But "there is now an imperious demand for learning, and the demand must be met. Colored men must be reared, well educated, in every department where they come into competition with the whites. Besides, as the people become more intelligent in the mass, their teachers must go forward in learning, or hinder the people."[11]

In keeping with such views, the new immediate abolitionists tried to improve the education of blacks. A few white abolitionists taught in black schools, as Lucy Colman did in Rochester, J. De Loss Underwood in Albany, and Dr. Abel Libolt in New York. More white abolitionists served on public school boards, all upstate where abolitionists were likely to be stronger than downstate, including Lyman Spalding in Lockport, Samuel D. Porter in Rochester, Spencer Kellogg in Utica, the Reverend Samuel J. May in Syracuse, and Ira Armstrong in Poughkeepsie. But in general, the immediate abolitionists' views were too extreme for the public, even upstate, and the influence they had over public schools was likely to be slight. Abolitionist Gerrit Smith grieved in 1844 that in New York State, abolitionists could not bring one public school in fifty under their influence.[12]

More directly, however, white immediate abolitionists affected black education by themselves creating schools, and doing so on a high level. In the 1830s the wealthy immediate abolitionist Gerrit Smith founded a secondary school for blacks in his home town of Peterboro, in central New York, and arranged to have leading black abolitionists help to choose its pupils. The discipline of this school was severe: students slept on straw, were refused coffee, tobacco, and intoxicants, and were required to work four hours a day at a trade or on a farm. In addition, in the 1830s to 1850s, the immediate abolitionists, including Gerrit Smith and the Tappan brothers, dared to develop two existing institutions, Oneida Institute, near Utica, and New York Central College, near Cortland, into interracial colleges. Because these colleges were interracial they became controversial, and we shall have occasion to examine them in detail later. These three immediate abolitionist schools were permeated with an animating mix of Puritan discipline, religious warmth, and zealous abolitionism; they helped to produce some of the strongest black abolitionists in the nation, including several who became teachers of black schools.

In addition to abolitionist schools, in the early 1800s charity schools, another type of schools for blacks, began to appear in New York

State. Charity schools were run especially by white, non-sectarian charity societies for the education of the poor.

The organizers of these white charity societies included prestigious family names like Clintons and Van Rensselaers. As men of benevolence, many of these men wished, like the abolitionists, to help blacks become better able to take care of themselves by teaching them the values of religion, work, and self-discipline. But generally being conservatives, they often felt more stake in preserving the social structure than the abolitionists did. They were not as likely as the abolitionists to wish to educate blacks to rise above their present status or to educate them to protest against inequality. They confined their level of concern almost entirely to elementary schools.

The white charity societies appointed only whites to the boards which controlled their black schools. If blacks donated funds to their black schools, as a few of them did, or if a black church donated the use of its building, the charity societies still did not acknowledge the assistance by appointing blacks to their boards. When it became apparent that blacks were not even on the board of a Brooklyn charity society whose only purpose was to run a black school, a white protested: "Can we expect a cordial cooperation in our exertions with the colored people themselves, when their own ministers and worthy men are thus treated?"[13] But such protests were rare. Whites tended to accept white control over most charity schools for blacks as inevitable, just as they did over most other schools for blacks, whether run by churches, abolitionists, or public authorities.

The Public School Society of New York City—the charity society which operated the largest charity schools for blacks in the state—acquired its black schools from the Manumission Society by transfer. The Manumission Society tried to make the transfer as smooth as possible. The Manumission Society urged its members who had been active in the supervision of its African schools to join the Public School Society if they were not already members. The Manumission Society even paid the membership fees for some of them, so that they could continue to have a hand in administering the African schools, and the Public School Society welcomed them. But black confidence in the Public School Society was difficult to establish. This society was not, like the Manumission Society, devoted primarily to black interests. Also it was larger, more impersonal. Moreover, some of the Public School Society's early policies on its new black schools disturbed blacks. The Public School Society decided that the black schools were of poorer quality than the white schools it had been running for many years, and it believed that it should raise them to the level of its white schools. To do so, it decided that some of the black grammar schools were only worthy of being classed as primary schools and discharged some of the black teachers.[14]

Nevertheless, New York City's only black newspaper at the time, the weekly *Colored American,* came to have some faith in the Public School Society. On June 24, 1837, it said editorially that the Public School Society trustees "are our friends. Many of them are noble minded men, who deeply sympathize with us in our disabilities and oppression." It added, perhaps too confidently, "They would willingly destroy the cord of caste, which disgraces our nation." It also said that the new teachers the society had appointed—virtually all blacks—were "the best of teachers." Indeed, the Public School Society was profiting from the Manumission Society's practice of identifying its bright black pupils and giving them experience in teaching as monitors; the Public School Society appointed some of them as teachers in its black schools.

However, the *Colored American* scolded the Public School Society for paying lower salaries to its black teachers than its white ones. It charged that the society had "always been unfortunate" in the appointment of some members of the committee which supervised the society's black schools. It published a letter from a black reporting that one of the trustees had arranged for segregated seating at a school function: he had shouted, "Tell them not to sit there," as a group of black ladies moved to sit where he had planned that only whites would sit. The black writer was shocked. He had himself attended the New York Manumission Society's black schools and was not accustomed to seeing segregated seating at school affairs. "But all this can very easily be accounted for," he added. "This trustee is, or was, the Recording Secretary of the New York [City] Colonization Society; and, as I suppose, seeing he could colonize none in Africa, he thought he would do it in the school house."[15] It is a question if the black community ever attained as much confidence in the Public School Society as it had had in the Manumission Society just before it transferred its black schools.

Not only in New York City, but also in upstate cities and towns, white charity societies ran schools for the education of the poor, both black and white. Upstate these charity societies were often called Lancaster societies because they used the Lancaster method of instruction.

The Lancaster method, whose major attraction was that it reduced school costs, was first introduced into the United States by the Public School Society in New York City in 1806 in its schools for whites.

The second school system to adopt the method was that of the New York Manumission Society in 1809 in its schools for blacks. Thereafter, it spread widely.

The major feature of the Lancaster method—named after the British Quaker Joseph Lancaster who promoted it—was that it employed few teachers for large numbers of children. It accomplished this by having each teacher select his best older pupils to become "monitors" or assistant teachers. The monitors were put in charge of groups of about six children each, which were stationed in various places in one large classroom. The monitors drilled the younger children in their lessons, as in reading, in writing on sand or on slates, and in reciting from memory. At best, the Lancaster system, besides cutting costs, kept the pupils active and participating, taught the older ones responsibility, and provided a built-in method of training teachers which was a special advantage to blacks who otherwise found it difficult to secure training as teachers. At worst, the system was choked with rules which were believed necessary when so many children were engaged in different activities in one large room, gave too much opportunity to the older children to mis-educate younger ones, and led to memorizing rather than thinking.

The Lancaster charity school societies often received grants of public funds from local and state sources, as the Manumission Society had also. They sometimes received these grants in a form which might make it difficult for them to refuse any poor pupil, whether black or white. For example, a state law of 1812, which provided that all school money due from the state to the city of Albany was to be paid to the Albany Lancaster Society, required the society to give free education to "all the children of every poor person residing in said city, and in no wise turn away any child that shall be, for that purpose, presented to them."[16]

While at first some of the Lancaster charity school societies may have taught black pupils in the same schools with whites, eventually when they had enough black pupils to justify it, they chose to run separate schools for whites and blacks the same as the Public School Society did in New York City. White charity societies ran separate schools for blacks in the period from the 1820s to the 1850s in at least five places upstate and three downstate.

Because most of the black charity schools were small, their costs per pupil tended to be greater than the white charity school costs, and the charity societies often found that their own funds were inadequate for their black schools. While their grants from public funds helped, and sometimes they asked for small tuition fees from parents who could pay, they often appealed to the public for contributions.

The Albany Lancaster School Society ran a school for whites in this building from 1817 to 1836. The society may have allowed a few blacks to attend this school. But from 1820 the society, finding it "inconvenient" to admit blacks "promiscuously to the same school with the white children," tried subsidizing existing black schools. In 1826 it created its own separate African school which met in the African church. *Howell,* Bicentennial History of Albany, *1886.*

In Hudson, when the Lancaster charity school trustees wished to open a separate school for blacks, they solicited funds in the community to make it possible. The city council contributed $50; the Presbyterian, Universalist, and Friends churches gave $25 each; the Episcopal church $20; the Methodist and Baptist churches $12 each. However, the pay that this made possible for the teacher, the black Miss Odell, a former pupil in the Manumission Society schools in New York City, was so low that she quit at the end of the year in protest. It was probably more than a year before Hudson's black charity school was able to reopen.[17]

In Poughkeepsie a number of different elements in the community assisted the Lancaster charity school for blacks. The Colored Female Sewing Society encouraged black children to attend the school—once they distributed two hundred pieces of children's clothing for that purpose. A young white Quaker, who was a private normal school teacher and an active abolitionist, assisted this society by lecturing at money-raising events. The *Poughkeepsie Telegraph,* a Democratic paper which might not be expected to be especially enthusiastic about black education, appealed to the citizens of the village to give funds to the black school because it had helped to produce an "extraordinary moral and intellectual improvement of our colored population," most of whom had been "degraded indeed." Poughkeepsie village contributed a substantial $200 a year to the school from public funds. Despite such help, the *Telegraph* warned that the school was in danger of dying for lack of funds.[18]

A white supporter of the black charity school in Catskill wrote that while one black had recently contributed $10, most blacks were "too poor or too careless of the advantages of education" to assist the school. If the school was to survive, the white supporter claimed, it needed "the liberality of our citizens generally."[19]

In Schenectady the Lancaster School Society reported in 1851 that, though the teacher of their black school was "competent," the city fathers had refused to supply them any more funds, their own funds were exhausted, and they had been reluctantly obliged to close the school for the present.[20]

A basic reason why it was hard to find enough money to support the charity schools for blacks was that some whites still questioned the wisdom of educating blacks. Many whites fear, a Poughkeepsie paper explained in 1837, that educating blacks would make them "insolent" and help them "forget that common consent makes them 'hewers of wood and drawers of water'." Another reason, according to the *New York Colored American* at about the same time, was that blacks "have as yet sacrificed nothing for the purposes of education." Unlike whites, blacks "have not even denied themselves the luxuries of life."[21]

Not only the inadequate funding, but also the colonizationist movement had a discouraging impact on the education of blacks, whether in charity schools or any other kind of school at the time. A leading colonizationist, President Nott of Union College, declared in 1829 that blacks are "a degraded and a wretched race. . . . Whether bond or free, their presence will be forever a calamity. Why then, in the name of God, should we hesitate to encourage their departure?" Convinced that the situation of blacks in America was hopeless, colonizationists naturally took action which would make their belief come true. Thus the New York Colonization Society memorialized the state legislature against giving blacks the equal right to vote in the state. Thus also when abolitionists—black and white, including New Yorkers like the Tappan brothers—tried to start a college for blacks in New Haven in 1831, a colonizationist paper opposed it, complaining that any endeavor to raise blacks "to a level with the whites, whether by founding colleges, or in any other way, tends directly in the proportion that it succeeds, to counteract and thwart the whole plan of colonization." New York City black pastor Peter Williams went to the heart of the matter when, in an address to blacks, he asked, how can the colonizationists have us removed to Africa except "by making our situation worse here?"[22]

About 1830 a young black, John Brown, who had already been studying medicine privately with physicians in New York City, applied to enter the New York College of Physicians and Surgeons. While he was allowed to attend lectures through the device of serving as an aid to one of the college's physicians, he was not permitted to become a regular student or take an examination for a degree. The president of the college, a colonizationist, said that no diploma could be given a colored man unless he would sign a pledge that he would not practice medicine anywhere but Liberia. Brown refused to sign such a pledge, and was never able to secure a medical degree.[23]

When, in response to incidents of this kind, the immediate abolitionists charged that colonizationists neglected the improvement of blacks in this country, the New York City Colonization Society replied that the improvement of blacks in this country "was not the object for which this society was formed," but that the society's members as individuals in fact were often the trustees of black schools.[24]

Whether it was healthy for blacks that colonizationists served as trustees of black schools is doubtful, but at any rate colonizationists often did serve as such trustees. For example, three officers of the New York City Colonization Society were trustees of the New York Public School Society, and similarly four managers of the state colonization society were trustees of the Albany Lancaster Society.

Colonizationists were intimately related to the education of blacks in other ways too. In Newtown, Queens County, Peter Remsen, a wealthy New York City merchant who generously contributed funds to the colonization movement, led in establishing a private school for blacks. In Jamaica, also in Queens County, William L. Johnson, an Episcopal rector who was a manager for life of the New York City Colonization Society, paid all the expenses of a black school for perhaps five or six years. Colonizationist Reverend James Milnor was president of the New York City Sunday School Union during the 1820s when about one fourth of the pupils in all its schools were black. In Rochester, a judge who was president of the local colonization society was also president of the local Sunday school union which sponsored an African Sunday School. In Brooklyn, Adrian Van Sinderen, the president of the local colonization society, was a director of the African Infant School Association. In the 1840s, William L. Stone, a manager of the State Colonization Society, served as New York City superintendent of schools and as such supervised at least nine black public schools. At least two active colonizationists, Gideon Hawley and John A. Dix, served as state superintendents of schools and as such supervised all the public schools of the state, whether black, white, or mixed.

The colonization movement dominated much of the state and the nation. Church bodies endorsed it. The New York legislature twice endorsed it. Newspapers praised it—the *Poughkeepsie Eagle* claimed on April 13, 1839, that colonization is "the noblest work of philanthropy that distinguishes the present age." Many teachers and parents of black children were inevitably infected with colonizationist attitudes to some degree, especially in the 1820s and 1830s when the movement reached its peak, and to some extent even as late as the Civil War when President Lincoln revived it. During the whole period from the American Revolution to the Civil War, the logical position on black education for the abolitionists was different from that for the colonizationists. For abolitionists to justify the abolition of slavery, it would help to show that the mass of blacks who were already free could improve themselves through schooling in this country. However, for colonizationists to persuade blacks to emigrate to Africa or elsewhere, it would help to show that the mass of blacks—if not the few who might become the leaders of colonies—could not improve themselves through schooling or otherwise in this country.

Not only the colonizationist movement and the inadequate funding, but also a number of other factors conspired to make it difficult for benevolent whites to provide quality education to blacks. The hint of benevolent condescension with which some of the white trustees ran the schools scarcely seemed likely to encourage the pupils to ambition. The parents were often illiterate or indifferent or both, and the pupils had little reason to expect that studying hard would lead to better economic opportunity. The Lancaster method of teaching might more easily develop martinets than intellects. The subject matter was likely to be limited, especially in the upstate schools. Eight years after its founding, the Albany charity school for blacks was still teaching only "spelling, reading, writing, cyphering, and geography," while its sister charity school for whites, a much larger school to be sure, was also teaching such advanced subjects as chemistry and American history.[25]

Nevertheless, in the period from the 1780s to the 1860s, benevolent whites contributed significantly to the education of New York State blacks. To teach in their black schools, benevolent whites often appointed very able and socially-aware black teachers who helped to offset the factors making for poor quality education for blacks. For example, among the teachers the Public School Society appointed in New York was "Dr." John Brown, who had been denied his medical degree because he refused to cooperate with colonizationist plans to sent him to Africa; and among the teachers the Lancaster charity society appointed in Poughkeepsie was Samuel R. Ward, who had escaped from slavery in Maryland as a child and had recently been an agent for a black protest paper. Both of these teachers were thorough-going abolitionists. Why conservative white trustees would appoint teachers whose social views were so different from their own is the subject of a later chapter.

Benevolent whites also contributed significantly in the numbers of pupils they reached. If we add together the largest number of pupils known at any one time in each of their black schools, excluding Sunday schools, the abolitionists taught perhaps 2,100 blacks, or perhaps six times as many as the Anglicans had taught in their known black schools, and white charity societies taught even more, perhaps 2,900.

Like the Anglicans, both the white gradual abolitionists and the white charity societies concentrated on elementary education, which, considering that at least into the 1820s the vast majority of blacks in the state still had virtually no schooling at all, was of course the level of their greatest need. The white abolitionists also contributed significantly by emphasizing, as the Anglicans had not, that black achievement in education showed that blacks were not inherently inferior, a factor of importance both in the effort to abolish slavery and in its effect on blacks' conception of themselves. The white abolitionists, especially those of the later immediatist variety, deliberately educated black leaders, including preachers and teachers, as the Anglicans had not, and the immediate abolitionists insisted on doing so on a high level. Moreover, the immediate abolitionists made a significant contribution by holding up the ideal of interracial education and carrying it into practice in the notable example of two interracial colleges.

In addition, benevolent whites, by using the inexpensive Lancasterian system of teaching, inadequate though it was, helped to demonstrate that universal education did not have to be prohibitively expensive. Thus they helped to prepare the way for the enormous expansion of public education which was to come in the state in the 1840s and 1850s for both blacks and whites.

SUNDAY BLESSING

$\mathbb{E}$ARLY IN THE NINETEENTH CENTURY, there swept across the nation an innovative form of education, the Sunday school

In its first years, the Sunday school was intended especially for those who went neither to church on Sunday nor to school during the week. So the Sunday school often taught not only religion but also reading, writing, and arithmetic.

In an age when public schools were still in their infancy, for many blacks the Sunday school provided the only means of basic education. Most blacks in the nation, North and South, could neither read nor write; many could not even count well enough to know how to use money. Blacks are "growing up in ignorance of . . . everything that belongs to civilization," said the *Long Island Farmer* of December 5, 1822. They "have nowhere to look for instruction but to the Sabbath schools."

Particularly beginning about 1815, Sunday schools sprang up in New York State. While in the colonial period there had been a few Sunday schools which were organized by Anglicans and usually taught by clergy, these new Sunday schools at first were usually organized by non-denominational Sunday school unions and taught by laymen.

As a major innovation, the Sunday school movement aroused conservative objections. Sabbatarians protested that schools on the Sabbath were a desecration of a Holy Day. Advocates of strong family ties objected that these schools would reduce parents' sense of responsibility to give religious instruction to their children. The clerical-minded objected that the schools were run by laymen. Some whites objected, as they had in the colonial period, to blacks being educated at all, believing it would make them more discontented with their lot than they already were.

35

But Sunday schools had the advantage of being cheap. Teachers taught without pay. Volunteering to teach in the Sunday schools became a popular outlet for the energy of the idealistic young.

Sunday schools also had the advantage of providing the established classes a means to influence the poor—to convert them to religion, to teach them orderly habits of work, and to reduce their danger to the stability of society. Particularly in the 1810s and 1820s, local white leaders —including both abolitionists and colonizationists—welcomed the opportunity to influence blacks because blacks in New York State, and elsewhere in the North, were in the process of being gradually freed from the restraints of slavery and often seemed to whites to be irresponsible.

Sunday schools met needs of the poor too. Many poor children could not attend weekday schools because they worked during the week. Moreover, if lower class parents felt alienated from churches because they could not afford to follow the custom of renting a family pew, they felt themselves welcome in the free Sunday schools. On Saturday night, parents scrubbed their children, and sometimes themselves too, for Sunday school, and the Saturday night bath, if not already an American institution, rapidly became one. On Sunday morning, the aspiring poor, both black and white, gladly trooped to Sunday school.

Black leaders urged blacks to take advantage of Sunday schools. In Rochester in the 1820s black grocer Austin Steward advised black adults to attend Sunday school to "learn, without loss of time or money, that of which none should be ignorant—to read." In New York in the 1820s the black *Freedom's Journal* decided that, "of all the blessings conferred upon us by the goodness of our Creator, we must consider Sabbath schools as one of the greatest." In the 1830s the New York Annual Conference of the African Methodist Church asked members and preachers to advocate Sunday schools "warmly and perseveringly."[1] By this time, some black churches were running their own Sunday schools.

Blacks from the beginning were attracted to Sunday schools, In 1820 the London Sunday School Union reported that in the United States, Sunday schools "are formed in almost every considerable town and village," and added, they "have spread particularly among the blacks."[2] In the period from 1810 through 1860, there were 110 known black Sunday schools in New York State. Adding together the largest known enrollment in each school and estimating the enrollment in the rest, we find that they probably reached more than 8000 pupils. Thus, black Sunday schools reached far more blacks in the state than the Anglican black schools in colonial days and even somewhat more than the black weekday schools run by benevolent whites at about the same time as the Sunday schools.

Some blacks eagerly grasped the opportunity provided by Sunday schools. A Sunday school in New York City reported that it placed a black girl "in one of the alphabet classes" and in three months she had "learned to read with facility." In another New York City Sunday school, some of its adult black pupils "blessed God with tears of joy when, at sixty years of age, they had reached the point when they could spell out a single verse in God's holy Word." In Albany, the pupils in a black Sunday school so appreciated the zeal of their white lady teachers in coming to school regardless of wet, cold, or illness that, according to the Albany Sunday School Society, "they received their instruction and their advice, as coming from the mouths of oracles." Farther west in Geneva, a little girl in a black Sunday school on one occasion recited 709 Bible verses; a Geneva delegate to a state Sunday school convention cited her achievement as a reply to "the common argument that colored children should not be taught on the ground that they have no capacity to learn." The young fugitive slave, James W. C. Pennington, who in 1829 had recently arrived in Brooklyn from the South and was eager to improve himself, considered it a "rare privilege" to attend Sabbath school. "I began to contrast . . . the condition of the children I saw sitting around me on the Sabbath . . . ," Pennington wrote, "with that of the . . . slave children [in the South] who had no means of Christian instruction. The theme . . . stirred the most agitating emotions I had ever felt. The question was, what can I do for that vast body of suffering brotherhood I have left behind?"[3] His Sunday school experience helped lead Pennington toward becoming a minister, a teacher, and one of the leading black abolitionists of the nation.

On the other hand, there were reports that some blacks did not make good use of Sunday schools. The Tarrytown Sunday school—about one-third of whose pupils were black—reported that the majority of the blacks were "inattentive." In Kinderhook, a young white teacher lamented that some of the black children she taught "are mischievous and heedless and try our patience to the utmost." In Rochester, the black Austin Steward mourned that black parents interested themselves but little in the Sunday school he taught; he explained, "Very few of the Negroes seemed to have any courage or ambition to rise from the abject degradation in which the estimation of the white man had placed him." In New York City in 1827 the black *Freedom's Journal* explained the lack of attention of the pupils in one black Sunday school by the "apparent carelessness and incapacity of the teachers." A few years later, Samuel Cornish, the editor of the *New York Colored American,* grieved that blacks attending Sunday schools did not apply themselves to learn. The reason was, he

Like most other private academies in the state in the 1830s, Flushing Institute, at
Flushing, Long Island, is not known to have accepted blacks as regular students.
However, an enterprising Institute instructor, Libertus Van Bokkelen, taught a
Bible class for black men at the institute on Friday evenings. In addition, Van
Bokkelen, assisted by students from the institute, organized a Sunday school for
black women and children which met elsewhere. Like many white teachers of
blacks, Van Bokkelen's career was evidently not harmed by his teaching of blacks.
He later became president of the National Teachers Association. *Courtesy of The
Queens Borough Public Library.*

explained, that blacks, having a position in society "comparatively without responsibility . . . have never felt the necessity of making themselves
adept in anything. But the times have changed. . . . They . . . are beginning to feel equal responsibilities with their paler faced brethren, and, no
doubt, for the time to come, will make closer application."[4]

The teachers of Sunday schools for blacks in the period being described here, from the 1810s through the 1860s, were usually white (55%),
male (66%), and born in the state. Of the white teachers whose name and
regular occupation are known, the largest group (55%) were businessmen
or farmers, the next largest group (28%) were professionals, while the rest

(17%) were skilled workers including bakers, hatters, and clerks. The white professionals included persons whose weekday occupation was teaching whites, yet they appeared not to hurt their status by taking on the extra burden of teaching blacks on Sundays. In Brooklyn, Ann Wetmore, whose weekday private school was patronized by the leading families of the village, on Sundays taught a school for blacks in her regular school room. Similarly, in Schenectady, two Union College teachers organized and taught a Sunday school for blacks. White Sunday school teachers were often of standing in the community, or if young people, from families of standing. In Flatbush, Long Island, in the 1850s, Mrs. John Vanderbilt, the wife of a judge, established a Sunday school for blacks; according to a local black pastor, she was assisted in her work by "ladies and gentlemen" from Flatbush's "best families." In Utica in 1816, the teachers of a Sunday evening school for blacks were the daughters of some of the most prestigious men of Utica, including merchants, a newspaper editor, and trustees of banks, academies, and churches. In the Finger Lakes region in Geneva, where the elite of the village were said to be especially distinguished for refinement, they were said to consider it more fashionable to teach Sunday school classes for blacks than for whites.[5]

Of the blacks who taught Sunday schools from the 1810s through the 1860s, for whom the information is available, most were males (74%), born in the state, and taught in Sunday schools related to black churches. Of the black teachers whose major occupation is known, 32% were professionals (especially teachers or pastors), 18% were skilled workers (such as barbers, printers, or dressmakers), 16% were businessmen or farmers, 7% were students, and 27% were unskilled workers (such as porters, whitewashers, or laborers). Thus, blacks who taught black Sunday schools represented a wider cross section of occupations than the whites who taught black Sunday schools did, particularly because the blacks included considerable number of unskilled workers as whites did not.

Sometimes blacks seemed to be proud when blacks rather than whites taught black Sunday schools. In Poughkeepsie, when the nondenominational black Sunday school changed from white to black teachers, a black correspondent of the *New York Colored American* interpreted this as an improvement. In New York City one of the most prestigious black churches, St. Philips Episcopal, appointed to teach in its Sunday school only blacks[6]—among them were the young druggist Philip A. White, who was on the road to becoming wealthy, and the dignified John Peterson, principal of a black public school.

However, other black promoters of Sunday schools for blacks

seemed to believe that there were advantages in having white teachers. During the Civil War in Flushing, Long Island, the lively young black William T. Dixon organized a black Sunday school which was held in the same black public school building where he taught during the week; he ran his Sunday school with eight teachers, seven of them white. In Troy over several decades the black churches often arranged that their Sunday schools be taught by whites, including some of the most respectable businessmen of the city.

White promoters of Sunday schools seldom gave black Sunday school leaders much recognition. They are not known to have chosen blacks as officers of Sunday school unions even when black Sunday schools were affiliated with the unions. An unusual example of whites inviting blacks to share with them in leading a major Sunday school function occurred in 1855 in New York City at a reception for one thousand visiting Sunday school workers from Massachusetts—perhaps it is significant that they came from a state where abolitionists were stronger than in New York State. The reception was held in New York's glass Crystal Palace on 42nd Street. Among the speakers was the black physician, James McCune Smith—then serving as the staff physician of the New York Colored Orphan Asylum—who told the story of the asylum's founding by Quakers two decades before. Afterward, a group of the asylum's orphans sang "We are a band of orphans" so appealingly that the audience clamored for them to sing it again; and a white pastor, who was a major figure in the New York Sunday school movement, told the great throng that the presence of the colored orphans in their midst was "an illustration of our Christian acknowledgement that 'God has made of one blood,' all these various children . . . to dwell together on the face of the earth." But he admitted that the "union of colors" at this great gathering was a sight "which I do not often see in New York."[7]

Sunday school unions, however, regularly included blacks in their annual marches through the streets. For instance, in 1826, just before slavery was finally abolished in the state, the New York City Sunday School Union arranged a march down Broadway to the Battery. About 5000 pupils participated, including an African Sunday School which carried a banner reading, "The Truth Shall Make You Free." But it was clear from comments on black participation in such marches that whites were sensitive about it. In Rochester in 1828, when an African Sunday school participated in a Sabbath School Union's procession, a Rochester newspaper commented that the "orderly" African Sunday school received "the same attention that was bestowed upon the others—thus giving a practical illustration of the principles of gospel humility." In a similar

The Reverend Daniel A. Payne, left, was driven out of the South for teaching his fellow blacks. While serving as a pastor in Troy in 1838, he taught a non-denominational Sunday school, for all ages, which is said to have attracted one-third of the blacks of the city. Payne later became an African Methodist bishop and president of Wilberforce University, Ohio. *Simmons,* Men of Mark, *1887.*

Lewis Tappan, right, the zealous abolitionist, superintended an interdenomina-tional Sunday school for blacks of all ages. The Sunday school met in 1837 in the basement of the interracial Broadway Tabernacle, New York. *Still,* Underground Railroad, *1872.*

Sunday school procession in Williamsburg, Long Island, in 1866, a jar-
ring incident occurred. When the scholars of a white Methodist Sunday
school were asked to march *behind* a black Sunday school, they objected.
Their teachers tried to persuade them to change their minds, but the white
children would not give in. They withdrew from the procession altogether. Horace Greeley's *New York Tribune* was angry: "If it was a sacri-
fice" for the white children to walk behind the blacks, asked the *Tribune*
editorially, "are not such sacrifices wholesome? Isn't humility worth in-
culcating? Isn't a self-denial a virtue? Pray, for what do they attend Sunday school, if it be not to learn these elementary principles of religion?"[8]

Whites often seemed uneasy about black Sunday schools. In
1815 in Flatbush, Long Island—where the proportion of blacks in the
population had recently been an unusually high 40%—a white "philanthropic society" opened a Sunday school for slaves. On short notice, upward of a hundred slaves came to the school, varying in age from ten to
sixty. The slaves have begun to learn how to count money and to write, reported the *New York National Advocate,* and so far have "conducted
themselves in the most becoming manner"; but, it warned, the project
could be defeated by "the misconduct of the blacks."[9]

Other whites seemed outright hostile to black Sunday schools. In
Albany about 1820 the whites who organized a Sunday school for blacks,
even though they included such respectable citizens as merchants, an
Episcopal rector, and an attorney, ran into continuous difficulty in finding adequate places for their Sunday school to meet. Several times the
school was on the point of closing because of it. The reason for the difficulty, reported the Albany Sunday School Society which sponsored the
school, was "the prejudice excited against the enlightening of this
people." In New York City in the 1860s Quakers discovered that when
they tried to run a Sunday school for blacks, they often had to shift its location, for "teaching 'them niggers' was . . . very unpopular." Hood-
lums sometimes pelted the teachers with stones.[10]

The methods used in Sunday schools varied. Many Sunday
schools memorized Bible verses and vied with each other to see which
schools could memorize the most verses; one Albany black Sunday school
claimed that it recited 6460 verses in seven months. While teaching reading was a key function in many Sunday schools, in a Sunday school in
Kinderhook, if adult pupils could not read, a teacher simply read aloud to
them. In one black adult Sunday school in New York, the white abolitionist merchant, Lewis Tappan, taught by discussion. In another such adult
school, the teachers were expected to do much of their important work by
visiting their pupils once a week in their homes; teachers reported that

their pupils always received them "with respect," and that they were often able to institute "a considerable reform in their domestic economy—filthiness and confusion succeeded by cleanliness and regularity."[11] Some Sunday schools featured singing—the perennially popular Sunday school song, "Jesus Loves Me," was written by two West Point Sunday school teachers in 1860. Some Sunday schools held annual outings or annual ceremonies recognizing the achievement of pupils. During the Civil War, a black Sunday school, several hundred strong, made one of its annual outings by sailing from New York up the Hudson River on a barge. In the company were returned soldiers who had been members of the Sunday school and teachers who ranged in age from sixteen to silvery gray. On the barge the younger pupils jumped rope. Arrived at a grove in Yonkers, many of the pupils took part in sports, and then the entire company locked arms, marched, and sang hymns.[12]

Sunday schools were intended, at different times and places and according to different observers, to fulfill varied if not contradictory purposes for blacks. They were expected to serve both the young and the old, to educate for both the secular and the religious life, to teach reading and manners, to teach morality and acceptance of the status quo, to drill in memorizing Bible verses and cultivate the intellect. A particularly sharp contrast in the purposes of Sunday schools is suggested by a comparison between the attitudes toward blacks of two sponsors of New York City black Sunday schools, one a white colonizationist, the other a black abolitionist.

The white Reverend James Milnor, Episcopalian, was president at different times of both the New York City Colonization Society and the New York City Sunday School Union. Like most colonizationists, Milnor had virtually no hope that blacks could become equal to whites in America. The black race, he said in 1826, while capable of appreciating civilization and receiving God's message of mercy, "constitute a separate class, marked by many features of decided inferiority in public estimation, and, in the common course of things, doomed perhaps to occupy for ever this degraded place." Even the North, he said, where slavery has "happily" been at least partially abolished, is interested in preventing an increase of a people who are "constantly fretting under . . . a denial of political rights to which they have no prospect of arriving, an exclusion from associations to which they can never look for an admittance."

Milnor's method for preventing an increase of blacks was the colonizationist method of persuading as many blacks as possible to return to their home in Africa and helping them do so. The role of the Sunday school for these blacks who were to return to Africa was to educate them so that they could take the benefits of Christian civilization to Africa and thus further justify sending them there. We rejoice, Milnor told his congregation in a sermon, that several blacks reared in our Sunday schools "have been enabled, under the auspices of the Colonization Society, to communicate the benefits conferred by you, to their brethren on the coast of Africa." The role of the Sunday school for those blacks who unfortunately remained in America was to help them to become less destructive of the social order. "We rejoice," Milnor said, "that some [blacks] reared under the happy influence of the Sunday schools which you support, now rank in our community among the friends of religion and good morals."[13]

In contrast to Milnor, the black Reverend Theodore S. Wright, in his black Shiloh Presbyterian Church, sponsored a Sunday school which was oriented to immediate abolitionism. Wright did not, like Milnor, accept the blacks' inferior status in America as inevitable. Instead, as a prominent abolitionist, he worked to improve it. He was active in the underground railroad, once helping to arrange for twenty-eight slaves to sail on a barge up the Hudson River to safety. He served on the executive committee of the American Antislavery Society. He worked for equal suffrage for blacks. He opposed segregation. Burn out prejudice, he pleaded in a speech to a state antislavery convention in Utica; "live it down, talk it down, everywhere consider the colored man as a man, in the church, the stage, the steamboat, the public house, in all places."

Wright's Sunday school superintendent was the black William P. Johnson, a shoemaker by trade, who was on the staff of the abolitionist *New York Colored American.* Superintendent Johnson's Sunday school had its own Juvenile Antislavery Society. When the Sunday school celebrated the 4th of July, according to Johnson, "instead of having a star-spangled banner unfurled, waving in the air, an emblem of liberty and equal rights, we had a more appropriate one, a large slave whip, which I thought ought to be hung in place of flags throughout our country."[14]

From the abolitionist point of view, most Sunday schools, North or South, were in effect pro-slavery because they did not teach against slavery. They were more like pastor Milnor's Sunday schools than like pastor Wright's. Abolitionists charged that the same pro-slavery men who controlled the political destiny of the nation also controlled the American Sunday School Union. In fact, the materials the union distributed to Sunday schools, while they condemned such sins as swearing and drinking liquor, carefully avoided the sin of owning human beings. When a Southerner complained in 1848 that a book with the union distributed to Sunday schools included a passage which condemned slavery, this cre-

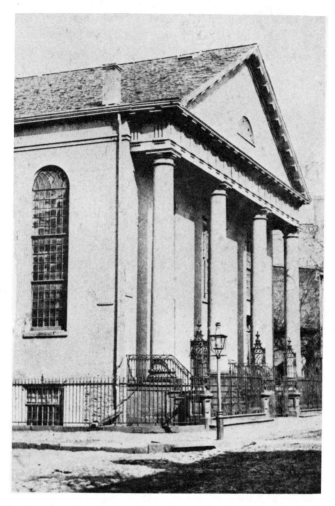

Shiloh Presbyterian Church, an influential black church on Prince Street near Greenwich Village, ran its own Sunday school. In the 1840s to 1860s when it occupied this building, its pastors included J. W. C. Pennington and H. H. Garnet. At a previous location its pastor was T. S. Wright. All these pastors were active abolitionists. *Courtesy of The New-York Historical Society, New York City.*

ated a furor, and the union withdrew the publication from circulation. Abolitionist Lewis Tappan loudly protested the withdrawal.[15]

Many Sunday schools for blacks, whether led by abolitionists or not, did not last very long. Attendance was often irregular. Pupils often progressed slowly. Teachers "often witnessed with pain," a writer in a Brooklyn paper reported, "the little improvement" which colored children make when they are "entirely deprived of weekday instruction." The remedy he suggested was establishing supplementary part-time schools during the week.[16] Some agencies which sponsored black Sunday schools did establish such supplementary schools. Other agencies, such as a Friends charity society on Long Island, abandoned their black Sunday schools entirely as inadequate education for blacks, choosing instead to support either full-time weekday schools which accepted blacks along with whites or even, when necessary, to found new full-time weekday schools exclusively for blacks.

Partly because many Sunday schools which blacks attended were short-lived, their records often do not survive. However, for the Sunday schools of the New York City region, because there were so many of them and because they were organized into strong Sunday school unions, some records about them have been preserved, and it is possible to trace some long-term trends.

In 1821, according to New York City Sunday School Union reports, blacks were attending Sunday schools in far greater numbers than their proportion of the population: 26% of the pupils in Sunday schools were black, while only 9% of the city population was black. At this time slavery still existed in the state, and opportunities for blacks to secure an education during the week were severely limited. After that time black enthusiasm for Sunday schools gradually waned. By 1856 the proportion of blacks in Sunday schools related to the New York City Sunday School Union had dropped to 2%, and the proportion of blacks in the population had also dropped—as white immigrants poured into the city—to about the same percentage. An additional factor in the drop in the proportion of blacks in Sunday school was that blacks were increasingly attending weekday public schools.

Early in the New York City Sunday school movement, by far most of the blacks attending were in racially mixed Sunday schools. However, within these racially mixed schools, there was considerable segregation by means of separate classes for blacks.

Moreover, there was a long-term trend in New York City Sunday schools toward more segregation. According to available Sunday school union reports, the proportion of blacks who were in separate schools for blacks rather than in racially mixed Sunday schools went up sharply from about one quarter in 1821 to well over a half in 1845. A factor in this climb was that blacks were increasingly creating Sunday schools of their own. Apparently also a factor was that the number of blacks qualified to teach Sunday schools was going up—they were being trained in the racially mixed Sunday schools, as well as in separate black Sunday and weekday schools, and once trained they helped to increase the proportion of blacks in separate Sunday schools.

Meanwhile in New York State as a whole, whether Sunday schools were racially mixed or segregated, the number of Sunday schools attached to churches grew. Moreover, both national denominations and local churches—black and white—were tightening their control over the Sunday schools related to them. By 1863, according to a New York City Sunday school leader, although there still remained a few non-denominational Sunday schools independent of any church, "every church has its Sunday school" and most Sunday schools have an "inseparable relation to the church."[17] Naturally, as Sunday schools became more nearly an integral part of the church, for this reason alone, as well because of the increase in the number of pupils attending weekday schools, Sunday schools tended to become more religious and less academic.

Black educational progress continued to be painfully slow. In 1865 a college-educated black, the Reverend Amos Beman, who taught both weekday and Sunday schools in Jamaica, Long Island, could still say pessimistically that few Jamaica blacks could read intelligently in the scriptures, fewer could write, and fewer still could understand even the simplest rules of arithmetic.[18] Nevertheless it was certain that by this time more Northern blacks could read and write and cypher than fifty years before, and that black opportunity for elementary education in weekday schools had increased. So black Sunday schools taught less reading, writing, and arithmetic. While in the South just after the Civil War, many blacks found their first opportunity to learn to read and write in Sunday schools, in New York State and much of the North after the Civil War, only a few black Sunday schools still continued significant academic functions. The religious Sunday school of course survived—it was to prove to be a remarkably resilient feature of American life, for both blacks and whites. But by the 1860s the great need for the Northern Sunday school as an agency of basic academic education for blacks was over.

BLACK INITIATIVE

WHILE IT WAS WHITES who were primarily responsible for creating most of the schools for blacks in nineteenth century New York State, blacks also took considerable educational initiative for themselves. They did so particularly in the first half of the century. Considering that blacks at this time were only just emerging from slavery in the state, their educational efforts provide a remarkable record of both their enterprise and their faith in education.

Who were the blacks who took the initiative in black education? Why did their thrust emerge in this period? What forms did their initiative take? What obstacles did they meet? It is difficult to ferret out full answers to such questions. Compared to the whites who led in providing education for blacks, blacks in this period lacked the status, skills, and continuity in organization which would make it easy for them to record and preserve the story of their activities. Only scattered information is available, as in church and school records, local newspapers, and in the black and abolitionist press. But we follow the story from the 1790s into the 1850s as well as we can.

In the 1790s what little education for blacks was available was often interracial. Even so, at this early period there was already an instance of black initiative. The black who was responsible for it was cake maker Kathy Ferguson of New York City. When Kathy was a slave of eight years of age, her mother had been sold away from her, and Kathy never saw her again. This searing experience, instead of embittering Kathy, taught her empathy with the many desolate children of the city. Once she had become an adult, and a philanthropic white had bought her freedom, Kathy Ferguson was able to take into her home unwanted children from the streets, both black and white, to raise them as her own. In 1793 this strong, compassionate woman, who never learned to read and write, gathered together her own foster children and other children of her neighborhood, both black and white, to form a Sunday school for religious instruction. When her white Presbyterian pastor became aware of her Sunday school, he offered her the use of his church building for her school. He also helped her find assistant teachers, including whites.[1]

Kathy Ferguson's school and church were interracial. But after the 1790s, with slavery under increasing attack and soon clearly on the way out, and yet with white prejudice against blacks continuing, if not increasing, New York State blacks moved toward establishing separate institutions of their own. They often did so as a protest against whites' unequal treatment of blacks. By 1800 blacks in New York City, in protest against segregation within the predominantly white churches—particularly their refusal to allow black preachers to preach as equals—seceded from a predominantly white Methodist church to create the state's first black church, a Methodist church. Then blacks moved—often with white help —to create black churches, usually Methodist or Baptist, in virtually every considerable community of blacks in the state. For example, they created the first known black church in Flushing by 1811, Brooklyn by 1819, Albany by 1820, Rochester by 1823, Newburgh by 1827, and Ithaca by 1833.

At about the same time, and for similar reasons, blacks were creating separate black institutions in other aspects of life too. In 1827, the year slavery was completely abolished in the state, with white help they established the nation's first black newspaper, the *New York Freedom's Journal.* Later they established other black newspapers in the state, as in Albany by 1831, Troy by 1839, and Rochester by 1847. At the same time they were creating black lodges, black temperance associations, and black mutual benefit associations for insurance purposes, as well as black schools.

To follow in detail examples of black initiative in the establishment of black weekday schools, we first look at what happened in Albany as well as the mists of history allow.

Albany in 1812 was a buzzing Hudson River port, the sixth or seventh largest city in the United States with about 9400 people. Of these, 8 percent were blacks, one-third of them still slaves.

In 1812 a group of Albany blacks bought a lot for a black school.

By 1816 several of this group, all free blacks, had been able, "chiefly by the liberality of the citizens of Albany," to build a school house on their lot, and probably already had a black school in operation there. In that year they petitioned the state legislature to incorporate them as the "Albany School for Educating People of Color," and the legislature did so. The trustees as designated by the act of incorporation were all black, including a shoemaker, grocer, cartman, and office sweeper.[2]

A few years later Albany blacks were again taking the initiative to assure that there was a meeting place for a black school. In 1820 the new non-denominational "Albany African Church"—which later became a Baptist church—solicited funds to erect a building for their church with the stipulation that it would contain a room for a school. Whites of many denominations contributed to the building. Perhaps it was about this time that the city loaned to the trustees of the church $500, "the payment of which was not to be demanded provided the trustees allowed the basement of their house to be used as a school for colored children." The church building was dedicated in January 1823. Almost immediately a school for black children was operating in the church, with, as the pastor of the church, the black Reverend Nathaniel Paul, said, "a worthy teacher of their own color." By December, however, the school had been discontinued, according to Paul, "for the want of pecuniary aid." Three years later, with the active cooperation of the church, a black school was again operating in the church's basement, this time run by the white Lancaster School Society.[3]

Turning to Brooklyn, we find more evidence of early black initiative for black schools. The black public school of Brooklyn was the earliest known black public school in New York State. Founded probably by 1817, this public school was unusual among the state's black public schools for the large degree of control which blacks acquired over it.

In the early 1800s Brooklyn, a rapidly growing village, had a high proportion of blacks compared to Albany or most of the state—in 1820 it was 16 percent. Perhaps it was partly because of this high proportion that a black public school was begun there so early, and that blacks took considerable responsibility for it. Evidently it was also because Brooklyn had enterprising blacks.

In 1815 Peter Cruger, a free black who was soon to be a leader in founding the black Methodist church in Brooklyn, advertised that a day and evening "African school" was being held at his house. The school taught, he said, "the common branches of education." Like other early black schools, this school was private, and Cruger, though he often worked as a whitewasher, evidently taught it himself. This school probably helped to prepare the way for the black public school soon to be established.

The next year, 1816, at a time when many taxpayers still opposed being taxed to support any school, the village of Brooklyn opened its first public school for anyone. While a school building was being constructed, the school opened in temporary, rented quarters. In announcing the opening of the school, the three school trustees, all whites, said that white children would be accepted at once, but black children would not be accepted until the new building was completed.[4] Thus the trustees acknowledged that the school would eventually accept black as well as white children, but made clear that they felt they could treat the black children differently.

By 1817 the new public school building was open, and blacks were admitted into the building, but they were placed in a separate room; their separate class was apparently called the "African District School." Their teacher was probably the black William M. Read. He had been educated in the Manumission Society's school in New York City, and was that school's only pupil to have become a teacher up to that time.

By 1818 there were 190 white pupils occupying rooms in the new school building, as well as 45 black pupils occupying their separate room. As in many early public schools, the trustees charged tuition fees of the children who could pay. They charged whites $1.50 per quarter, but the blacks only $1.00, which probably meant that the teacher of the blacks was paid less than the teachers of the whites. These fees covered all expenses, including books, stationery, and fuel to heat the rooms. Pupils who could not pay, whether white or black, could be admitted free.

In 1827, the year slavery was finally abolished in the state, the Brooklyn black public school was forced out of the district school building. At that time a black society, the African Woolman Benevolent Society, undertook to construct a building for the black school. As a black writer explained later, "From some reasons unknown to us," blacks "were deprived of the use of that room [in the regular district school building], and were driven to the necessity of building the present school house we now occupy."[5]

Though the school was now housed in a privately owned building, it was still a public school, and, at first, part of one of the town of Brooklyn's regular school districts.[6] However, perhaps part of the time while the school was still in the district school building, and certainly later while it was in the new separate building, blacks were largely responsible for administering the school. Early in 1827, before the Woolman Society's building was opened, the *Brooklyn Long Island Star* editorially praised the "intelligent portion of our numerous colored population" for their efforts "to improve the condition of their brethren generally," giving as examples that they had a church, a library, and "several schools" of their own. In 1830 a white, though he admitted that the black school which met in the Woolman Society building received public funds, called it an "example of enterprise" on the part of a "few pious and intelligent colored people." In 1831-32 the three African Public School "managers," as they called themselves, were blacks: two of them were laborers, and the third, Henry C. Thompson, was a polisher of shoes and a manufacturer of blacking who at one time had been president of the African Woolman Society.[7] For 1841-43 the three "trustees" of "African Public School No. 1" were appointed, like all other public school trustees, by the Brooklyn Common Council,[8] but they were still all blacks, this being the only clear instance available at any time in nineteenth century New York State of the existence of legally-chosen black trustees for a black public school. These black trustees included a former teacher of the school, George Hogarth, who by this time had become a national official of the African Methodist Episcopal denomination, and Sylvanus Smith, a hog driver who was the father of several bright girls who were to become teachers in black schools.

Both before and after this school moved to the Woolman Society building, public school officials gave the black school public funds. But as often with publicly-supported schools at the time, whether they were run for whites or blacks, the funds were not adequate. In the 1830s the black managers tried to raise the rest of the necessary funds by charging tuition fees of $1 per quarter, as the white trustees had earlier, but one-third of the pupils never paid any tuition at all. The managers also tried to raise funds by holding school exhibitions in the African Church. Patrons bought tickets at 12½ cents to hear the black pupils recite pieces and sing.

A consistent supporter of the black school was the white newspaper, the *Brooklyn Long Island Star*. However, the *Star's* usual view of blacks was disparaging. For example, the *Star* not only printed but also praised a letter which claimed that blacks have "a natural want of intellect." The *Star* opposed giving blacks the equal right to vote. When the new immediate abolitionist movement was coming into prominence in the 1830s, the *Star,* like most New York State newspapers, denounced it as "fanatical" and instead supported the colonizationist movement to send blacks back to Africa. Nevertheless, when the African school held one of its many school exhibitions, the *Star* observed that the exhibition "proved that the colored population were more capable of receiving education than is generally accredited to them" and offered to forward any contributions to the school.[9]

A black who appealed through the *Star* for a larger share of public funds for the black school wrote that if the school had more funds, it could teach many more blacks "who are destitute, and unable to pay." He also threatened that if the African school was forced to close, the African children would attend the white district school, implying that blacks believed that they had a right to attend there if they had no school of their own. "We are aware," he added, "of the disagreeable feeling that is likely to take place, if we were to send our children to the regular district school of this village";[10] he assumed white parents simply did not want their children attending school with blacks. By the early 1840s, the black school was receiving more public funds, and the average attendance had gone up to eighty.

Brooklyn's black public school continued largely under black control until 1843 when Brooklyn, having become a city, reorganized its public schools from the district system into a unified system under an all-white board of education.

While in an ultimate sense, whites, as the overwhelming majority of voters, were always in control of Brooklyn's black public school, in an immediate sense, as far as available evidence indicates, from at least 1827 to 1843 blacks were primarily responsible for administering its finances, for maintaining a building for it, and for selecting its teachers. In no other place in the state are blacks known to have taken a similar degree of responsibility for running a black public school at any time in the first half of the nineteenth century.

From at least 1827 to 1843, this considerably black-controlled school was apparently always a one room school with one teacher. Of the five known teachers of the school, all were males, all blacks. Of the five, four were known to have been involved, either before or while teaching this school, in such black protest activities as the movements to abolish slavery in the South or to secure equal suffrage for blacks in the state.

Of the teachers whose educational level is somewhat known, one, Augustus Washington, had gone through what might be considered the equivalent of one year of college at the abolitionist-supported Oneida Institute; a white letter-writer in the *Star* cited Washington as the kind of colored gentleman you would want—contrary to custom—to have sit with you in your pew at church and at your table at home. A second teacher, George Hogarth, was afterwards described by his black associate, Bishop Daniel Payne, as earnest, intelligent, and having "business tact," but having less educational attainment than "a lad well drilled in a common grammar school." A third, William J. Wilson, in later years when he was still teaching in a black public school in Brooklyn, became a sprightly writer for black newspapers. The white-controlled *Brooklyn Daily Eagle* remarked editorially that Wilson's writing was better than that of Brooklyn white school officials who year after year judged the qualifications of teachers.[11]

Brooklyn's unusual experiment in a large measure of black control evidently produced a school of at least fair quality by the standards of the time. In guiding the school, its black trustees could take into account the special needs of black pupils in a world of unequal opportunity. However, a long-term weakness of this school, as of many black schools at the time, was that it did not reach most of the black children of the community.

By the 1830s New York State blacks had taken the initiative for the education of their children not only in Albany and Brooklyn but also in several other places in the state.

They were encouraged to do so by the new Colored National Convention movement, which held its first conventions in Philadelphia in the years 1830 to 1833 and the next in New York City in 1834. Among the leading New York State black teachers who took part in these conventions were George Hogarth of Brooklyn, James W. C. Pennington of Newtown, Long Island, and Austin Steward of Rochester. The conventions helped to prepare blacks to see their problems on a large scale and to plan and act together for their own benefit.

The Colored National Convention of 1833 regarded the increase in the number of black schools and black churches in the nation as a sign of improvement for blacks. In keeping with this attitude, the convention chose as one of its first major projects to try to establish a college for blacks, in New Haven, Connecticut. The black Reverend Samuel E. Cornish, former editor of the *New York Freedom's Journal,* became the general agent to collect funds for the proposed college, and the white Arthur Tappan, New York City abolitionist merchant, became a major supporter. The project failed largely because of white repugnance to higher education for blacks.

New York State blacks did not take the initiative in the 1830s in any educational projects for New York State that were as ambitious as the New Haven college project, and perhaps because of this, they did not run into such fierce opposition as the New Haven project did. But New York State blacks did increasingly lead in establishing schools for blacks.

In 1830 in Troy, blacks took the initiative in organizing a black school which was evidently private. Parents of the pupils were to pay tuition if they could, but Alexander Thuey, a black carpenter, provided board for the black teacher, and William Rich, a black barber who was to figure in the black convention movement, promised to be responsible for making up to the teacher, a black woman, any deficiency in her salary. A white woman, the wife of the first mayor of Troy, donated fuel and stationery. The school struggled along in this manner until about 1833 when the city corporation, recognizing the need for better facilities for the colored people, bought a lot, moved a building to it, and left it to Rich and Thuey, as a committee, to raise the funds to put the building into condition for the black people to use as both a church and school. Rich and Thuey did so, raising the money from both blacks and whites.

From then on for several years blacks ran their own charity school in this building. They believed, as they resolved at one meeting, that "the colored people of Troy consider it a sacred duty to send their children to school, and pay for the schooling themselves. The moral effect of the school will in a great degree be lost if they depend upon the white people to do it." They stumbled from time to time. Once they chose an unsatisfactory teacher. Moreover, they had continuous trouble finding enough money. To push parents to pay tuition fees if they could, they held public meetings in which they read aloud reports of which parents had paid and which had not. To help those parents genuinely unable to pay, for several years they raised funds among themselves—from meetings, from a black female benevolent society, and from subscriptions. They succeeded well enough so that the American Antislavery Society's national paper claimed that Troy blacks supported churches and schools "in proportion to their numbers and their means" better than whites.[12]

In Rochester, blacks joined with whites in working for the creation of a black school. Thirty-two blacks, supported by local school officials and some others, petitioned the state legislature for a separate black public school explicitly because, when black children attended predominantly white public schools, the white children "despised . . . and completely discouraged them."[13] An Assembly committee supported the proposal, saying, in a devastating statement, that a black scholar attending school with whites "is reproached with his color; he is taunted with his origin; and if permitted to mingle with others in the joyous pastimes of youth, it is of favor, not by right. Thus the law which may declare him free . . . is a dead letter. His energies are confined; his hopes are crushed; his mind is in chains, and he is still a slave."[14] The legislature enacted the necessary law, and in 1832 Rochester established a separate public school for blacks.[15] In Rochester, as in Albany, Brooklyn, Troy, and many other places in the state, blacks and whites were cooperating in creating black schools.

Soon afterward, blacks in Lockport, a booming Erie Canal port near Buffalo, were agitating for both a separate black church and a separate black school. They formed an organization to promote their cause, explaining in a resolution in 1835 that they did so because "the customs of the country do not permit us, neither indeed do we desire, to join in society with those of a different complexion."[16] By 1840 they had raised enough money, with white aid—including a gift of land by a businessman who was a Quaker and president of the local antislavery society—to build themselves a building to be used jointly as a church and school. The Lockport board of education provided a teacher. In Lockport, too, blacks and whites were willingly working together to establish black schools.

The idea of creating separate black schools was very much in the air in the 1830s. The black teacher and minister, James W. C. Pennington of Newtown, proposed that blacks form an education society to encourage the creation of more black schools. "We have many young men and women who have gone through the schools of New York and are abundantly qualified to teach," he argued in the *New York Colored American* of June 2, 1838. "There are also places where the people would make efforts to support teachers if they knew where to look for them. The society would do much by finding those places and by recommending teachers." But so far as available evidence indicates, no such society was formed.

Meanwhile, in New York City, where at the time blacks were a relatively large community of about 14,000 people (7 percent of the population), blacks were taking leadership in black education through the popular device of organizing charity societies. In 1833 with a few of their white friends, they founded the Phoenix Society which was intended to "promote the improvement of the colored people in morals, literature, and the mechanic arts." Of its six major officers, five were black, the president being the black Bishop Christopher Rush of the African Methodist Episcopal Zion Church, and the treasurer being the white godfather of many black and abolitionist projects, the wealthy silk merchant Arthur Tappan.[17] The absence among its officers of current leaders of the New York Manumission Society suggests that the Phoenix Society was aware from its beginning of weaknesses in what the Manumission Society was doing for black education and intended to correct them.

The Manumission Society's schools in New York City did not reach beyond grammar school. Before 1831 neither it nor apparently any other agency in the city provided an academy or high school for blacks. Yet scarcely any blacks could enter the city's white academies or high schools, all of which were private. Many whites even doubted that blacks should study beyond grammar school. In 1831, when blacks, led by the popular black rector Peter Williams, had organized a private high school in New York City for the study of the classics,[18] Editor William L. Stone of the *New York Commercial Advertiser,* a colonizationist, had asked: "What possible good can a classical education yield them? Will we feel any better because the man who waits on our table can read Vergil and Horace?"[19] Peter Williams' classical high school—taught by two whites—was apparently short-lived.

But particularly to meet the growing need for black teachers and preachers, some blacks persisted in asking for another classical high school. In 1833 the Phoenix Society established one. It met in "spacious rooms" in the second story of a building on the corner of Canal and Mercer Streets—this was evidently the same place where Peter Williams' high school had been held, suggesting that the new school was a continuation in some sense of the older one. By December 1833, in an appeal for funds, former editor Sam E. Cornish, now agent of the Phoenix Society, wrote that the society has in operation "a classic school of ten or twelve promising youths."[20]

In addition to the high school, the Phoenix Society conceived a variety of devices to encourage the education of blacks, some of them devices which a primarily black agency might more effectively employ than a white agency like either the Manumission Society or the Public School Society. To encourage a larger number of black children to attend school, the Phoenix Society urged black women to loan children the necessary clothes, but if the children didn't attend school, to take the clothes away from them. To improve the general intellectual climate for blacks, they planned a lecture series, circulating libraries in each ward, and the encouragement of "mental feasts"—that is, social occasions at which blacks read and discussed literary papers of their own composition. To stimulate black youths to secure an education, they planned to help young mechanics find work, "giving a preference to those who have learned to read, write, and cypher."[21] In 1833 the Colored National Convention endorsed the Phoenix Society as a model for other societies to follow in promoting the education of blacks.

But the need for funds proved a chronic problem for the Phoenix Society. In 1836 David Ruggles, a grocer and protector of fugitive slaves in New York City, wrote to the upstate wealthy abolitionist, Gerrit Smith, asking help for the society. We are trying "to initiate on a more permanent basis a school for the education of our children in the classic mathematics and higher department of English," Ruggles wrote. "But, sir, you are aware that we [blacks] are surrounded by difficulites, hampered by disabilities, doomed to struggle. We are cut off from those occupations that secure wealth. . . . Our generous and philanthropic friends the abo-

litionists are everywhere so encumbered by their subscriptions and dona-
tions for the societies for . . . complete emancipation . . . that we have
delicacy in soliciting their aid for a subordinate project."[22]

Soon afterward, the school, now called the Phoenix High School
for Colored Youth, had two teachers, one being the principal, a young
white who had studied at Yale and Amherst Colleges. The fact that both
the high school organized especially by the Reverend Peter Williams in
1831 and this one organized by the Phoenix Society, though both primarily
black-organized, employed whites as their major teachers suggests either
that blacks believed that white teachers were desirable to give these high
schools prestige, or that black teachers with sufficiently high teaching
qualifications were not available.

By the spring of 1837, the high school was barely surviving. Its
male department was "suspended" for the present, only the female department continuing.[23] In a few months the society had to abandon all its
school rooms for lack of the $300 necessary to pay the rent, and for a time
even the female department, which consisted of "thirty-five or more
young misses," was closed, in what the *Colored American* of July 1,
1837, called a "grievous calamity." Afterward, the female department
briefly revived in new, presumably cheaper rooms in the basement of an
interracial church, the Presbyterian Broadway Tabernacle, and then
again melted away.

But some New York City blacks persisted in wanting a black high
school. In 1839 they organized another one, called the New York Select
Academy. It offered such advanced subjects as geometry, natural philos-
ophy, botany, ancient and modern languages, and bookkeeping. Unlike
the Phoenix Society, its trustees whose race can be identified were all
black; at least two of them had been trustees of the Phoenix Society. The
academy met first in the basement of the black St. Philip's Episcopal
Church, later apparently in the same place in which the Phoenix High
School had recently met, the basement of the Broadway Tabernacle. The
trustees contributed the cost of the rent, but they charged tuition to meet
the other costs.[24] Unlike the high schools organized by the Reverend Williams and the Phoenix Society, the two known principals of this academy
were both blacks—Thomas S. Sidney, who had attended Oneida Institute, and "Dr." John Brown, who had unofficially attended the New
York College of Physicians and Surgeons.

Regardless of its having black teachers, the New York Select
Academy, like the previous high schools, did not attract enough students
or funds to survive long. After it had been open five months, the *Colored
American* mourned that the patronage was not enough to give even a

scanty salary to its two teachers. This high school, too, soon disappeared.

In their effort to take educational initiatives, blacks repeatedly faced a severe lack of funds. This problem derived in considerable part, as Ruggles had said, from blacks being shut out from lucrative jobs because they were black. It also derived, some black leaders claimed, from blacks misusing what money they had. It was criminal that blacks did not better support their own best institutions, the much-respected black New York City pastor, Theodore S. Wright, cried out in the *Colored American* on October 5, 1839. "Our schools dwindle and die, our churches are crippled and drag . . . and our learned men are driven from the country for want of our contributions, while our porterhouses, gaming tables, and theatres receive from our pockets their tens of thousands. . . . What are we waiting for? Do we expect or wish our white brethren to drag us from our poverty, ignorance, and degradation . . . without effort . . . on our part?"

Blacks seemed to run up against a lack of funds, especially in trying to establish high schools. Blacks themselves had tried three times to establish such schools in New York City and once also in nearby Jamaica, Long Island, as well; and the white abolitionist Gerrit Smith had also tried similarly in his manual labor school upstate in Peterboro. The continued failure of such black high schools to last very long suggests that founding black schools on the secondary level was unrealistic for the times. It was only on the level of elementary education that many black parents, as well as much of the white public, could see clear enough advantages in educating blacks to be willing to find the necessary funds.

In 1840 at the opening of a decade in which New York State blacks were to move farther than ever before toward establishing separate black schools, blacks held a state civil rights convention—the first time, they believed, that blacks in any state had done so. Of the six convention officers, three already had been, or were soon to be, teachers of black schools: the president, Austin Steward of Rochester, and two of the secretaries, Henry Highland Garnet of Troy and Charles L. Reason of New York. The convention issued an address which boasted—with exaggeration —of black educational progress: "A spirit of intelligence pervades our entire people," it said. "There are but few families in which books are not a common and necessary commodity." The address also boasted of black support for black separate schools, both public and private: "Although to a considerable extent, we have been excluded from the advantages of the common school system; yet we have been enabled, not only to sustain

Jermain W. Loguen, a black minister who taught black schools in Utica, Syracuse, and Bath. *Loguen,* Reverend J. W. Loguen as a Slave, *1859.*

them [common schools] among ourselves, but likewise in many instances, select [private] schools of our own."[25]

About this time a fugitive slave, James Wesley Loguen, was creating private black schools in upstate New York. His experience illustrates that of many individual black teachers who established small, private black schools of their own, especially before black public schools became numerous.

Born a slave in Tennessee, Loguen had run away to Hamilton, in Upper Canada, where he supported himself by farm work, and at the same time, learned to read in Sunday schools. Later, Loguen worked in Rochester as a hotel porter, and being attentive to guests, he made considerable money, which he methodically saved. When he met a black student from the abolitionist-supported Oneida Institute, who was teaching in Rochester during his vacation, Loguen determined to use his savings to improve himself by attending Oneida Institute. During the winter vacation of his third year at Oneida Institute, probably 1840, Loguen taught school—the winter vacations were three months long, and it was the custom for older students to employ these months in teaching. Loguen started a school for blacks in Utica.

Utica was a center of abolitionism. It was not only close to Oneida Institute, which at the time was the only higher institution in the state where black students were received as the equals of whites, but also Utica itself was the seat of the state antislavery society. This meant, Loguen found, that Utica attracted "an intelligent and spirited colored population." Yet he also found that, while Utica's blacks were taxed to support the common schools, black children were "excluded" from them —presumably he meant more by custom than by law. Loguen offered to teach the black children in a private school, and the principal black families encouraged him to do so. He hired a room. The first day only three scholars came, but soon there were forty. They learned rapidly, Loguen said. At the end of the term, the school held a public exhibition in a large hall. The children prepared pieces to recite and compositions to read "and presented themselves" on the stage, Loguen said, "in all the pride of juvenile humanity" before a mixed back and white audience. The exhibition was a rousing success. Speakers thanked Loguen for his good work, and he "now began to feel," he wrote, "the delight of living for use—the only real delight God allows to man."

In 1841 Loguen moved to Syracuse where he found the needs of the black people even greater than in Utica. By this time licensed as a minister, he preached in a black Methodist church. He reported that the minds of his congregation "were on the lowest natural plane." Loguen was discovering that the educational progress of blacks was less than the colored state convention had claimed. The blacks of Syracuse, he said, "deprived of social and mental culture . . . formed a . . . girdle of moral and intellectual darkness about the city." He started a school for black children, teaching them on the most elementary level to read, write, and cypher.

Loguen had some encouragement from Syracuse whites. For instance, the Presbyterian pastor, who was silent on slavery, nevertheless offered to take Loguen into his household and help launch him in his work for blacks. But Loguen declined. Having temperate, steady habits, he had continued to save his money. Now he drew his money from a bank, bought a house for his family, and proudly remained for much of his life a tax-paying citizen of Syracuse. He did, however, use the building of the Congregational Church—which had recently been formed by anti-slavery members seceding from the Presbyterian church to protest its neutrality on slavery—for an exhibition of the work of his school. As in Utica, both whites and blacks attended the exhibition, and they encouraged Loguen in his teaching.

However, other Syracuse whites hampered Loguen. Because the room he was using for a school had become too small, he set about building a school house. By the time he had the building up, whites in the neighborhood were so upset that a black school was coming there that he was obliged to move it. He dragged it with oxen to a less offensive site, near a factory.[26] Even separate elementary education for blacks by no means always had the practical encouragement of whites, whether upstate or downstate.

In 1846 a group of New York City blacks began the most ambitious educational enterprise yet undertaken by blacks in the state. At that time, public opinion was gradually changing from the idea that charity societies, such as the Public School Society, should operate charity schools for the poor to the idea that local government should operate public schools for all children, rich and poor. Now that New York City had a board of education, created in 1842, which already operated a few public schools, it was being charged that the reason for the existence of the Public School Society was disappearing. Particularly Catholics, whose power was rising with the increase in Irish immigration, argued that despite its name, the Public School Society was really a private corporation and Protestant, and it should no longer receive public funds to support its charity schools unless Catholics received comparable public funds for Catholic schools. During this controversy, while the number of pupils attending the board of education's public schools went up, the number attending the Public School Society's charity schools went down, its expenses per pupil increased, and it tended to neglect its black schools.

In this situation, black leaders—who had never become completely trusting of the Public School Society's management of its black schools anyway—organized a charity society of their own, the Society for the Promotion of Education among Colored Children, to run black charity schools. Among those who took leadership in bringing the new society into being, at some risk to their careers, were two well-known teachers in the Public School Society's black schools, John Peterson and Charles L. Reason.

While the members of this new society, like those of the similar Phoenix Society, included both blacks and whites, unlike the Phoenix Society all the trustees of this new society were required by its charter to be black. The original trustees included at least two porters, three clergymen, four skilled workers (one tinman, one cooper, and two barbers), and six businessmen. Among these trustees were leaders in the New York State colored convention movement, in the immediate abolitionist movement, and in newspaper publishing for blacks. A number had been active in the now defunct Phoenix Society.

While the treasurer of the Phoenix Society had been white, the treasurer of this new society was the black Dr. James McCune Smith. Because whites often distrusted blacks' ability to handle money—Lewis Tappan wrote that "almost every colored man I have ever known is loose about money matters"[27]—the treasurer was a key figure in the ability of the new society to work with the white school authorities. Dr. Smith, though only in his thirties, had aleady helped to edit two black newspapers and to lead blacks in their drive for the equal right to vote in the state. He was known for his independence and responsibility. He was an excellent choice for treasurer.

Dr. Smith had a sober perspective on what schools in his city could accomplish for blacks. The present generation of black adults are "badly educated," Dr. Smith wrote privately to his white abolitionist friend, Gerrit Smith. Black children needed to be "better and more thoroughly taught than their parents were," he said. But there was only "faint" hope that the children would show significant progress because they had such poor models to follow in the black adults of the city. Black adults are rushing to their political, moral, and social death, he declared. They are given to wasteful celebrations, and to drink in "splendid rum palaces," but can't find money for improvements; "they have stabbed freedom to the heart." Seriously improving the education of blacks was a work "of centuries," Dr. Smith believed, but meantime he promised to "fling whatever energy I have into the cause of colored children."[28]

At about this time, according to the state colored convention, there was not one high school in New York City which blacks could enter. To provide one, in 1847 the Society for Education among Colored Children established a black high school such as New York City blacks had already established three times in the 1830s without lasting success. There was at the time only one other black high school known to exist in the whole of the North, in Cincinnati. But the quality of both the New York

James McCune Smith, M.D., of New York City, was a leading black activist and
intellectual before the Civil War. He promoted black schools and helped to administer them at the same time that he struggled to open white schools to blacks.
New York Public Library Picture Collection.

and Cincinnati high schools was questionable. Said a committee of the
colored national convention in 1847: Neither of these two high schools
for blacks "will compare favorably with the ordinary high schools established among the whites." The New York City high school was abandoned in 1848, like the others that preceded it, the reason being, the society explained, lack of funds.[29] Again an attempt at a black high school
had failed, as indeed such attempts would continue to fail in New York
State through the nineteenth century and even as late as the 1910s.

    The Society for Education among Colored Children received no
public funds for its high school, but it did for its elementary schools. The

society's charter provided that the society could operate elementary schools for blacks under the supervision of the New York City Board of Education. It could charge tuition fees, but children unable to pay were to be educated free. The society was to receive public funds for its elementary schools in the same way that other charity societies, such as the Public School Society, did, in accordance with its number of pupils.

By 1848 the Society for Education among Colored Children was operating two elementary schools for blacks—one on Center Street in the basement of the black St. Phillips Church, where black-run schools had often been held before; the other on Thomas Street. All, or nearly all, of the teachers the society appointed were black—among them the much respected Charles L. Reason—as were most of the teachers in the other black schools in the city at the time. In 1848 the number of pupils enrolled in the new society's schools was 652, and the number went up each year until in 1852 it reached 975.

The city's black elementary schools which were being supported by public money were now being administered by four different agencies, three of them under white control (the board of education, Public School Society, and Colored Orphan Asylum trustees) and one under black control (the Society for Education among Colored Children). Not surprisingly, the New York City Superintendent of Schools complained that "rather conflicting organizations" ran the black schools and proposed that, for efficiency, one organization should run them all.[30]

The Society for Education among Colored Children believed that it at least should administer more of the schools than it did. In 1848 it applied to the Public School Society for the transfer of one of its black schools to the new society. The Public School Society was willing to consider going further: in 1850 it appointed a committee to consider transferring all its black schools to the Society for Education among Colored Children. The Public School Society reported later, however, that the transfer "on consultation, appearing somewhat premature, the subject was dropped for the present." But the society hoped, it said publicly, that the transfer would eventually be made. "The time, it is to be hoped, is not far distant," it explained, "when this portion of our population will be able to attend to their own educational wants; and, perhaps, the sooner the burthen or duty is laid upon them, the sooner they will be able to meet its requirements."[31]

Meanwhile, Protestant-Catholic conflict over the securing of public funds for non-public schools encouraged the trend to public schools as a way to avoid the conflict. In 1853 the New York City Board of Education finally absorbed all the Public School Society's schools, both black and white, and the Public School Society ceased to exist. At about the same time, the board of education in effect also absorbed the two schools of the Society for Education among Colored Children. In the case of the Public School Society's black schools, the board of education retained many of the black teachers; in the case of the Society for Education among Colored Children's schools, the board retained only a few of the black teachers. Anyway, with the demise of the Public School Society, the need for a black-controlled society to run its own black schools to compensate for the weakness of the Public School Society had gone.

During the five years it operated black schools, the Society for Education among Colored Children enrolled more black children in its schools than any other black-controlled organization in the state up to 1900. During this time, the society won the respect of the city and state school officials enough for them to continue to grant it public funds. It won the respect of black parents enough for its enrollment to increase steadily. It won the respect of the Public School Society enough for it at least to negotiate on the possibility of turning over all of its black schools to the black society. Altogether this was quite an achievement for a black society in the mid-nineteenth century.

In the state as a whole, according to the information available, at various times in the period from the 1800s to the 1850s, the eight known black-organized charity societies (in New York, Williamsburg, Troy, and Albany) taught at most at any time in each of their known schools a total of about 1450 pupils. In addition in the same period, at a conservative estimate, perhaps 900 more pupils were taught in the state in the two known black-organized church weekday schools (in Brooklyn and New York) and the thirty known black-organized private schools. Thus, the black-organized charity, church, and private schools together taught about the same number of black pupils as the white-organized abolitionist schools, but less than the white-organized charity schools.

In the rest of the nineteenth century, blacks continued to establish schools of their own—including several private schools and a notable black orphanage in Brooklyn which had its own school—but because of the growing availability of public schools to blacks, blacks did so on a reduced scale. In terms of size, in the whole nineteenth century, the contribution of the black-organized schools, of all types, was modest, as this comparison suggests: there were only 142 teachers known by name in black-organized schools for blacks, but 703 in white-organized schools for blacks (see Table 11 in Appendix). Nevertheless, from 1800 into the 1850s the achievement of blacks in helping to promote black education was impressive considering that it was only during this period that all blacks became free in the state and considering the formidable impediments they met, such as their relative poverty and inexperience, the lingering resistance of some whites to significant education for blacks, and the preference of many blacks for immediate pleasure rather than the dubious long-range struggle to improve their lives through education.

Though blacks were sometimes reluctant to rely on white help, in their promotion of black education blacks were often forced to depend on whites in some degree. The blacks' relative lack not only of wealth but also of education and experience, usually forced them to it, as they themselves recognized. In 1828 a black New York City paper said that, in promoting schools, blacks must work with whites: "The colored population of the Northern and Middle States, as a body," it explained, "have not the ability to accomplish anything of consequence of themselves." Even as late as 1846, the black New York City physician, James McCune Smith, admitted that blacks alone were too weak to insist on the creation of black schools wherever in the state they were needed, but with their white friends, he believed they might succeed,[32] as indeed they often did.

New York State's black leaders, far from being passive about black interests, as the stereotype has often described nineteenth century blacks to have been, played a significant educational role. In these years when belief in universal education was only beginning to take hold in the state, blacks struggled to persuade whites to recognize black educational interests. Blacks pointed out where black schools were needed. They offered the use of buildings of their own. They appealed for public or private funds. When they perceived it to be necessary or desirable, they themselves established black schools and sometimes took considerable responsibility for financing them. While some of the black-run schools failed, blacks often kept them going long enough to prove to openminded whites that there were black pupils who really wanted schooling and were capable of learning. Some of the black-established schools provided education for blacks who otherwise might not have attended school at all. Others provided respectable alternatives to existing white-run black schools. Still others prepared the way for black public schools.

PUBLIC RESPONSIBILITY

$\mathbb{P}$UBLIC EDUCATION WAS LATE in developing in New York State compared to New England. The early population of New England was overwhelmingly English and Puritan, making it possible to create a consensus on what education should be. By contrast, in New York State from colonial times, the population varied ethnically and religiously so that there could be little agreement on what education should be.

It was only in the 1790s that New York State began to encourage public education by offering to give matching grants to towns for public schools. Even after that, public schools were often considered to be intended for the poor, so that proud parents, both blacks and whites, avoided them as demeaning. However, in the 1820s when the state gave the vote to all white males, it gave impetus to the argument that public education was necessary to prepare men to vote. In the next decades, as faith in democracy grew, the working classes increasingly turned to public schools as a means of increasing their opportunities, and the upper classes, gradually recognizing the limitations of charity and Sunday schools, looked to public schools to stabilize society by drawing together children of varied religious, national, and class backgrounds.

There was no state law in the 1790s, nor for some time after, which either required or forbade blacks to be admitted to public schools. Black attendance was simply a practice which developed in some places where whites tolerated it and did not develop elsewhere because whites were prejudiced and blacks were indifferent or afraid.

In the early 1800s what gradually emerged in most of the state as the usual public school was a "district school," that is, a one-room school serving a small neighborhood and governed by trustees elected by the voters of that neighborhood. The district school system was best suited to rural regions, as nearly all of New York State was when the system arose, and in rural regions it survived with little change into the twentieth century. In cities, by the 1840s or 1850s, as public schools became popular, the district system was often transformed into a city-wide system, under a board of education.

Since taxpayers constantly attacked public schools, the school trustees might be more concerned with running the schools cheaply than offering substantial education. The trustees might keep the schools open only for the minimum period required to receive state aid, which in the 1830s was three months. They might be tempted to hire as teachers those who were willing to work for the least wages. To cut costs, rural trustees often arranged for the teachers to take turns living with the families of the children they taught, a custom likely to cause trouble when white teachers were supposed to live in black families. Black children may be kept out of school, a Dutchess County school commissioner reported euphemistically in 1845, because their parents "have no room in their scanty apartments for the teacher who is required to board round."[1]

Public schools were normally financed by a combination of three means: property taxes on the residents of the district, state aid on the basis of the number of pupils, and tuition payments by the pupils. If pupils were not able to pay tuition—as black pupils were often not—they could be admitted free as "charity scholars." But trustees could be stingy in admitting charity scholars, and the poor could be too proud to accept such charity; doing so was usually regarded as degrading, thus preventing some poor children, black and white, from attending school at all. Compulsory attendance was not enacted by the state until 1874 and even then for many years was not generally enforced.

The right of blacks to attend public schools became only gradually established. In 1824 the state superintendent of schools wrote that although there is no legal impediment to the admission of black children into the public schools, "yet it is believed that from habit or prejudice, or from some other cause," few blacks attend public schools; he stopped short of saying that blacks had a legal right to attend. In 1827 a state law specifying the qualifications required for voting in school district meetings said nothing about race;[2] at least it could be interpreted to imply that blacks had the right to send their children to the public schools the same as anyone else. In 1841 a general state education law provided that the public schools were open to "all" children of school age. Meanwhile the state superintendent of schools in his judicial rulings was at last making explicit the right of blacks to attend public schools. He did so in 1841 in a case arising in Rochester; he did so again in 1847 in his officially-published interpretation of the education law, saying: "Colored children are entitled equally with all others to the privileges and advantages of the district schools."[3] This remained the basic state education policy into the twentieth century.

When blacks attended public schools with whites, sometimes they got along satisfactorily together. Members of the Albany school board recalled in 1872 that in their own childhood they had attended Albany County district schools with blacks, and "recited with them in the same class and under the same teacher, with none to gainsay or remonstrate."[4]

But many reports about the presence of blacks in predominantly white public schools were not so favorable. As we have seen, a state Assembly committee on education reported in 1832 that the black pupil in racially-mixed schools is "reproached with his color, he is taunted with his origin." In 1845 a Dutchess County school commissioner said that black children in district schools are subject to "almost constant petty annoyances." In 1846 a white New York City cartman said that for white and black children to attend the common schools together forced "the children of the poor into companionship against which the soul of every pure minded man revolts, as his stomach would against a dish of carrion." In Kinderhook in 1858, according to a local newspaper, so many white parents threatened to take their children out of the district school because blacks attended it that the school was likely to break up altogether.[5] In the 1860s a Queens County school commissioner said, "colored children are found in a majority of the district schools," but "are not much" to the schools' "advantage, as they prevent many [white] people from sending their children to these schools." At about the same time in a district school in Genesee County, a black boy, though he was not a behavior problem himself, became such a "laughing stock" that the teacher could not keep order and the trustees dismissed him from the school. The upstate black activist Austin Steward, who had himself taught separate black schools, wrote in the 1850s that there was so much prejudice against blacks in racially-mixed schools, "that the poor, timid colored children might about as well stay home as go to school where they feel that they are looked upon as inferior."[6]

Even in the racially-mixed schools, seating was sometimes segregated, and at times this caused humiliation to blacks. A black Connecticut pastor, just after having traveled in New York State in the 1830s, said of the North at large that a way for teachers to control white children was to threaten them "with being made to sit with the niggers." In a revealing incident in Westchester County near Peekskill in 1872, a teacher punished a white boy by requiring him to sit with a black child, which seemed such a terrible punishment to the white boy that he absolutely refused to sit there.[7] The effect of this incident on both the children could have been scarring.

Under these circumstances, it is not surprising that black parents, white parents, and white school officials often asked for separate public schools.

As early as 1824 the state superintendent of schools recommended the creation of separate public schools for blacks. Beginning in 1841 New York State enacted general laws permitting local school authorities to create separate black schools.[8] However, while Pennsylvania and Ohio required a separate black school in any locality where there were more than twenty black pupils, New York State, like Massachusetts, never required separate schools under any circumstances.

In 1845 the state superintendent of schools estimated that there were 11,000 black children in the state of school age, that is, five through fifteen. Of these, the proportion attending regular district schools with whites was "extremely limited," he said, and not over one quarter attended separate black schools, leaving many who attended no school at all. He urged the creation of more separate black schools, saying they would benefit both black and white children.[9]

At least until the 1840s, the majority in the state who favored black education at all seemed to agree that separate black schools were desirable wherever there were enough black children to make them practical —the majority seemed to agree, black and white, abolitionists and colonizationists, school officers and parents, even though some of them regretted the necessity of separate schools. The Buffalo superintendent of schools declared that blacks needed separate schools because blacks "require greater patience on the part of the teacher, longer training and severer discipline than are called into exercise in the district schools; and generations must elapse before they will possess the vigor of intellect, the power of memory and judgement, that are so early developed in the Anglo-Saxon race." On Long Island, a white newspaper was pleased that the blacks who attended Jamaica's recently-established black public school were "totally different" in "appearance and attainments" from the street blacks; Jamaica's "street denizens" are a "shiftless set" who should learn that whites, by providing a black public school, have opened up for them "the way to elevation." One of the state's major black abolitionists, Dr. James McCune Smith, called for more black public schools. When he found in 1846 that, of the first seventeen blacks in Westchester County to receive grants of land from philanthropist Gerrit Smith for set-

Colored Public School, Williamsburg, Long Island, about 1855. *Armbruster, Eastern District, 1912.*

tlement in Northern New York, only one could sign his name, he wrote Gerrit Smith: If in the next ten years there are as few black schools in rural areas as there are now, no matter how much progress blacks make in acquiring land, we will still continue to "form a lower grade in the classes of mind which make up our state."[10]

Gradually black public schools, operated by regular school districts, spread over the state, existing at various times from the 1810s to the 1940s in at least twenty-four different counties, in forty-three different cities, towns, or villages.

As we have seen, black public schools often came into existence through black initiative. In some places blacks, with the encouragement of whites, petitioned school officials to create black schools, as they did in Rochester, Lockport, and Buffalo. In many places blacks cooperated with public school officials by allowing their church buildings to be used at least for a time for black schools, as they did in Auburn and Haverstraw.

The Colored Public School of Geneva, New York, occupied this building from 1853, when the building was built, to 1873, when the colored school was abolished. *Courtesy of The New-York Historical Society, New York City.*

Sometimes, as far as available evidence indicates, black public schools came into existence primarily through white initiative. In Catskill the school was created when the white teacher of a district school insisted that both his black and white pupils would be better served if they were separated. In Newburgh the initiative was taken by a philanthropic white lawyer, working with the local school trustees.[11]

Sometimes previously existing black schools seemed to prepare the way for black public schools, showing the public that blacks could usefully learn and could do so in separate schools. For example, Sunday schools for blacks seemed to prepare the way in Geneva and Rochester, private schools for blacks in Hillburn and Utica, and black-organized charity schools for blacks in Williamsburg and Troy. In the Long Island communities of Amityville, Huntington, and Jerusalem, the black public schools evolved directly from black schools established by a Quaker society; even for several years after these schools had become public, the Quaker society continued to donate funds to heat the buildings, pay the teachers, and shoe the pupils. The state superintendent of schools admitted in 1847 that because black parents were often too poor to pay the usual tuition fees, rural colored public schools can seldom be adequately funded "but through the efforts of charitable and benevolent individuals."[12]

In other places, especially larger ones, black public schools evolved directly from existing white-organized charity schools for blacks.

In Poughkeepsie, the Lancaster School Society opposed having its charity schools, both black and white, replaced by public schools. When, nevertheless, Poughkeepsie citizens finally voted in 1843 to create a new, unified public school system for the whole village, the Lancaster School Society thereby lost its public funds and abruptly closed its black school. The society simply "turned the children into the street," a Poughkeepsie newspaper charged.[13] To set up a new black public school, the new board of education chose a sympathetic, three-man committee, two of its members being active abolitionists. But it wasn't until a year later that the committee had acquired the necessary funds to rent a room and open the school.

In Schenectady the transition from the Lancaster society's black school to a public black school was smoother. The Schenectady Lancaster school trustees, unlike those in Poughkeepsie, favored the creation of public schools to take the place of their charity schools. In 1854, when Schenectady's public schools came into existence, two members of the Lancaster school trustees became members of the new public board of education. The new board promptly repaired a building for a black school, and the black children continued to have a separate school to attend without interruption.[14]

New York City by the late 1840s already had two small public schools for blacks, located in suburban Yorkville and Harlem. But in 1853, when the white-organized Public School Society turned over its many charity schools, both those for blacks and those for whites, to the board of education, there were soon nine black public schools scattered about Manhattan. As in Poughkeepsie and Schenectady, there was no significant argument about whether the black schools ought to be continued as separate schools—it was simply accepted as inevitable. As in Schenectady, the transition was smooth, without interruption of school sessions to the children.

In many places, as black charity schools were transformed into black public schools, blacks and their friends hoped that the quality of the schools would improve. The change sometimes meant a shift from the use of Lancasterian-style pupil-monitors to the use of older and better qualified assistant teachers. It also sometimes meant a change to more financial stability, with more adequate tax support.

Like white public schools, black public schools gradually moved toward becoming tuition-free. When black charity schools were transformed into black public schools, the schools usually became free if they had not been entirely so before. Elsewhere when the black public schools had been part of the district school systems, the black pupils, like other pupils, had been expected to pay tuition fees; however, when the schools were reorganized under a unified board of education system, as in Rochester in 1841, Brooklyn in 1843, Newburgh in 1852, and Jamaica in 1853, all the public schools became free. In more rural places, children in public schools were sometimes still expected to pay tuition fees in the early 1860s, as in the black public schools in Huntington, Long Island, and Fishkill Landing, on the Hudson River. In 1867, however, the state ceased to permit tuition fees. Meanwhile, a slow trend was developing to provide pupils with free textbooks. Poor children—both black and white—were finding it easier to attend school.

Once a black public school existed, school officials usually required all the black children living in the district to attend that school. The desire to keep black schools large enough to keep their cost per pupil in control would be likely to prompt such a requirement, if nothing else. But in some places at some times such requirements were only half-heartedly enforced. For instance, in Albany, Buffalo, and Brooklyn in the 1850s, if a black pupil lived far from the black school, or was regarded as especially bright, or his color was almost white, school officials might allow him to attend white schools. Such exceptions sometimes caused tensions. Blacks pushed to extend such exceptions, and whites pushed to close them off. But everywhere up to at least the 1870s, and in many places long after that, officials were likely to maintain that they had a right, if they wished, to require all black pupils to attend black schools.

By 1855 most of the non-public weekday black schools of the state—whether abolitionist, charity, church, or private—had been closed or transformed into public schools. At that time state school officials, using statistics which were admittedly not accurate, reported that there were 5,243 pupils in black public schools in the state, most of them in New York City.[15]

Unfortunately, after 1855 state education reports do not give the numbers of children in black public schools, but they do give the expenditures for such schools. From those reports it is probable that the numbers of children in black public schools rose only slightly from 1855 into the early 1870s. Expenditures for black public schools hit their peak year in 1874, and then, as the movement to abolish black public schools gained momentum, gradually declined.

During the nineteenth century, school officials appointed as teachers in the black public schools mostly blacks (69%) and females (also 69%). However, the proportion varied sharply by region. The highest proportion of blacks among the teachers was downstate (97 percent in Manhattan), where the black population was heavy, while in the Hudson region the proportion was 55 percent black, and in the central and western part of the state was only 23 percent black. Similarly, the highest proportion of females was downstate, and the lowest proportion was in the central and western parts of the state. In Manhattan, Brooklyn, and Flushing, a pattern was to appoint blacks not only as regular teachers but also as principals. In Troy a pattern was to appoint a white male principal with one black female assistant teacher. In the latter part of the century, in the one-room black schools of Hempstead, Roslyn, and Lockport, a pattern was to appoint poorly paid, inexperienced young women, whether black or white, some of them just out of high school.

Was there a tendency for the salaries of the teachers in the black schools to be less than the salaries of the teachers of the white schools in the same school systems? Meaningful comparison is difficult because, though schools often did not have clear policies, they seemed to allow salaries to vary by such factors as the teacher's sex, race, experience, educational level, and number of pupils. In Albany and New York in certain years about the middle of the century for which salary schedules are available, there seemed to be a pattern of lower salaries for teachers in the black schools than in the white schools, while at the same time in Brooklyn there seemed to be a pattern of equal salaries. By the 1870s there was a pattern of equal salaries in New York City too. In the state at large, there were regional variations. Using the limited records available from 1840 to 1917 to compare three different regions, four towns on Long Island (including Roslyn and Hempstead) together had the worst record, giving most of the teachers in their black schools the lowest salary of any of their

"Kept In." Artist Henry, a Carolina-born white, was known for his story-telling subjects. He usually painted downstate in Manhattan or upstate in the artists' colony of Cragsmoor, in Ellenville, Ulster County. *New York State Historical Association.* Painting by Edward L. Henry, 1888.

teachers. Five places in the Hudson region (including Troy and New Rochelle) together had only a slightly better record, giving nearly half of the teachers in their black schools the lowest salary. Two western places (Lockport and Buffalo), where most of the teachers were whites, had the best record, giving nearly all of the teachers in their black schools for whom such information is available, better salaries than at least one other teacher.

Neither blacks nor their white allies made a great issue about discrimination in salaries in the black public schools. One reason probably was that since salaries depended on many variables, discrimination was

difficult to prove. Another was that in fact, in terms of the easily measured annual expenditure per pupil, school officials usually did well by
their black schools. This happened in part because black schools compared to white schools tended to be small—and they were somewhat small
even in the largest cities like Brooklyn and New York because the black
population was considerably scattered. The smaller size of black schools
produced a higher proportion of teachers to students in black than in
white schools. This helped to bring it about that public school officials in
New York State, unlike those in the South, spent more per pupil on their
black schools than on their white schools.[16]

High costs per pupil of course disturbed taxpayers. High costs
were likely to cause pressure to keep the salaries and building costs in the
black schools down. High costs were also likely to cause pressure to close
black schools altogether, and some did not last very long. That the black
public schools persisted for many decades in some places despite such
high costs attests to the determination of school officials, taxpayers, and
parents to have separate schools.

When school officials were locating black schools, strict separation of the black and white children did not always seem important. In
Lakeville, Queens County, school officials placed two one-room public
school buildings side by side, one for whites, one for blacks. In Fishkill
Landing, officials put the black school in a little annex next to the white
school. To house the black school in Hempstead, officials deliberately
built an addition onto the white school. In fact, the association of whites
and blacks in the same school building was not always in itself regarded as
contaminating even in communities which had separately-organized
black and white schools. It was possible, though not usual, for white and
black schools to occupy different rooms in the same building, as at various times they did in Poughkeepsie, Flushing, Haverstraw, Catskill, and
Brooklyn, while proposals to do the same were turned down in New Rochelle and Roslyn. In Troy it was possible for the school board to have its
offices upstairs in the building which the board built expressly for the
black school and named after a leading local black. Somewhat the reverse
was also possible: in New York City, space in a building recently built by
a black mutual benefit association for its own meetings, a four story
building, was rented during the day for use as a white public school.

Black public schools were placed in an astonishing variety of
buildings. In Roslyn for a time the school met in a former store; in Buffalo, in a tenement. In Hempstead the school was temporarily held—to
the delight of the children but not the teacher, one can imagine—in a fire
station. In Kinderhook, when the teacher was a young white lady, she

simply taught the school in her father's house. In suburban Harlem about 1860, a private dwelling fitted up with the "best approved style of seats" became a popular school.[17] Black schools often met in association with churches, as in the basement of a black church in Schenectady, the basement of a white church in Troy, and in an old building behind a black church in Poughkeepsie. Black schools were held where noise could regularly be disturbing, as on the second floor over a factory in Hempstead, under a market in Buffalo, and in the wing of a market in Troy.

To offset the high cost per pupil in the black public schools, if for no other reason, school officials were sometimes negligent about black school buildings, including their facilities and locations. It was not unusual for both blacks and whites to complain about black school buildings —they complained more about buildings than teachers' salaries. A black teacher in Flushing protested that his building, which was forty-six years old, "let in as much fresh air as chose to enter without invitation."[18] A black teacher in New Rochelle said that the building the board hired for his school was unsuitable, and when a committee of the board investigated, it decided that the building was so dilapidated that it was not worth repairing. A white newspaper in Kinderhook reported in 1859 that the local black school was temporarily closed for lack of funds for fuel and insisted that black scholars had as much claim to heat as white scholars. A taxpayer in Hudson complained that the local black school was located not only near hogpens and stables which drained onto the school yard, but also in "the worst neighborhood in the city" where for a person just to be seen "would cause the finger of suspicion to be pointed" at him; the neighborhood tends, the taxpayer added, "to counteract all the efforts of the teacher."[19] *Frederick Douglass' Paper* charged on March 9, 1855, that the New York City school board, "with the course usual in such cases all over the country," have built many "palatial schools for white children" but "have not erected a single school house for colored children: old buildings, dwelling houses altered into cramped-up school houses, basements, and rear buildings are good enough for colored children." Similarly, the *New York Tribune* of March 8, 1859, complained that in New York City, while schools for whites are in good locations and are "commodious and elegant," because of prejudice the black schools "are nearly all, if not all, old buildings, generally in filthy and degraded neighborhoods, dark, damp, small, and cheerless, safe neither for the morals nor the health" of the children.

The state superintendent of schools seemed to be supporting such charges when he pointed out in 1856 that school trustees "have no right to give to colored children teachers or facilities for education in any respect

Kindergarten and first two grades of the Colored Public School of Hillburn, Rockland County. The school, established in 1888, survived as a black school to 1943. *Schomburg Center, New York Public Library.*

inferior to those of the whites." He added that it was unjust for school officials to apportion money to a black school on the basis of the number of black children attending the school, while they apportioned money to white schools on the basis of the number of white children in the district whether they attended school or not.[20]

The general state school law, however, did not specifically require equal support for black schools compared to white schools until the Civil War shook public opinion into more concern for black rights. In 1864 for the first time the state school law provided that the black schools in any district were to be "supported in the same manner and to the same extent as the school or schools supported therein for white children," and that districts must provide to the black schools "facilities for instruction equal to those furnished to the white schools."[21] This equal support principle remained in the general school law into the twentieth century.

Over a long period there seemed to be some improvement in both the salaries and buildings of the black schools. The improvement may have come about in part because of the new equal rights principle in the school law, but probably more because of improvement in the salaries and buildings for all public schools. It also probably came about because some whites were increasingly willing to concede blacks equal rights. This willingness derived from such factors as the decline of the movement to colonize blacks in Africa; the upheaval of the Civil War and Reconstruction, including the federal Constitutional amendment which at last gave blacks in New York State, as elsewhere, the equal right to vote; and the cumulative effect of the long black campaign against separate schools which maneuvered some whites into defending black schools by improving them.

In New York City in the late 1850s in response to complaints, school authorities undertook a large program of constructing, relocating, and improving buildings for black schools. Troy in 1866 built a sturdy two story, brick building for its black school, with plenty of room for the number of pupils to grow. In Brooklyn in 1883, after a black had been appointed to the school board, the board replaced a dilapidated wooden structure with a sturdy brick building. In the 1890s, when Dan Beard, the illustrator and future Boy Scout founder, was chairman of the Flushing school board, Flushing built a new black public school. As the pro-segregationist Mrs. Beard afterward recalled, "For fear the Negroes would say it was a poorer school than the other four schools in the town, it was built especially good—a little better than the others, if anything."[22] The author's study of teachers' salaries in the twenty years following the adoption of the 1864 law requiring equal support indicates surprisingly that teachers in the black public schools in the state had higher average salaries than teachers in all public schools in the state, and furthermore that the *black* teachers of the black schools had higher salaries than the *white* teachers of the black schools. These results are considerably affected by the fact that most teachers in black schools tended to teach in the larger places in the state where the salaries were likely to be higher, and that, in particular, in New York City and Brooklyn where the salaries were especially high, the teachers were virtually all black.

By the 1880s and 1890s, the state's minimum requirement for school sessions was lengthening beyond seven months, the qualifications demanded for teachers were rising, and the opportunities for blacks to educate themselves as teachers were improving. In the black communities of Brooklyn and New York, black teachers were considered well paid and held in high esteem. The black principals Sarah Garnet, Charles Reason, and Charles Dorsey, along with some other black teachers, moved in the most prestigious black circles socially, intellectually, and politically. In an article on the wealthiest blacks in the metropolitan area, the *New York Times* of July 14, 1895, named sixteen blacks, including five who were or had been teachers. Leading blacks claimed that the buildings, salaries, and quality of education of Brooklyn's black public schools were equal to those of Brooklyn's white public schools.

Among the various kinds of black separate schools in nineteenth century New York State, the public schools reached the largest number of children over the years and had the most significant long-term impact. Keeping this in mind, as we turn to black educational issues, we consider especially issues related to black public schools. We consider such issues as who should teach black schools, how the black teachers should be educated, how much freedom the black teachers had, and to what extent blacks achieved control over black education.

MOBBING A TEACHER

IN THE SEVENTEENTH AND EIGHTEENTH CENTURIES in the colony of New York, blacks were not educated to be teachers. The question of whether blacks should teach whites simply did not arise.

In the early nineteenth century, however, with the gradual end of slavery in New York State, as well as elsewhere in the North, and the increasing establishment of separate schools for blacks, blacks were being educated as teachers. In this situation the question of whether they should be allowed to teach whites naturally arose.

In keeping with the general white belief in the inferiority of blacks, the custom became established at this time that blacks were not to teach whites. This was similar to the custom which was also established about the same time that black pastors would not serve white congregations.

However, occasionally there were black teachers who did teach whites, providing exceptions to the general rule that blacks should not teach whites. The story of a few of these teachers who did teach whites helps to explain how the general rule could be bent and what could happen to teachers who flagrantly violated it.

Some black teachers evidently taught whites secretly. The Reverend James W. C. Pennington, who had taught a black school on Long Island, was once invited to teach white children secretly. He reported disdainfully in 1841 that while teaching a colored school he was once "earnestly solicited to go into a white family evenings, and give their children lessons. But O! it would not do to let this be known, nor for those children to go to his school."[1]

Nevertheless, a few black teachers openly taught whites in their black schools. This seemed to happen especially as a matter of convenience for the whites, when the white children lived nearer to a black school than to a white one, and especially when the children were still young. It happened in Brooklyn, in the neighborhood of Weeksville, where the principal of a black public school was Julius C. Morel, the mulatto son of a Carolina slaveholder. In 1851 twelve whites were among the forty children attending his school. By the late 1860s, when Morel was still principal and the only other teacher was white, the school had eighty-nine children, nearly half of whom were white. But when a committee of the Brooklyn school board became aware of what was happening, the committee claimed that it was unhealthy for blacks and whites to have such an "intimate relationship." Even the interest of the black children demanded that they be separated from the white children, the committee said, for black teachers take such pride in having white children to teach that they bestow "special attention on them, to the neglect of colored children." The board directed that the white children be dismissed from the black school on condition that they could be accommodated in the white schools near their homes. However, several years later there were still seventeen whites in this same black school, as well as five whites in another black-taught Brooklyn school intended for blacks.[2]

Another such situation occurred in 1860 in a black public school in Harlem on 120th Street. At that time there were so few black children in Harlem that only about twenty black children attended the school, making it too expensive to maintain for blacks alone. On request, the school trustees gave permission to the black teacher, Mrs. Caroline W. Groves, to open her school to white children if their parents wished to send them. Mrs. Groves, whom a black newspaper called "one of our best colored teachers," was so popular, and her school so pleasantly situated in a private home, that she soon had twice as many white as colored pupils, and had to turn away twenty more whites.[3] In both Brooklyn and Harlem the usual rule that blacks should not teach whites could be bent when white parents desired it.

Blacks could also occasionally teach whites when the subject they taught was music. Whites had long recognized music as a special preserve of blacks. As Washington Irving had indicated in his *Legend of Sleepy Hollow,* which was first published about 1820, it was not strange for Hudson Valley blacks to provide music at white parties and to direct the dancing. It even became acceptable for blacks in New York State, as well as elsewhere in the North, to teach music and dancing to whites; for blacks to do so was regarded as quite different from blacks associating with whites as equals. In the 1850s in Newburgh, a locally-born black musician, Dubois B. Alsdorf, established a private academy where he taught dancing and music, including the guitar, violin, and piano. The academy was intended especially for whites. It was continued by various members of his family for over one hundred years, until the 1950s, a remarkable record for such an enterprise, whether run by blacks or whites.[4] In the 1850s in Rochester, a black musician, who had already taught music in white schools, was teaching singing to an evening class of black adults when he was offered what *Frederick Douglass' Paper* called "a handsome salary on condition that he would not teach 'his own kind of people', but devote all his time to those of a more favored complexion." However, the paper explained, he "refused the offer like a man, and is resolved to do what he can for the elevation of his race."[5]

Whites might tolerate blacks teaching whites in predominantly black schools if white parents were so foolish as to wish to send their children there, and whites might tolerate black musicians teaching music to whites for it was widely recognized that blacks had special talent in music. But for blacks to be appointed to teach a public school intended primarily for whites was another matter. Yet this did happen in the 1830s in Hunter, a town of thinly scattered settlements in the Catskill Mountains.

The trustees of Hunter's school district No. 1 employed a black man to teach their school even though it was attended almost entirely by whites. Why they made this decision available records do not explain. Since many of the community came from New England, where there were few blacks, they may have been less prejudiced against blacks than many other inhabitants of New York State. Maybe, too, the black teacher was willing to come cheap—cost was often a major consideration for school trustees. Or perhaps they had trouble finding teachers who were willing to live in this isolated, rough, mountain settlement where a principal occupation was stripping the bark from hemlocks to use in tanning hides.

In any event, some of the residents of the school district objected to a black man teaching their school. When the trustees nevertheless insisted on keeping him, the residents took their complaint all the way to the state superintendent of schools.

The state superintendent happened to be the wealthy lawyer John A. Dix, a prominent Jacksonian Democrat who was an active colonizationist. In 1833 he made a formal decision in the case. It was legal, he declared, for trustees to appoint black teachers in predominantly white schools. But, as might be expected of a colonizationist, he advised against employing blacks. Whether Americans should or should not make distinctions between blacks and whites, he said, they do so. Blacks "are disqualified by the laws of the United States for the performance of services in the militia, and by the constitution of this state for the exercise of the

As state superintendent of schools in the 1830s John A. Dix administered all the public schools of the state, whether black, white, or mixed. At the time Dix, like many York Staters, was discouraging blacks in their hope to improve themselves in America by urging them to return to Africa. *Courtesy of The New-York Historical Society, New York City.*

right of suffrage, without a qualification of property. Under these circumstances the trustees of school districts, whose duty it is to cultivate a spirit of harmony and good feeling, by carrying into effect as far as is proper the wishes of the inhabitants, should abstain from employing them in the capacity of teachers."

Superintendent Dix suggested what opponents could do if the trustees persisted in keeping a black teacher. They could vote the trustees out of office at the next annual election. Or they could refuse to send their children to the school—school attendance was not compulsory, as he said, and if a number of parents didn't send their children to school, he made clear, it would force up the tuition costs for those who did send their children.[6]

How long the black man stayed on as teacher in Hunter available records do not say. Under the circumstances, it is not likely that he stayed very long.

In the 1850s another black who taught whites in an upstate rural community ran into more serious trouble—he was mobbed. This black teacher, William G. Allen, was light skinned. By ancestry he was only one quarter African, the rest European. But by the illogical American custom, if anyone had any discernible black ancestry, he was considered a black.

Allen was the son of Virginia parents who were too poor to help him get an education. The leading abolitionists Gerrit Smith and Lewis Tappan gave him funds to help him study at the abolitionist-supported, interracial Oneida Institute. After graduating, Allen first joined Henry Highland Garnet in editing a black paper in Troy, then studied law in Boston, and then was appointed to teach language and rhetoric at a predominantly white college. It was an extraordinary act for any white American college to appoint a black to teach at this time or for a long time to come.

The college which dared to appoint Allen was the abolitionist-supported New York Central College, at McGrawville, Cortland County, in the heavily abolitionist central part of the state. The college was non-sectarian, but supported especially by a group of dissident antislavery Baptists. Since the demise of Oneida Institute, Central College had taken its place as the only abolitionist-oriented college in the state. Because the college was often poor, some non-Baptist abolitionists, including Gerrit Smith, contributed funds to keep it alive.

Allen was not the first black to teach at Central College—preceding him was Charles L. Reason, who both before and after taught in the black schools of New York City. In fact, Reason was the first black

New York Central College, McGrawville, Cortland County, about 1860. This abolitionist-supported college was the first predominantly white college in the nation to have black professors. One of them, William G. Allen, caused a scandal by falling in love with a white student. *McGraw Public Library.*

appointed to teach in a predominantly white college in the United States. The circumspect Reason had managed to teach at Central College without incurring spectacular hostility.

However, Professor Allen, while teaching at the college, fell in love with one of his students, Mary E. King. Unfortunately for Allen, she was white.

In 1853 when they decided to be married, Mary's father, Lyndon King, the pastor of a Wesleyan Methodist church near Fulton, Oswego County, gave his consent. It probably made it easier for the pastor to give his consent that the Wesleyan Methodists were an antislavery denomination, and that he was an active abolitionist himself.

However, Mary King's brothers opposed her marrying a black. So did her stepmother. And so, when the engagement became generally known, did the neighbors. Under this pressure, the Reverend King changed his mind. He no longer would approve of a black marrying his daughter. He even forbade Allen to visit his house.

After this interdict, when Allen came to town to see Mary, he was only able to see her at the house of such friends as Mr. and Mrs. John C. Porter, local white teachers who were graduates of Central College. But it became known that Allen was seeing Mary at the Porters'. One night while Allen and Mary were there, a mob of several hundred whites surrounded the house. They had tar and feathers ready for Allen. They shouted, "down with the house," "bring him out," and "kill him."

Inside the house, Professor Allen, Mary, and the Porters were terrified. When a committee from the mob came to the door, the Porters felt forced to let them into the house. The committee told Allen that he could escape death only by letting Mary go home.

Allen, listening to the cries outside, became convinced that the committee meant what it said. He consented for Mary to go home. The committee led Mary out of the house and into a waiting sleigh, and amid the cheers of the mob, the sleigh drove off.

Then the mob began to shout for "nigger" Allen to come out too. The committee went back into the house. They convinced Allen that his safety, as well as the safety of the house, required that he leave at once, and they promised to protect him. The committee ushered him out of the door and formed a guard around him as he walked. Still some of the mob closed in, as Allen recalled it, "some of them kicking me, some striking me in the side, once on the head, some pulling at my clothes and bruising my hat, and all of them hooting and hallooing." The committee finally succeeded in leading Allen to a sleigh which took him out of town.

Several weeks later, Mary pretended to be going to Pennsylvania to take a teaching position. In fact, she met her lover in New York where they married and then set sail for safety in Britain.

At about this time at an abolitionist convention, Gerrit Smith introduced a resolution which called Professor Allen "accomplished and worthy" and condemned the mob attack on him as showing that slavery had corrupted the American heart.[7] New York Central College continued to defy public opinion by appointing as professors not only John Porter, who had lost his previous teaching post for identifying himself with Allen, but also another black professor, George B. Vashon, to take Allen's place.

However, the college maintained its principles at a cost. Having become notorious, the college found itself in increasing financial trouble. In a few years, despite maneuvering by Gerrit Smith, it went bankrupt and closed. Public opinion was reasserting the rule that blacks should not teach whites, and particularly not when a black teacher fell in love with a white pupil.

From the 1830s through the 1880s slightly more of the known cases of blacks teaching whites in the state occurred upstate rather than downstate, even though there were far more blacks teaching downstate. No doubt it was easier for blacks to teach whites upstate because there, before the Civil War, the evangelical movement had released a strong social reform impulse, helping to make abolitionism stronger there than downstate. No doubt it was also easier for blacks to teach whites upstate because the proportion of blacks in the population was lower, and hence there had been less occasion for prejudice to develop.

Other states were earlier than New York in giving long-lasting appointments to blacks to teach in predominantly white public schools. In Salem, Massachusetts, as early as the 1850s a nearly white-appearing young lady from a wealthy black family was appointed to teach in a public school and continued to teach for several years without significant protest. In the 1880s there were several reports of blacks teaching successfully in predominantly white public schools, as in Portland, Maine; in Boston; in Cleveland; and in Detroit and Bay City, Michigan. It was notable that such instances usually seemed to occur not close to the Mason-Dixon line but in northerly locations where relatively few blacks lived, much as within New York State, more of the attempts of blacks to teach whites occurred upstate rather than downstate. But the general rule that blacks could not teach whites continued to prevail throughout the nation. In fact, in 1883, after a local black girl was appointed to teach whites in a public school in Patterson, New Jersey, near New York City, whites—both pupils and parents—drove her out.[8]

It was not until the late 1890s that the deeply felt white antipathy against blacks teaching whites began to weaken visibly in public schools in New York State. At that time, a few blacks were deliberately appointed to teach in traditionally white public schools in Manhattan and Brooklyn, as we shall see later in detail, and once appointed they stayed. Why such long-term appointments came first downstate rather than upstate, contrary to the general tendency we have been noting for upstate New York to be more advanced in equal rights for blacks, we will consider in a more appropriate place. By the 1890s school segregation in general in the state was seriously weakening. Even so, these few blacks met considerable hostility in their teaching of whites.

All through the nineteenth century, it was seldom possible for blacks to teach whites in New York State, or anywhere else in the nation, and if they did so, they were taking a risk.

SHOULD WHITES TEACH BLACKS?

IN THE COLONY OF NEW YORK, the teachers in the Anglican schools for blacks were, as we have seen, all whites. Anglican officials were aware of the possibility of educating blacks to be teachers of blacks—some even suggested it—but there is no available evidence that they did it.

By the late 1790s in its school for blacks, the New York Manumission Society, while largely depending on white teachers, employed one black teacher. In 1805, the American Convention of Abolitionist Societies —in which the Manumission Society played a major part—declared that it was an advantage for black children to be taught by blacks; it will help to "kindle a spirit of emulation" in the black children, the convention said.[1] Soon after this time, the Manumission Society was educating a few blacks to become teachers. By the 1830s, with black prodding, a regular pattern of appointing black teachers in the publicly-funded schools had been established downstate—this pattern was established earlier in both Brooklyn and New York than in either Boston or Philadelphia. Nevertheless, especially in upstate New York, a substantial portion of the teachers in black schools continued into the twentieth century to be white.

In the North at large it was sometimes suggested that it was degrading to whites for them to teach black children. In Rhode Island in the 1820s a white was reported to be so ashamed that he taught a black school that when he was on the street he did not want his black pupils to acknowledge in any way that they knew him. In Ohio before the Civil War, whites who taught blacks were often regarded with such contempt that local whites would not rent rooms to them.[2] In New York State there was some similar evidence. The Swedish writer, Fredericka Bremer, visiting Rochester in the 1850s, admired the force of character which permitted a

Quaker woman, who privately taught the children of Frederick Douglass, to stand up under the odium "she must have to bear from the prejudiced white people." A committee of the Brooklyn Board of Education in the 1860s opposed the mixing of black and white children in schools for one reason because the white teachers would feel that having black pupils would reduce the status of their schools. In the 1910s a New York City teacher openly declared that she felt degraded by teaching black pupils.[3]

Regardless of what was said, does direct evidence indicate that the position of white teachers was significantly degraded by their teaching black schools in New York State? In Lockport, a white public school teacher asked to be transferred from a white school to a black school, which suggests she did not expect to be hurt by doing so. In Hudson, a white teacher, at the same time that she taught a black school, was sufficiently esteemed by whites to edit a local education journal which was put to use by the white Columbia County Teachers Association. In Roslyn, Long Island, a young white woman, after having taught a black public school for eight years, felt herself to be sufficiently respected so that she could invite white Presbyterians to her house one evening to form a Christian Endeavour Society, which they did. In Albany, an ambitious young mathematician, Joseph Henry, not only served as a trustee of the Albany Lancaster Society which operated a separate school for blacks, but also urged his wife to accept an invitation to take charge of the Schenectady African school for a week as a "work of benevolence"; such ties to black schools did not prevent Henry from later becoming head of the Smithsonian Institution in Washington.[4]

It was possible for whites to teach both a black school and a white school at the same time, as if doing the one did not hurt their opportunity to do the other. In both Troy and Rochester, whites were principals of black public schools while they taught public evening schools for whites. In both Schenectady and Flushing, whites who taught weekday schools for whites also at the same time taught Sunday schools for blacks. Moreover, it was common for whites after having taught in a black school to transfer to teaching in a white public school in the same town, as would not be likely to be the case if teaching in a black school had seriously hurt them. Such transfers occurred at least eight times in Lockport, fourteen in Buffalo. In sum, it is not at all clear from direct evidence that, in New York State, whites at large seriously lost status by teaching blacks.

However, no matter what happened to the status of white teachers, the question whether whites should teach in black schools was a controversial issue in New York State through most of the nineteenth century, especially from the black point of view.

Blacks who insisted that blacks rather than whites should teach blacks emphasized different arguments at different times. Early in the nineteenth century, William Hamilton, the black carpenter who was to become a major figure in persuading the New York Manumission Society to shift from predominantly white to predominantly black teachers, argued that white teachers did not expect enough of black pupils. "It has been the policy of white men," he said in an address to black youths in 1827, "to give you a high opinion of your advancement when you have made but smattering attainments. They know that a little education is necessary for the better accomplishing the menial services you are in the habit of performing for them. They do not wish you to be equal with them —much less superior. . . . They will take care that you do not rise above mediocrity."[5]

By mid-century, a more common argument was that given by the black abolitionist editor, Samuel R. Ward, who had himself taught in black schools in both New Jersey and New York. He emphasized that blacks should insist on black teachers because blacks ought to support black talent. He urged blacks to insist on black teachers even if they had to establish black private schools to get them. Public school officials "ought to know that if *they* won't encourage black talent, *we* will," he wrote. But Ward was not quite absolute in his call for black teachers. "Great care needs to be taken, in the early education of our people, to enable them to overcome the evil influence begotten by slavery," he continued. "We are harsh, coarse, and uncouth in our manners; we are deficient in refinement and good taste . . . we are low and vulgar in our religious ideas and our religious actions. . . . I lay it down as a rule of almost universal application, that none but a black person, or, if a white person, one thoroughly identified with our people, either can or will enter upon this work according to its demands."[6]

Blacks were by no means united on insisting on black teachers for black schools. For example, the *Christian Recorder,* the national organ of the African Methodist Church, argued that for blacks to insist on black teachers was to strengthen "the color line" which was in fact the "death line" for blacks. Moreover, school officials often believed that black parents preferred white teachers. In Brooklyn in 1863, when attendance at a black school dropped, a white school board member declared that it would improve attendance at the school if it had white teachers because black parents preferred white teachers. Lending support to this belief, a black school principal explained that some black parents preferred white teachers because they believed this would help to prepare for abolishing black schools.[7]

Samuel R. Ward as a young man in the 1830s taught black schools in Newtown, Long Island, and Poughkeepsie. He later became a pastor and editor. *Penn, Afro-American Press, 1891.*

Similarly in New York City, when attendance at black public schools was lagging in 1865, some white school officials proposed to improve attendance by employing white instead of black teachers. But the black *New York Weekly Anglo-African,* which was edited by Robert Hamilton who was himself a teacher of music in the New York City black schools, insisted that there was no proof that a change to white teachers would fill up our schools. "We find it difficult to trust white men to educate our youth," the *Anglo-African* explained. "It is not because they are not abundantly qualified in the letter, but their defect is in spirit and sympathy. There are many whites among our professed friends who do not believe in the square, civilized doctrine of human equality."[8]

Nevertheless, school officials who believed that having white teachers would improve attendance were probably correct for certain times and places. For example, in Troy in the 1830s, the black teacher of a black charity school was so unsatisfactory that enrollment dropped until the school had to be closed. As soon as the school reopened with a white teacher, attendance improved. In New York City in the 1880s when attendance at the black-taught schools for blacks was dwindling, a black columnist explained it by saying it was "almost characteristic" of New York blacks to believe that whites were more capable of teaching their children than blacks were.[9]

That blacks were significantly divided on the wisdom of insisting on blacks to teach in black schools is further suggested by the fact that in the schools which blacks themselves organized they chose a significant number of white teachers. As we have already noted, in the 1830s blacks in organizing black high schools of their own, even in New York City where one would expect many black teachers to be available, sometimes appointed white teachers; in the 1840s to 1860s, blacks in black-organized Sunday schools in Flushing and Troy often chose white teachers. In such cases blacks probably chose white teachers for a combination of such reasons as that they desired prestige for their schools, they found competent black teachers unavailable, and they opposed segregation on principle. In the state in the nineteenth century as a whole, of all the teachers whose race is known whom blacks appointed to teach in black-organized black schools—including private schools, charity schools, Sunday schools, and orphan asylum schools—14 percent were whites.

Despite an inclination among considerable numbers of blacks to accept some white teachers, or even prefer white teachers, a solid portion of New York State's black leadership continued through most of the century to plead for black teachers for black schools. The black *New York Freeman,* edited by T. Thomas Fortune, said on September 26, 1885, that it had always protested against white teachers in black schools. Having white teachers tends "to discourage the honest efforts of our young men and women" and hold up "to the world the unkind insinuation that we are unable to do anything unless we have some second-rate white scrub to boss the matter. White churches and schools do not employ colored brains, and until they do we shall protest against the shoddyism on our part which thinks it is too learned or fastidious to set at the feet of thoroughly prepared scholars of the [colored] race."

Following such beliefs, substantial numbers of New York State blacks campaigned in their local communities to secure black teachers for black schools. They did so in several different places, both upstate and downstate.

As we have already seen, in the early 1830s New York City black leaders clamored for more black teachers in the Manumission Society's black schools. To push their cause, they held public meetings, urged parents not to send their children to the schools, and visited school officials. They finally succeeded in persuading the Manumission Society to oust the long-time white principal Charles Andrews and to look for more black teachers. Soon thereafter most of the teachers in publicly-funded black schools of the New York City area were black and they remained so through the rest of the century.

In Buffalo in the 1850s, according to the superintendent of schools, several public meetings of blacks indicated an almost unanimous preference for a black principal in the black public school, and in response the superintendent appointed the future Episcopal bishop, James T. Holly, whom the superintendent called a "colored gentleman of talent and education." But Holly's discipline was said to be poor and the parents fell into dissension about him. Holly stayed only a year.[10] While the Buffalo black public school continued to exist about twenty-seven years more, it is doubtful that it ever had another black teacher.

In Troy in the summer of 1855, when a white was appointed to teach the black public school, many black parents objected. Previous teachers of the school had often been black; black parents wanted a black teacher again, they said.

Black parents became so excited over this issue that many of them refused to send their children to the school. One day in September out of an enrollment of fifty-three, there were only two scholars present in the school; another day only three. The parents were boycotting the school—using a method already used by black parents in school crises in New York, Rochester, Boston, and elsewhere. As a Troy paper put it, the black people were "refusing to send their children to be instructed by a white man." Some also were objecting because the white teacher, Patrick Farrell, was Catholic and was so recent an immigrant to this country, one black said, that he could not pronounce English correctly and could not have "much sympathy with our children, or understand our peculiar wants."[11]

The Troy Board of Education, confronted with the boycott, explained that Farrell had only been temporarily appointed because no suitable black teacher could be found. However, by October, the board's committee on licensing teachers had examined a young black candidate, Allen M. Bland. He was born in the South, had attended the preparatory department of Oberlin College, and had recently taught a black school in New Jersey. Among his children was a small son who was later to be the author of "Carry Me Back to Old Virginny." The committee recommended Bland for a certificate which would permit him to teach the Troy black school, but the board took no action at once.

Meanwhile, the black community had time to develop a split. In November, blacks sent the board of education two petitions of almost an equal number of signatures, one asking for the appointment of the black Bland and the other asking for the retention of the white Farrell. Representatives of both black groups came to a board meeting to present their case. For keeping the white Farrell, the spokesman was barber William S. Baltimore of a prominent Troy black family. Baltimore had been active in black protest: he had signed the call for the colored state convention of 1840, spoken twice at celebrations of emancipation in the British West Indies, and had been local agent for Frederick Douglass' weekly, the *North Star*. For appointing black candidate Bland, the spokesmen included a black Presbyterian pastor and the black barber William Rich, one of the major leaders of the state Negro convention movement.

It was not until December that the board, on a fourth ballot, finally chose Bland as principal of the African school.[12] Though frequently harassed by his black enemies, who at times charged that he punished pupils too severely, Bland stayed on for seven years.

Perhaps influenced by the success of the drive for a black teacher in Troy, a group of black parents in nearby Albany tried to persuade the Albany school board to appoint black instead of white teachers in Albany's black school. According to an Albany black Baptist pastor, the black parents were following "the good old motto":

> Colored schools, colored teachers,
> Colored churches, colored preachers.

When the black parents did not succeed in getting black teachers at once, the "greater part" of the parents, the pastor reported in 1859, kept their children at home, boycotting the school. By autumn the school board responded by appointing a black woman as assistant teacher, but since the board still retained the white principal, the black parents were not satisfied. In early 1860 the pastor was still cheering on the campaign for black teachers, saying that "agitation and perseverence" would eventually win. After a black committee threatened to make public a report on the issue, the next year the board reluctantly appointed as principal the black

Thomas Paul, a graduate of Dartmouth College. Thereafter attendance increased at the school only slightly, but Paul stayed on as principal for eight years, an unusually long time for a teacher in an upstate black school.[13]

In Poughkeepsie in 1872, shortly after blacks had acquired new confidence from having at last achieved the equal right to vote in the state, a delegation of blacks appeared before the local school board to present a petition asking that a black rather than a white teacher be appointed to Poughkeepsie's one-room black school. The delegation represented a considerable cross-section of blacks: two laborers; a cartman; a black Methodist pastor; a dyer; and Abraham Bolin, a school janitor, all Republicans. In response to the delegation, the school board instructed its committee on teachers to hire a suitable black teacher. However, a month later the committee reported that it had not yet found a suitable black candidate, and instead the board soon hired a white.

About a year later, an African Methodist bishop, Joseph J. Clinton, wrote janitor Bolin saying he would like to have his son employed to teach the black school in Poughkeepsie. Bolin sent the bishop's message to the school board; it consented to examine young Clinton, and he came to Poughkeepsie for the purpose. The board's Committee on Examination pronounced him well qualified, black janitor Bolin urged his appointment, but some blacks considered him too young, and the board delayed a decision.

When young Clinton had already been waiting in Poughkeepsie for several weeks with the hope of securing the black school post, Bolin appeared on Clinton's behalf before the school board. The board had promised to provide a black teacher, Bolin said, and young Clinton wanted to know if he would be employed or should go home.

A lawyer board member asked Bolin, who served as janitor of both a white school and the black school, if he had any fault to find with the white teacher of the black school.

Bolin himself had children in the black school. "My children don't learn as fast as they ought to," he replied.

Another lawyer board member teased Bolin about being janitor at the school they were debating about: the question of a teacher, he said, "might be referred to the Resident Engineer." The board laughed.

One board member, a Civil War hero who had become Republican postmaster of Poughkeepsie, had recently spoken to Poughkeepsie blacks, appealing for their votes. Now in this meeting he spoke warily in their behalf. It would not be right to dismiss the white teacher "at the edge of winter," the postmaster said. But if she believes that the school should have a colored teacher, and if the colored people want Clinton, then he would favor appointing Clinton.

Though janitor Bolin persisted in pleading for the appointment of a black, later the board, considering that the white teacher had entered in good faith into her position, decided to keep her.[14] At least Bolin had not allowed his job as janitor to make him obsequious to the lawyers, bankers, and physicians of the school board.

Brooklyn blacks also campaigned for black teachers in black schools. In 1869 when the Brooklyn school board appointed a white teacher to a black school, though it usually did not, black spokesmen appeared at a hearing before the board to object the appointment. One of the black spokesmen, Baptist pastor Simon Bundick, claimed that the daughters and sisters of colored taxpayers were obliged to accept menial positions, that colored women needed good positions as in teaching, and that competent colored teachers could be found. Another of the black spokesmen, the nationally prominent Baptist editor, Reverend Rufus L. Perry, said that a black teacher, unlike a white one, would be likely to live in the black community, and that the social influence of an educated black teacher was very desirable for the black community.

However, other black spokesmen appeared before the board in behalf of keeping the white teacher. They said the objection to her because of her color was "ridiculous," and that she was competent. The principal of the school, a black, confirmed that she was competent.

A committee of the board concluded that since the white teacher was doing well she should be kept, but conceded that as a matter of policy, since most colored people preferred a colored to a white teacher, "each being equally competent," the board in future would give "preference to colored teachers in colored schools."[15] Through the rest of the century, the Brooklyn Board of Education almost always appointed black teachers to black schools.

In Stapleton on Staten Island, as in most of the New York City region, blacks were accustomed to having black teachers in their school. Once when the black teacher became ill, school officials broke custom by choosing a white woman as a substitute. The black pupils objected to having a white teacher, and their parents supported them. One day out of an enrollment of forty children, only three attended school. The boycotters are "perfectly right," said Thomas T. Fortune's black newspaper, the *New York Globe* of May 5, 1883. But white papers disagreed. The *New York Sun* of April 27 said, "It is Negroes who now display the race prejudices." And the *New York Evening Telegram* of April 25 avowed that the boycott "shows that our colored fellow citizens are asserting their natural right to be as foolish as their white brethren have been in times past." However, the Staten Island black parents soon obtained what they wanted. School officials replaced the white substitute teacher with a black one.

Altogether, among these seven campaigns to secure black rather than white teachers in black schools, each in a different locality in the state, in four of the campaigns some blacks favored a white teacher, or at least opposed the appointment of a particular black teacher being considered for appointment. However, the blacks who desired the appointment of black teachers were directly successful in five out of the seven campaigns. Such campaigns helped to cause a substantial rise in the proportion of blacks among the teachers in black schools in the state, from 33 percent in the first decade of the nineteenth century to 76 percent by the last decade (see Table 7 in the Appendix).

During the nineteenth century as a whole, New York State blacks were often vocal on issues that concerned them. They were vocal not only on national issues like the abolition of slavery and state issues like the equal right to vote, but also on local issues like who should teach in the black schools. Blacks sometimes spoke out and acted firmly in campaigns for the appointment of black teachers, and they did so even in their own home towns, where their jobs might be threatened or patronage for their businesses might fall off. They were often not the obsequious Uncle Toms that later generations have imagined them to be. And they often won what they asked for, including black teachers.

PREPARING TEACHERS

NEW YORK STATE'S BLACK LEADERS often argued that the teachers of black children were not well qualified. They especially argued so in the early and middle part of the nineteenth century. The black *New York Freedom's Journal* complained that "dull and stupid instructors" who would not be allowed to teach whites were allowed to teach blacks. The black Reverend J. W. C. Pennington charged that "adventurers" among black teachers had hurt the education of blacks. Black editor Samuel R. Ward mourned that few black teachers "have the interests of the rising generation sufficiently at heart to be well qualified."[1]

For their part, school boards in New York State—whose vision was doubtless blurred by the usual white prejudice—often reported it was difficult to find qualified black teachers. A committee of the Rochester board said in 1849 that it was an "almost utter impossibility" to secure them. At various times both the Troy and Poughkeepsie boards said, as we have seen, that they were forced to appoint white teachers in their black schools because they could not find suitable black teachers. The New York City board lamented in 1874 that it had "great difficulty" in providing schools for blacks with "cultivated teachers of their own color" and gave this as an explanation for the poor showing of black pupils scholastically.[2]

In much of the nineteenth century, education for teachers, whether they were black or white, was thin, aimed at keeping teachers just above the level of their pupils. It was a popular view that almost anyone who had acquired elementary knowledge was competent to teach, but officials concerned about schools kept pushing for higher standards.

In the first half of the century, many teachers, both black and white, were only in their teens or early twenties and regarded themselves as teaching temporarily. Many of them began to teach when they had only just completed grammar school—in the 1830s and 1840s nearly half of the black teachers in black schools for whom the information is available had only attended grammar school. But other teachers were already being prepared for teaching by attending academies for a year or so. In the normal departments of academies, they were given intensive drill in the elementary subjects they were expected to teach, as well as a little instruction in teaching methods. They were taught to live by a severe discipline imposed from both within and without, including elaborate school rules, personal soul-searching, and self-consciousness about their behavior and dress. They were taught to accept the increasing split between male and female roles, assuming that men were inherently more materialistic and dominant while women were more delicate and self-sacrificing, and that it was natural that women teachers be paid half of what men teachers were paid.

Students from poor families found it difficult to attend academies both because they required tuition fees and because students often had to live away from home to attend them. In any event, few academies allowed blacks to enter. From 1840 to 1860, of the more than 150 academies in existence in the state, only eight can be cited as either certainly or probably open to blacks—two downstate in Huntington and Flushing and six upstate in Clinton, Varysburg, Whitesboro, Newburgh, Nyack, and Rochester.

From about the middle of the century, as public high schools began to come into existence, private academies began to be transformed into high schools or otherwise to disappear, and high schools sometimes organized their own normal departments. At first blacks were often refused at high schools as they had been at academies. However, as early as the 1860s at least one black girl had secured her teacher education in the public high school in Troy, and in the 1880s at least three had in Flushing.[3]

Meanwhile, early in the century the Lancasterian method of preparing teachers was in vogue, particularly for teachers of poor children. In New York City in the 1820s and 1830s in accordance with Lancasterian practice, the Manumission Society selected a few of its black pupils to become monitors or assistant teachers in its black schools. Lancasterian theory, emphasizing economy, held that to prepare teachers, it was necessary to give them teaching practice but scarcely any teacher education.

By 1834, however, when the New York Public School Society took over the Manusmission Society's black shools, the Lancasterian system was being criticized for the "mechanical" teaching it fostered, and support for special education for teachers was growing. From soon after this time the Public School Society ran two part-time normal schools, one for whites and one for blacks, and later the New York City Board of Education continued these two normal schools.[4] Though the black normal school—which was the only significant separate normal school for blacks in the history of the state—was much the smaller of the two, school officials made some effort to make the black normal school comparable to the white one.[5] Both normal schools usually met only on Saturdays so that beginning teachers could attend them. Both schools at first, like the academies, devoted nearly all their time to drilling in subject matter, but gradually they abandoned the Lancasterian system, and as the age and preparation of their pupil-teachers advanced, they gave some attention to teaching methods, especially methods which were less mechanical than Lancasterian methods.

For some thirty years, the black John Peterson headed the Saturday Colored Normal School. Peterson, who came from a poor family, graduated from Charles Andrews' Manumission Society school and never received any formal education beyond it. After continuing to study under Andrews privately for about two years, he became an assistant teacher in Andrews' school and from that position gradually rose to become one of the city's most beloved black principals. Peterson was modest, courtly, and sure of his Christian faith—in his later years he served as assistant pastor of the black St. Philips Episcopal Church in addition to teaching school. Like other teachers of normal schools in the state at the time, Peterson gave his normal school a moral and elevated tone, and like them, he emphasized that teachers should drill pupils thoroughly in the fundamentals. He was not a great scholar, but according to his former pupil Alexander Crummill, "rarely has there been a schoolmaster who exercised such a strong personal influence upon his pupils as he. His pupils took up unconsciously his tones, his manner, his movements, his style, and his faults, so that oft times, they were copies of their old master."[6]

By the late 1850s, Peterson was assisted as head of the Saturday Normal School by Charles L. Reason. Like Peterson, Reason was born in New York City and attended Andrews' black school. At the age of fourteen, Reason became a monitor or assistant teacher in that school. Over a period of years he studied with private tutors. At one time he tried to enter the Episcopal General Theological Seminary in New York City, but because of his color the seminary refused to admit him except as a listener, a status which he declined as demeaning; he withdrew his Episcopal Church membership in protest. Nevertheless, apparently without any more formal education than grammar school, he eventually became a

Charles L. Reason taught black schools in New York City most of the time from 1832 to 1892, frequently as a principal. *Simmons,* Men of Mark, *1887.*

principal of a New York City black school and succeeded Peterson as head of the city's Saturday Colored Normal School. Like many normal school teachers, Reason conveyed to his normal pupils a high sense of the purpose of teaching and a conviction of the virtue of discipline. He impressed his pupils, as one of them who became a teacher afterward recalled, as being intolerant of mediocrity. More of a scholar than Peterson —as suggested by his having at one time taught in the predominantly white New York Central College—his major impact on his pupils was in developing in them a love of study for its own sake. The black President Daniel Payne, of Wilberforce University, said that he had never seen a better teacher.[7]

In the 1850s, the New York City Board of Education required all its teachers in the lower ranks to attend one of its Saturday normal schools. In the 1860s, many of the city's grammar schools, both white and black, offered "supplementary classes" for prospective teachers, and the graduates from these classes could also attend the Saturday normal schools. The number of pupils in Peterson's and Reason's black normal school—they were mostly female—ranged from about sixteen to thirty.

At times all the students in the Saturday normal schools, whether black or white, wrote the same examinations prepared by city school officials. At times they heard the same lecturers, including Assistant Superintendent Norman A. Calkins, who by the 1860s had become nationally known for championing new teaching methods. What Calkins advocated, as well as much of what the normal students heard and read by this time, was intended to lead them away from the robot method of teaching which the Lancasterian system had popularized. Calkins appealed to the example of the Swiss educator Pestalozzi who had maintained that a child should be taught not by making him a passive recipient, but by calling his powers into action. Calkins advocated the "object" method of teaching, based on Pestalozzi, which emphasized the advantages of giving small children direct experience of real objects—such as animals and plants—rather than abstractions; it encouraged more classroom discussion and less dependence on books and memorizing.[8]

Despite the influence of such new methods, the mechanical, clockwork style of teaching tended to persist in New York City as well as elsewhere in the state through much of the century. Public apathy, political obstruction, and overcrowded classrooms encouraged it to persist. So also did the system by which school officials graded teachers on the basis of the performance of their pupils in annual public examinations: such grading tended to push teachers into preparing for the examinations by devoting much of their time to drilling their pupils in singsong recitation of multiplication tables, definitions, and set answers to questions, rather than encouraging each pupil to develop his own capacities.

In New York City, school officials, while retaining their confidence in Peterson and Reason personally, were often dissatisfied both with the Colored Normal School and the colored schools generally. In 1857 they reported that the "general proficiency" of the Colored Normal School was "not satisfactory." In 1864 the city superintendent complained of the poor qualifications of the black teachers in the black schools and recommended that "white teachers of superior qualifications" be appointed in place of black principals, but his recommendation was not carried out.[9]

Before the Civil War, blacks who sought advanced education to help them become teachers found that not only few academies but also few colleges were open to them. Several black men who afterward became teachers in New York State were only allowed to study at colleges without being admitted as regular students: they were tolerated only in the guise of janitors, visitors, or special assistants to professors. But at least nine black men who afterward became teachers in the state studied as regular students at Oneida Institute, the abolitionist-supported interracial school near Utica which gave the equivalent of a two-year college education. Oneida educated more blacks who became teachers in the state than any other college, until in 1844 it was forced to close in considerable part because of white hostility to its policy of accepting black students as equals.

In 1844 New York State followed the example of Massachusetts by establishing its first full-time normal school, a tuition-free one, at Albany. In the 1850s a young black woman apparently studied at Albany state normal and afterward became a teacher in the black public school in Poughkeepsie;[10] but up to 1890, far more whites who were to become teachers in black schools had studied at Albany normal than blacks had. By the 1860s, the state had opened several other tuition-free state normal schools, including one at Oswego which became famous for popularizing the "object" method of teaching, but only one black is definitely known to have attended Oswego normal before the 1890s—she afterward became the head of the normal department at Wilberforce University in Ohio.[11] Through most of the nineteenth century, blacks were seldom admitted as equals with whites into New York State's normal schools or colleges, helping to lead, as we shall see, to recurrent attempts to establish a black college in the state.

As part of the trend toward normal schools, in 1870 New York City established a tuition-free, full-time normal school for girls, and with high aims, called it the Normal College. Its first president was the Irish-born Thomas Hunter (it was later named Hunter College in his honor). President Hunter believed, more than most normal school administrators at the time, in a thorough liberal arts education for teachers. In teaching children, he recommended that teachers avoid giving corporal punishment, avoid drilling in memory work, reduce the use of texts and lecturing because they encouraged children to be lazy, and instead emphasize the direct exercise of children's observation and reasoning powers.

In 1873, shortly after the Normal College opened, a new state law required equal opportunity for all races in public education. Before it became apparent that the new law was not to be strictly enforced, black Principal Reason decided to take advantage of the law by trying to enter his best pupils in the Normal College, even though he was undercutting his own Saturday Normal School by doing so. Reason prepared several of his girls to take the written entrance examination, and other black principals followed suit. President Hunter dared to admit a considerable

Albany State Normal School, second building, built 1885. By 1890 at least two blacks had graduated from the normal school and afterward taught in black schools in Jamaica, Roslyn, and Flushing, Long Island. At least ten whites had also graduated there who afterward taught in black schools, as in Albany, Buffalo, New York, and New Rochelle. *Howell,* Bicentennial History of Albany, *1886.*

proportion of the black applicants—nine out of fifteen in one group—including some with the lowest passing scores.[12] Meanwhile, because the Normal College was now open to blacks, in 1874 the New York City Board of Education discontinued its Saturday Colored Normal School.

President Hunter received the black girls at the Normal College gingerly. The first ones he carefully separated, placing not more than two in a class. He observed that the faculty accepted the black girls less easily than the students did—to keep the more obstreperous faculty in line, he assigned the blackest girls to their classes.

As generations of black girls succeeded each other at his college,

New York City's Normal (Hunter) College as completed in 1874, on Park and Lexington Avenues, between 68th and 69th Streets. *Courtesy of The New-York Historical Society, New York City.*

President Hunter became convinced that the general average of black students was below that of whites. Black students did poorly in "studies requiring reason and judgment," he decided, but better in music and drawing and in subjects which "mainly depended on memory and imitation." The most intelligent white scholars, he explained, had the advantage of having educated ancestors for generations, which was unfortunately not true of black scholars.

President Hunter, like many white educators at the time, believed he saw a difference in the ability of the black students who were very Negroid and those who were nearly Caucasian. For instance, he reported that one girl, whom he described as having "the negro face in all its barbaric deformity," with a "flat nose, thick lips, retreating chin and forehead," took eight years to finish her four year course; according to Hunter, she was such a poor student, that if she had been white, he would have asked her parents to withdraw her from the college. Another black girl, however, who won a prize for the greatest progress in French studies, seemed to Hunter to have an "almost perfect Grecian face," with a straight nose, high forehead, and "only a slight kink in her hair." Hunter decided that, "had her color been a shade or two lighter, she would have been pretty." President Hunter found an occasion to ask her about her ancestry. The girl replied that she was descended from an Abyssinian king. When the president hinted his doubt that this could be true, she tossed her head, flashed her eyes, and insisted, with the air of a princess, that it was true according to family tradition preserved on a Carolina plantation. Whether she was really of royal descent or not, President Hunter recalled afterward, she was certainly three quarters white. That seemed to him to explain why she was the only black student he had ever known in his long career at the college whom he considered to be an "able scholar."[13]

A close look at one black school toward the end of the century gives us a more favorable impression than President Hunter gave of education for black teachers. The principal of this school—a Brooklyn primary and grammar school combined—was Charles A. Dorsey who was said by the black *New York Freeman* to be "at home in the school room, teaching always with ease and dignity."

Dorsey was born of well-to-do parents in Philadelphia. When Quakers established their Institute for Colored Youth there, he was the first pupil they enrolled. Later, Dorsey attended the abolitionist-supported New York Central College, at McCrawville, while there earning pocket money in winter by cutting wood. In 1859, to complete his college study, he entered another abolitionist-supported institution, Oberlin College, in Ohio. After graduation in 1861, he first taught at a black school in a log house in southern Ohio. Then hearing that there was a vacancy for a principal in a black school in Brooklyn, he applied for it, passed the Brooklyn superintendent's written examination for a principal's license, and in 1863 was appointed.

By 1887, the nine other teachers who taught with Dorsey in his Brooklyn school were all black women. Among the ten teachers, the only one who had graduated from a liberal arts college was Dorsey himself. Two had graduated from President Hunter's Normal College. One had taught in a New York City black school and at the same time attended the Saturday Colored Normal School there. Four had merely graduated from high schools. The other two teachers were reported to have attended various "schools" (in Utica, New York City, and New England), which might mean that they had only attended grammar schools.

It is noteworthy that, despite a modest influx of Southern blacks into New York State at this time, all ten teachers in Dorsey's school were

Principal Dorsey and his black public school in Brooklyn in the early 1890s. Blacks were proud of this school, both for the quality of its instruction and for its brick building, built in 1883. *Long Island Historical Society.*

born in the North and had acquired their entire education in the North where educational standards were higher than in the South. It is also noteworthy that five of these ten teachers had studied at one time or another with either Charles Reason or John Peterson, both of whom were widely known for preparing blacks to teach.

The level of education of the black teachers in Dorsey's school compares well with that of the white teachers in Brooklyn about the same time. Although in the 1880s there were already in existence in the state at least nine full-time public normal schools, of all the new teachers appointed in Brooklyn in 1887, both black and white, only 22 percent had received "professional training." Even if, among the teachers in Dorsey's school, only those having graduated from liberal arts colleges or full-time normal schools may be said to have had "professional training," still at least 30 percent of the teachers in his school had such training.[14]

In Brooklyn, the school superintendent claimed that the examinations required for appointment to teaching were of a higher standard than similar examinations in New York City and in most large cities of the nation. It would not be difficult to make them of high standard since in the early 1880s the number of candidates seeking teachers' licenses in Brooklyn each year was about five hundred while the number of teachers appointed was only about one hundred. Some of the examinations did indeed appear to be rigorous. A black woman who took the examination to qualify as head of a department competed with ten white teachers. She was one of only three candidates who passed, and she became head of a department in Dorsey's school.

Blacks were proud of Dorsey's school. Black lawyer T. McCants Stewart claimed that Dorsey had raised his school "as high as any of the other schools of Brooklyn."[15] The pride which blacks took in this and several other black schools in the state in this period is in contrast to the shame which they had felt for many of their schools earlier in the century.

In comparison with other submerged groups in the New York metropolitan population at about the end of the century, blacks were showing that they had a moderate drive for professional education. Certainly a substantial number of blacks had more such drive than most recently arrived Italians who, being predominantly of peasant background, usually were illiterate, and in accordance with Italian family tradition wanted their older children to drop out of school so that they could contribute immediately to the family income. However, blacks had far less drive for professional education than the also recently-arrived East European Jews whose religious roots gave them a passion for education. As early as 1900, Jews, in an extraordinary feat, constituted a majority of students at the city's free public colleges where blacks often felt overwhelmed by their competition. Jews were on their way to providing, well beyond their share in the city's population, half of the city's public school teachers. The black struggle for status in American life was not intense enough, not hopeful enough, to call out from blacks as great resources of energy for higher education as the similar struggle called out from Jews.

During the nineteenth century as a whole, among all the teachers in the black schools in the state whose level of education is known, most of the black teachers (68%) reached only as far as grammar school, academy, high school, or part-time normal school, while most of the white teachers (58%) had achieved a full-time normal or college education. However, the proportion of black teachers in black schools who were known to have had a grammar school education declined from 50 percent in the 1830s to 20 percent in the 1860s, and to 0 percent in the 1910s.

As the nineteenth century came to an end, it was beginning to be apparent that an increasing number of black teachers—often from middle class families long settled in the North—were as well prepared as whites in comparable teaching posts. By 1890 at least four blacks had attended Albany State Normal School, and fifty-six had attended New York City's Normal College. In the year 1898–1899, a few "colored" students were reported to be in such widely scattered public normal schools as Plattsburgh and Potsdam in the north, and Brockport and Fredonia in the west. In the 1890s at least four black women, all veteran teachers in New York City black schools, earned graduate degrees in New York University's recently founded School of Pedagogy—the earliest professional school for teachers on the graduate level in the United States. Though resistance to admitting blacks to many higher institutions in the state continued, the number of blacks attending Columbia University's new Teachers College, a fount of the new "progressive education," was about to zoom. In the 1890s perhaps only five blacks attended, but by the 1910s there were at least twenty-eight, and by the 1920s, 174.

In the nation as a whole, in the 1890s and early 1900s blacks were losing civil rights. Nevertheless, in New York State in 1896, in recognition of the trend toward equal education for black teachers, as well as the gradual decline in school segregation in the state, a young black woman, Susie Frazer, began to serve the first regular, long-term appointment of a black to teach in any predominantly white school in the state—she was a graduate of New York City's Normal College who was appointed in Manhattan. In the next few decades the number of such appointments would go up dramatically.

As the twentieth century opened, for large numbers of teachers, particularly in the burgeoning cities, teaching was no longer a temporary occupation for youths, but a life-time career. Teacher licensing was increasingly being used to raise standards for teachers. The trend from one-room, ungraded schools to larger graded schools encouraged specialized preparation for teaching. Teachers were being trained to think more critically; they were attaining better salaries and more freedom in their teaching; and the public was said to honor teachers more than ever before.

By this time teacher education was taking timid steps toward "progressive education." Led by such Columbia University professors as Nicholas Murray Butler and John Dewey, teachers were beginning to be taught that education should take on social work functions for the care of the whole child, including his health and his choice of a vocation; and that education should not only pass on the social heritage to new generations but, as a major social force in itself, help reshape society to achieve democratic goals. The way was being prepared for schools in Northern cities to give less attention to the mastery of limited subject matter and more attention to the increasingly varied needs of children, including the children of the "new immigrants"—such as the Jews and Italians—who were already pouring in from Europe, as well as the blacks who were beginning to pour in from the South.

Meanwhile, in the South the education of black teachers was being redirected to provide the special kind of industrial education that Booker T. Washington, the head of Tuskegee Institute, believed was suitable for most blacks: an education which emphasized teaching blacks to become better carpenters, farmers, and domestics more than to become the equals of whites.

There were some signs that education for blacks in New York State was also moving toward industrial education and doing so sometimes in association with the new progressivism. From the 1880s into the early 1900s, as the apprentice system gradually died out, some industrial education was becoming popular for public school pupils, both black and white. Moreover, in the 1890s the formidable black clubwoman Victoria Earle Mathews established on New York's upper East Side the White Rose Mission, modeled on Tuskegee Institute, to train black women as domestics, and Booker T. Washington helped her raise funds for the mission. In the early 1900s black Principal William L. Bulkley ran in mid-Manhattan a flourishing public industrial evening school, intended especially for blacks; the success of his school induced the city school board to establish other vocational schools in other black neighborhoods. Though Bulkley was more of a follower of the pro-liberal-education W. E. B. DuBois than of the pro-industrial-education Washington, Bulkley described his school as similar to black industrial schools in the South.[16]

It is also true that shortly after 1900 a considerable number of black teachers who had been trained in Southern industrial schools were imported into New York State to further special industrial education projects for blacks—one of these projects on Long Island was designed with the hope that it would develop into a Northern Tuskegee. However, these special projects were not undertaken by public schools, but by private institutions for blacks, like charity schools or orphan asylums; and most of them did not last long.[17]

The impulses to industrial education in New York State did not seem to interrupt the main trends in the education of black teachers. The main trends in the period of the 1880s to 1910s were toward their education at higher levels, under the influence of the progressive spirit, as the equals of whites; and to the extent that they were still being educated to teach blacks rather than all races, they were not being prepared as much to give blacks a separate kind of education as essentially the same kind of education as for all races.

About this time, two black teachers symbolized the trends under way in the state in the preparation of black teachers, as well as the new roles for teachers to which these trends led.

Soon after the Civil War, Maritcha Lyons—the daughter of a New York City porter who had risen to being the proprietor of a boarding house—began to teach in Dorsey's school in Brooklyn. At that time she had only graduated from high school. But as she continued to teach in Brooklyn, she took advantage of opportunities around her to improve herself. She read in the libraries of the local teachers' association and the Brooklyn Institute. She attended meetings and lectures, including lectures by Nicholas Murray Butler in psychology. She read teachers' magazines. "It was the era of a revolution in ideas regarding the aims, work, and management of schools," Miss Lyons recalled afterward. "Into all this I plunged." By the 1890s she has become the head of a department in a racially-mixed school in Brooklyn, with white as well as black teachers under her; and from then on for many years she supervised normal school students doing practice teaching at her school—students from "all the various nationalities to be found in a cosmopolitan city."[18] In a dramatic reversal of the usual roles, a black teacher was helping to educate white teachers.

In the late 1890s William L. Bulkley, a light-complexioned man who had been born a slave in South Carolina, arrived in Brooklyn looking for a teaching post, He had scrounged for the funds to permit him to study—he had lit gas lights and sold steam cookers. He had succeeded in studying in Paris as well as earning a doctorate in languages at Syracuse University, one of the six Ph.D.s earned by blacks in the nation up to 1900. In Brooklyn he was appointed to teach seventh grade in a white school over the protest of white teachers. Nevertheless he persisted; school officials stood by him; and eventually, according to the *Brooklyn Eagle,* he won recognition as a "model teacher in every way." By 1901, he was appointed principal of an officially desegregated, formerly black school in Manhattan, on West 41st Street, a school which was still predominantly black, but had a racially-mixed faculty. He was soon reshaping the school in keeping with the "progressive" idea that schools should be community centers. He encouraged teachers to walk into back alleys and climb dark stairs to visit the homes of their pupils. He arranged con-

Dr. William L. Bulkley served as principal of predominantly white public schools in Manhattan from 1909 to 1923. A black activist, he was a founder of both the National Urban League and the National Association for the Advancement of Colored People. *National Urban League,* 40th Anniversary Year Book, *1951.*

ferences for teachers and parents. He opened not only evening industrial classes, as we have seen, but also classes to teach reading and writing to adult illiterates and a kindergarten to relieve working mothers. At the same time he was also active with white social workers and philanthropists in trying to open up new types of jobs to blacks, an activity through which he helped to found the national Urban League. In 1909 Bulkley was appointed principal of a Lower Manhattan public school where most of the pupils were white—the first significant appointment of a black as principal of a predominantly white school in the state.[19]

Black teachers in New York State were gradually throwing off the weight of generations of contempt and neglect for their educational capacities. Their doing so was helping them to move—if slowly—into newly responsible educational roles, in equal association with whites.

HOW MUCH FREEDOM
FOR BLACK TEACHERS?

I̲N THE NINETEENTH CENTURY NORTH, from the black point of view, black teachers were potentially important leaders of the black liberation struggle. Since few other suitable employments were open to educated blacks, teaching attracted some of the ablest of them. It was crucial to blacks to see whether whites would permit these black teachers to develop their leadership in the direction of protest against racial inequality.

During the nineteenth century, New York State whites often seemed determined to "keep blacks in their place." In the first half of the century, the prevailing white view was that it would be better to send blacks back to Africa than to permit them to become the equals of whites here. From 1821 to 1870, whites denied blacks the equal right to vote in the state. All through the century whites usually confined blacks to menial employment. Under such circumstances it would not be surprising if the dominant whites in the state would try to prevent black teachers from openly protesting against inequality. Did whites in fact do so?

From the limited evidence available, of the teachers who taught in the separate schools for blacks in New York State in the nineteenth century, 390 of those whose names are known can be identified as blacks.

How many of these 390 black teachers were protesters? That is, how many of them took some significant action against inequality or discrimination on the basis of race? To be counted here as protesters, they must have taken such action either before or while teaching in a black school. Thus school officials, in hiring them for the first time or in hiring them again, could, if they cared to investigate, know of their protest activity and reject them. This was, of course, before any general development of a system of tenure to protect teachers against arbitrary dismissal.

Of the 390 black teachers, 104 or 27 percent can be called protest-ers.[1] It is possible that a larger share of the black teachers are called pro-testers than their true share in the total number of black teachers because, as protesters, they were likely to be better known. However, considering that in the 1840s—when the proportion of protesters among the black teachers reached its height—in the whole country only about fifty blacks would come to a colored national convention, and only about 1500 would subscribe to any antislavery paper,[2] for anywhere near 27 percent of the black teachers to be protesters is significantly high. Also considering that 61 percent of the black teachers were women,[3] who in much of the nine-teenth century were expected to leave public criticism to men, for 27 per-cent of the black teachers to be protesters is remarkably high.

Many of these New York State protesters taught in black public schools, while smaller numbers taught in charity, private, Sunday, or other kinds of schools for blacks. In any event, 70 percent of the protest-ers taught at least for a time in a school under white control. Moreover, in view of the weak position of blacks politically and economically, it is likely that whites could have prevented the black protesters from teaching even in the schools run by blacks if they had chosen to organize to bring pres-sure for that purpose.

Comparing the black teachers who were protesters with those who were non-protesters, the protesters were more likely to be born out-side of New York State. Moreover, the more distant the region of birth, the more likely the teachers were to be protesters. This suggests that many teachers who came to New York State from the South or the West Indies may have done so in protest against racial conditions in their home re-gions. It suggests too that the kind of people who had the initiative to move out of their home regions were also the kind of people who had the initiative to protest. The protesters were more likely to have been pre-pared for teaching by college education, while the non-protesters were more likely to have been prepared only by a normal school education. In terms of numbers, most protesters as well as most non-protesters taught downstate, where the proportion of blacks in the population was higher, but the proportion of black teachers who taught upstate and were protest-ers was higher than the proportion who taught downstate. Indeed, the farther one moved upstate toward the north and west, the higher the pro-portion of protesters became. Probable factors in this geographical dif-ference were as one went farther upstate, one found fewer blacks, less prejudice, more abolitionists, more Republicans, and more white institu-tions open to blacks.

What were the ways in which these black teachers protested?

Were their protests serious enough so that the white school officials under whom most of these teachers taught might be expected to be alarmed if they were profoundly determined to "keep blacks in their place"?

One of the ways in which the black teachers protested was to act as local agents of protest papers, taking subscriptions and collecting money for them. In doing so, black teachers allowed their names to be publicly listed as agents of the papers concerned, so that school officials could easily know of their action. George Hogarth, while teaching in Brooklyn, and Nathan Blount, while teaching in Poughkeepsie, allowed themselves to be listed as agents of what was widely believed to be a seditious paper, Garrison's *Boston Liberator.* Several teachers allowed themselves to be known as agents of the anti-slavery and anti-segregationist weekly, the *New York Colored American.*

Black teachers even edited or published abolitionist or black protest periodicals, and thus were among the leaders of militant black opinion in New York State. William C. Nell, who had already assisted William Lloyd Garrison in publishing the *Liberator* in Boston, came to Rochester to assist Frederick Douglass in publishing the *North Star,* and at the same time taught in a Rochester black public school. During the Civil War, Robert Hamilton edited the *New York Weekly Anglo-African,* one of the major organs of black militancy, at the same time that white officials allowed him to teach in the black public shools of anti-Lincoln, anti-draft New York City. Other black teachers who helped edit or publish protest periodicals included James T. Holly who had been an editor of the Windsor, Canada, *Voice of the Fugitive* before he taught in the black public school in Buffalo; and James W. Randolph who had already joined underground railroad operator Stephen Myers in editing the *Albany Telegraph and Journal* before he taught in the black public school in Albany.

One of the persistent drives of militant blacks in the period from 1835 to 1870 was the drive to secure the equal right for blacks to vote in the state by abolishing the special requirement that black voters must own property. Three times this issue came before the voters of the state in referendums, in 1846, 1860, and 1869. Despite the intensely emotional nature of this issue for whites, considerable numbers of black teachers in the largely white-controlled black schools openly took part in the campaign for equal suffrage. Among the black teachers who led in organizing meetings and planning strategy for the campaign in the 1830s, and were still doing so in the 1860s, were two of the most respected black public school principals in the state, Charles L. Reason and John Peterson of New York City. In the 1840s the one-legged militant, Henry Highland Garnet, who was teaching the public black school in Troy at the time, was

The Reverend Henry Highland Garnet, a passionate advocate of equal rights for blacks, was nevertheless allowed to teach black schools in the 1840s in Troy and Geneva. *Simmons,* Men of Mark, *1887.*

chairman of the black state central committee for equal suffrage, and as such spoke at least twice before committees of the legislature. Blacks are determined, he told them, to keep "blowing the ram's horn until the massive walls of injustice shall fall."[4] Troy school officials could scarcely have missed knowing that Garnet gave such militant speeches.

Among the major agencies of black protest in the period 1830 to 1870 were state and national Negro conventions. They provided an opportunity for black leaders to issue declarations of protest against slavery and segregation, including segregation in the schools; to call for equal rights in voting and jobs; and to plan strategy. Several New York State black teachers were major convention officers. Among them, Austin Steward was president of the state convention but afterward taught school in Canandaigua; J. W. C. Pennington was president of the national convention but afterward taught in both Newtown, Long Island, and Poughkeepsie; and Amos G. Beman was twice president of the national convention before he taught in Jamaica, Long Island. Serving as secretaries of either national or state Negro conventions, and most of them serving at the same time they were teaching, were Henry Hicks (who taught in Albany), Henry Highland Garnet (Troy), William C. Nell (Rochester), William J. Wilson (Brooklyn), and Ransom F. Wake, Benjamin F. Hughes, Charles L. Reason, and Robert Hamilton (New York City). The activities of these conventions were by no means secret. Their proceedings were often summarized in newspapers and then later published in detail as pamphlets. White school officials could easily discover who took part in them if they wished.

Black teachers often gave speeches against slavery—even women teachers sometimes did so. Before she taught in black schools in New York City and Williamsburg, Long Island, Maria W. Stewart gave passionate speeches against slavery to blacks in Boston. She did so in the early 1830s when for a woman to speak publicly on any subject was regarded as offensive, even if not on the inflammatory subject of slavery. The young Elizabeth Waters, both before and while teaching the colored public school in Newburgh in 1859, spoke against slavery on tour with a Southern-born black preacher. Using a magic lantern, they showed pictures of slavery, sang slave songs, and spoke in both black and white churches.

John Brown's raid on the arsenal in Harper's Ferry won fervent support from some New York State blacks. While Brown was awaiting execution in Virginia, a group of black women in Brooklyn wrote him a public letter calling him "a model of true patriotism"; one of the authors of the letter, the black public school teacher Mrs. Sarah J. S. Tompkins, read the letter aloud in a Brooklyn public meeting. At about the same time the black principal of one of the Brooklyn black public schools, Junius G. Morel, said in a public meeting that the "true" way to eradicate slavery was John Brown's way. After John Brown was executed, the black principal of a black public school in New York City led in arranging a mammoth concert by some of the children of her school for the benefit —as her newspaper advertisement said—"of the bereaved relations of that most noble, self-sacrificing hero, John Brown, and of those engaged with him." Similarly in Troy, the black principal of the black public school, Allen M. Bland, publicly raised funds for a monument to honor the "noble" black associates of John Brown who were either killed during his raid or later hanged with him.[5] All four of these black teachers who publicly supported John Brown continued to teach in public schools in the state for years thereafter, without any sign of consequent trouble.

Black teachers published protest letters, pamphlets, magazine articles, and books. William Levington, while teaching a black school in Albany in 1822, published an address in which he protested against slave owners as "barbarous and vicious men."[6] In 1859 and 1860 a new black protest periodical published in New York City, the *Anglo-African Magazine,* frequently advertised the names of its writers. Among them were five blacks who were teaching at the time in black public schools in the state, and two more who were soon to do so. In the 1870s and 1880s, Cordelia Ray, a teacher in a New York City black public school, not only was a correspondent for a black protest paper, but also published a poem praising the black revolutionary Toussaint L'Ouverture, saying we must "guard with love" his name.[7]

Among the black teachers were several former slaves who had made the drastic protest of running away from their masters. As fugitive slaves they were likely to be bitter against the slave system, yet they were permitted to teach in black schools in New York State. A fugitive who escaped from slavery in New York State itself was Austin Steward; he established himself as a grocer in Rochester, and afterward was allowed to teach in both Rochester and Canandaigua. A fugitive who escaped from slavery in Tennessee was Jermain W. Loguen; he was allowed to teach in Utica, Syracuse, and Bath. J. W. C. Pennington wrote a book telling the story of his escape from the oppression of slavery in Maryland: how he deceived pursuers, hid in barns, and to stay alive ate hard corn from the fields. After publishing his book, he nevertheless was allowed to teach public schools in both Newtown, Long Island, and Poughkeepsie.

Before 1860, considerable numbers of black teachers were active in abolitionist societies. Henry Highland Garnet, shortly before becoming a teacher in Troy, give a rousing address to the annual meeting of the American Antislavery Society in New York City, in which he protested that the black role in building America was scarcely mentioned in history books. Nathan Blount, while teaching in the tax-supported Poughkeepsie black school, was chosen as a member of the Dutchess County Antislavery Society's executive committee; as such he signed a call to an antislavery convention which appeared in the *Poughkeepsie Telegraph* of November 14, 1838, so that his school officials could hardly have missed it.

The Reverend James W. C. Pennington, though a fugitive slave and active aboli-tionist, was allowed to teach black schools. *Armistead,* A Tribute for the Negro, *1848.*

Later black teachers were active in other kinds of protest groups. During the Civil War, Edmonia Highgate, either while or just before she taught the black public school in Binghamton, gave speeches to raise

Mrs. Sarah J. S. Garnet was the daughter of the prosperous Indian-Negro, Sylvanus Smith, of Brooklyn. She taught black public schools in Brooklyn and Manhattan from the 1850s through the 1890s at the same time that she struggled for black rights. Crisis, *October 1911.*

money for an abolitionist-oriented freedmen's relief society which advocated equal rights for freedmen in the South. In the late 1860s, New York City black principal John Peterson and Brooklyn black principal Junius

C. Morel were national officers of the controversial, Garnet-founded African Civilization Society which sent blacks to West Africa to promote black self-determination. In the 1880s Charles A. Dorsey, while principal of a black public school in Brooklyn, was host at his home to a society committed to abolishing the still-lingering slave trade in Africa; he also served on the executive committee of the New York branch of T. T. Fortune's aggressive Afro-American League. Mrs. Sarah J. S. Garnet, the second wife of Henry Highland Garnet and longtime principal of a New York City black public school, was in the 1880s the "moving spirit" in the National Vigilance Committee which promoted awareness of black history and black rights.[8] In the 1890s Mrs. Garnet, and such other metropolitan area black public school teachers as J. Imogen Howard and Marithcha Lyons, were active in the Women's Loyal Union, an organization which defended black women's rights.

Black teachers sometimes protested specific acts of discrimination. Principal Reason at one time protested a case of segregated seating in a restaurant, at another time the exclusion of blacks from a lecture. William C. Nell, who was then or was soon to be teaching in a black public school in Rochester, accompanied editor Frederick Douglass to a Rochester banquet for newsmen where they were both refused admittance because of their color; they protested at the door until a banquet official took a vote among the newsmen, who decided to admit them after all. Elizabeth Jennings, a teacher in a New York City black public school, rode in a New York horse car intended for whites; on being ordered out, she clung to her seat until she was dragged out; as school officials could easily discover, she took the case to court. Principal Charles Dorsey was on a committee which visited the manager of a Brooklyn theater to protest its segregated seating.

Altogether, according to available evidence, among the 102 black teachers who can be identified as protesters either before or while teaching in black schools in New York State, 18 were agents of abolitionist or black protest periodicals; 14 edited or published such periodicals themselves; 32 campaigned for equal suffrage or other civil rights legislation; 40 helped organize or attended state or national Negro conventions; 22 lectured against slavery or racial discrimination; 6 were themselves fugitive slaves; 12 aided in protecting fugitive slaves from being sent back to the South; 25 published protest letters, pamphlets, articles, or books; 50 identified themselves with abolitionist, equal rights, or other protest organizations; and 17 protested specific acts of discrimination.

This protest activity was often substantial, persistent, and conspicuous, and it sharply challenged majority white opinion. Nevertheless, evidence that whites objected to the appointment of black teachers because of their protest activity is rare.

As we have seen, many public conflicts occurred over whether the teachers in the black schools should be blacks or whites. One might expect that if whites were ever to charge that blacks should not be appointed as teachers because of their efforts to upset the racial status quo, they would take the occasion of such public conflicts to make the charges. But no instances of such charges are available.

Before the abolition of slavery throughout the nation in 1865, one might expect that public objections would be made to the appointment of black teachers who were educated in institutions that were known for their abolitionist orientation, such as the two upstate colleges, Oneida Institute and New York Central College; or Oberlin College, Ohio; or the Quakers' Institute for Colored Youth, Philadelphia. While blacks who had studied at all these institutions were appointed to teach in the black schools of New York State, no instance of serious public protest against their appointment can be reported. In fact, the black Charles L. Reason had even taught at both the Institute for Colored Youth and New York Central College when in 1855 he was appointed principal of a New York City black public school without, as far as it is known, any white objections.

One might expect that it would be easy for whites to object to the teaching appointment of the black John J. Zuille because he was said to have been fired from his previous job as a foreman in a predominantly white printing shop for being defiantly antislavery. But Zuille was appointed to teach a black public school in New York City in 1853 without, as far as is known, any public objections.[9]

In the 1840s in Williamsburg, Long Island, there was a spat over the school board's failure to appoint the black William J. Hodges to teach a black public school when he had been led to expect that he would be appointed. There was ample opportunity for black parents involved in the dispute to claim that he was not appointed because he was a protester against racial discrimination, as indeed he conspicuously was. But they did not make such a claim, and Hodges himself explained that he was not appointed because the trustees were Methodists while he was not.[10]

In the 1830s in New York City, a group of black youths, especially pupils in the Manumission Society's schools, organized a literary society for themselves and began to meet regularly in a Manumission Society school building. However, when they decided to name their new society after the abrasive abolitionist William Lloyd Garrison, a white official of the Manumission Society requested one of the Manumission Society's black teachers, Prince Loveridge, to ask the black youths to drop the name Garrison, threatening that if they did not they could not continue to meet in the school building. When Loveridge reported this to a meeting of the black students, they shouted their protest and voted to keep the name Garrison even if they had to pay for a room for their meetings elsewhere. One might expect that the Manumission Society would punish Loveridge for allowing this to happen, but it did not. In fact, the Manumission Society soon hired him as its agent to improve attendance at the black schools, a sensitive position in which he was an intermediary among school officials, parents, and children.[11]

If whites objected to black protesters being teachers, one would expect to find evidence of protesters being let go from their jobs and having difficulty finding new ones. Evidence of black teachers being let go from their jobs because of their protests is rare, and in fact, among the black teachers in the state who left their teaching posts, a higher proportion of protesters than non-protesters found another teaching post in the state.

The only case of a black teacher being punished for his protest activity that I have discovered is that of William J. Wilson, and even his case is not altogether clear. By the late 1840s, Wilson had become principal of a Brooklyn black public school, with three women teachers under him. Nevertheless, while he continued as principal, Wilson was a conspicuous protester. He participated openly in at least two colored national conventions. He was on the board of managers of the Colored State Suffrage Association. In a speech to blacks which was published under his name in a prominent black protest periodical he praised the New York City slave insurrection of 1712 as a "noble" revolution for freedom and urged blacks to do everything they could to abolish slavery in the South.[12] When Northern blacks were imprisoned for trying to protect fugitive slaves from being returned to the South, Wilson spoke at meetings to raise funds for them.

In 1863 after he had been teaching about twenty-one years in Brooklyn's black schools, Wilson's position as principal came under attack. His position was attacked for three reasons, according to the usually carefully-spoken black physician, Dr. James McCune Smith. One reason was that Wilson had personally offended a Brooklyn black pastor. The second was that an unscrupulous black teacher from Staten Island, who wanted Wilson's job for himself, circulated a petition among the parents of Wilson's school asking his removal.[13] The third reason was the only one clearly related to Wilson's protest activity. According to Dr. Smith, "Mr. Wilson made one or two strong anti-slavery speeches of marked ability in Cooper Institute Hall in the winter of 1862–63. These excited the wrath of a Copperhead-Celtic member of the Board of Education, and he openly avowed his determination to remove him for that cause."[14]

When Wilson's case was brought before the Brooklyn board, there seemed to be additional factors working against Wilson which were unrelated to his protest activity. It was charged that attendance at his school was poor, that he neglected discipline, and that his pupils were making slow progress. But before the board decided whether to remove Wilson, he resigned.[15] While Wilson's protest activity played a role in his leaving Brooklyn, it is not clear that it played a crucial role.

Aside from the dubious case of Wilson, it is remarkable that evidence is not available that by being protesters, black New York State teachers seriously jeopardized their jobs.

The great freedom with which New York State black teachers agitated against discrimination suggests that the Northern black schools and the social context in which they operated were in basic respects unlike those of recent generations in the South.

In the South in the black public school system which emerged after Reconstruction, black teachers found it difficult to be outspoken critics of the racial status quo. Employed as they usually were by white school boards who were fiercely determined to separate the races, black teachers could not easily protest discrimination. In the late 1800s and early 1900s, Booker T. Washington's Tuskegee Institute and similar schools in the South educated black teachers to acquiesce, at least in public, in the inferior status of blacks. From then on, for several decades, the great majority of black teachers in the South smothered their protests. In the 1930s Carter G. Woodson found that Southern black teachers, mindful of their precarious tenure, seldom asked for changes which were not approved by a large majority of the citizens in the communities in which they taught; and, similarly, Roy Wilkins reported that they were not usually willing to take cases of discrimination to court because they not only feared losing their jobs but even bodily injury.[16]

In New York State, by contrast, while most whites regarded abolitionists as dangerous fanatics, white school authorities were able to tolerate black abolitionists as teachers—even some of the most militant and prominent black abolitionists in the nation. While the majority of New York State citizens up to 1870 opposed allowing blacks the equal right to vote, nevertheless whites tolerated, as teachers in black schools, blacks who worked conspicuously for that right. As long as a considerable number of legally segregated black public schools survived in the state, up to 1900, most whites in the state regarded blacks as inherently inferior, essentially as most whites did in the South. Still, unlike in the South in recent generations, white school authorities in New York State were able to accept black teachers who insisted that blacks were not inferior, who identified with black militant movements, and who struggled for equal rights in legislation and in practice. Even allowing for differences in time and place, the contrast cries out for explanation.

Possible factors to help explain why whites in New York State were tolerant of black teachers who engaged in protest can at least be suggested. Factors that seem plausible, but have only limited merit, are the following:

1. Perhaps school officials in New York State were often unaware that black teachers were engaging in protest. School records in fact do not indicate that school officials concerned themselves significantly with the protest records of the black teachers they hired. Yet most of the protest activities we have cited were easily known to the public. A simple reading of the local white newspapers, or black newspapers, or abolitionist newspapers, or a simple enquiry from local politicians or black parents would surely have elicited information about the protest activity of most of the black teachers.

2. Perhaps white school officials, being often from the upper classes[17] who had less to fear from blacks competing with them for jobs or social status than whites of lower classes did, were not as hostile to black demands for equal rights as most citizens were. Yet in the South similar factors do not seem to have made school officials tolerant of black teachers who engaged in protest.

3. Perhaps school officials in New York State, living as they did in a region of greater diversity of religious and ethnic background than the South, had pragmatically learned, more than school officials in the South, that for schools to avoid crippling controversies, they had to be broadly tolerant of the teachers they employed. However, it is possible to cite a considerable number of examples of New York school officials' intolerance—not of black teachers because of their protest, but other kinds of intolerance. For instance, as we have seen, a state superintendent of schools advised local school officials in the 1830s that it was unwise to appoint black teachers to white schools simply because they were black; and at least until the 1890s, the overwhelming majority of school officials in the state would not even consider appointing blacks to teach whites. In Albany and elsewhere in the state, according to an abolitionist claim, many *white* teachers lost their jobs just because they were abolitionists.[18] In Fulton, two white teachers reputedly lost their jobs because they supported the black Professor Allen who wished to marry a white. In the 1840s a state superintendent ruled that school officials could refuse to appoint an Irish teacher simply because he was Irish; in the 1850s a state su-

perintendent ruled that school officials could refuse to appoint any teacher "because of the feelings or prejudice of the inhabitants."[19] In New York City in the 1850s teachers were often not appointed or promoted because of their place of birth, politics, religion, or national background. In the 1870s a New York City superintendent of schools was forced to resign because he had become an avowed spiritualist.[20] Such examples do not encourage the belief that school officers in the state had moved very far in learning pragmatically to be tolerant of their teachers.

More compelling reasons for New York's tolerance of black teachers who were protesters seem to be these:

1. Despite occasional claims that the North was at least as prejudiced against blacks as the South, the North was less prejudiced. In New York State, with comparatively few blacks in the population and the proportion either declining or remaining nearly stationary through the nineteenth century, most school officials did not feel great discomfort in allowing black teachers to protest. The prejudice of New York State whites in responsible positions, while real, can be exaggerated.

2. White school officials, like white leadership generally, often ignored black protest. Some officials may have done so in part because they felt guilty about it, didn't know how to deal with it, and hoped that by ignoring it, it would go away. Other officials may have felt able to ignore it because it came from blacks who were inferior, uninfluential, and could be isolated; as one of New York State's black teachers, the protester Austin Steward, himself observed, upper class whites could tolerate a black protesting against racial discrimination when they could not tolerate a responsible white doing so. Still other white school officials, especially those with political, commercial, or religious ties to the white South, may have been led to ignore black protest during the abolitionist period, as Benjamin Quarles has suggested, by taking their cue from Southern slaveowners.[21] The slaveowners battled *white* abolitionists openly, but they tried to ignore *black* abolitionists whenever possible because they desperately desired to believe that blacks were contented. For white supporters of the status quo, North or South, to acknowledge that a significant proportion of blacks were militant protesters could help undermine confidence in the nation's social system and threaten the Union itself.

3. Finally, if school officials were to employ well-educated black teachers at all they could scarcely avoid employing protesters. The better educated teachers were more likely to be protesters than non-protesters, as we have seen. They were so in part because the schools and colleges they attended often encouraged them to become protesters—schools or colleges which were likely to admit blacks were likely to be sympathetic to

black protest, while other schools and colleges simply refused to admit blacks. In addition, many of the well-educated black teachers were likely to be protesters simply because the milieu of New York State's more articulate blacks was one of protest against slavery, segregation, and inequality. Often during the nineteenth century, New York State—as the site of black conventions, the seat of black publications, and the home of outstanding black leaders—was the center of black protest for the nation.

Because of such factors as these, New York State black teachers were remarkably free to develop their leadership as protesters against slavery, segregation, and inequality. Assisted by their freedom to protest, many of the teachers became models of such protest to their pupils, and themselves became major figures in the long black struggle for greater opportunity.

WHO LED ON BLACK SCHOOL ISSUES?

IN NINETEENTH CENTURY NEW YORK STATE there were, as we have seen, blacks who were willing to lead campaigns to put black rather than white teachers into the black schools. There were also blacks with a vision of an America of equal opportunity who struggled to open white schools to blacks. Who were these and other blacks who led on educational issues?

Were these blacks largely from the black bourgeoisie, that is, the business and professional class which has traditionally provided a large share of leadership in America? The black sociologist Franklin Frazier made the mid-twentieth century black bourgeoisie infamous for what he considered their failure to lead the black community on real issues, and instead their escape into their own make-believe world of status-seeking social life.[1] Did the black bourgeoisie fail to lead in black school affairs in the nineteenth century too?

What of the skilled workers? Did the ubiquitous black barbers pour their feelings about black schools into the ears of their white customers as they drew razors over their soapy throats?

Were black pastors more or less outstanding as leaders in school issues than black barbers? The black abolitionist William C. Nell, once himself a teacher in a black school in New York State, claimed that black pastors monopolized leadership among blacks.[2] Was this true in New York State school issues?

Which occupational groups of black leaders were more active in the different aspects of school matters? Was one group more active in school issues involving little conflict and another in those involving considerable conflict?

Was there any significant role for black women as community

leaders in school affairs? For black students? When white school boards chose black leaders, were such black leaders likely to be from the same occupations as when blacks chose their own leaders?

It is not claimed that definitive answers to such questions can be given from the limited information available. Nor is it claimed that black leaders were necessarily effective. They were often hampered by such factors as racial prejudice, problems of cost, and division of opinion among blacks. In 1855 the perceptive black physician James McCune Smith complained that American blacks lacked real leaders of their own, and always had, because the black masses refused to support them; blacks are attracted more to white leaders than to black ones, Smith mourned.[3]

Keeping in mind the scarcity of information available, as well as limitations on the effectiveness of black leaders, we proceed as well as we can to note who among blacks took significant community action in regard to educational issues.

A few blacks led in trying to improve attendance or scholarship at New York City black schools. They did so in various group actions stretching from 1828 to 1887. Those we count either put themselves forward in such actions, or were chosen by other blacks because they believed they would be persuasive. Such black leaders visited in black families, urging parents to send their children to schools. They gave speeches and published articles for this purpose. They awarded prizes to pupils who achieved outstanding scholarship. Of the sixty-one black leaders of this kind whose occupation can be identified, 72 percent were professionals and businessmen, far higher than their approximately 4 percent in the black working population in the state, while 28 percent were skilled and unskilled workers, far less than their approximately 96 percent in the black population. The largest single occupational group among these leaders—39 percent of the whole—was pastors. Thus the role of pastors, while by no means a monopoly, was substantial indeed.

Other blacks became leaders as prominent visitors—either as speakers or otherwise playing a significant role—at black schools. Invited by the black principals, they often sat on the platform at public examinations or graduation exercises. They often exhorted the children to study to contribute to the progress of the African race, and generally served as models of black achievement toward which the children could strive. Among such visitors at black schools in the New York metropolitan region, as reported in black newspapers in the years 1883 through 1892, there were 106 blacks whose occupations can be identified. Of them, 80 percent were professionals, 20 percent businessmen. There were no unskilled or even skilled workers among them. Somehow black principals did not seem to find any representatives of such numerous black groups as barbers or waiters as suitable visiting speakers for their scholars. There were only three women visitors; one was the head of a school in Liberia, another the wife of a wealthy caterer, and the third was the poet Frances E. W. Harper. The outstanding individual occupation among the visitors was again pastors, and they were such a high proportion (61%) of the whole that one could argue that in the category of prominent school visitors, pastors approached a monopoly.

Being a leader in either of these two activities related to schools— helping to improve school attendance or serving as school visitors—was not likely to bring blacks into direct conflict with either whites or other blacks. When blacks were leaders in more controversial issues, however, they were likely to come into conflict with whites or other blacks. Here the occupational grouping of the black leaders becomes noticeably different.

Blacks led campaigns for black rather than white teachers in the black schools, and, as we have seen, this was likely to be a matter of sharp conflict. Available information on who the leaders were in these campaigns comes from Brooklyn, Manhattan, Staten Island, Poughkeepsie, Albany, Troy, and Rochester. In these campaigns, of the thirty-five black leaders who can be identified by occupation, the proportion of pastors is a fairly low 23 percent, suggesting that pastors found it more difficult to act on this controversial issue than on such matters as improving attendance or visiting schools. The proportion of journalists is also 23 percent, thus bringing a new occupational group to the fore. Since there were fewer journalists in the black population than pastors, this suggests that journalists were more willing to act on controversial matters than pastors.

We test another area of school conflict to see if again the proportion of pastors was fairly low compared to what it had been in areas of little conflict, and to see whether journalists or any other occupational group also come to prominence. This is the area of the long, hard-fought campaign to open white schools to black pupils and abolish black schools. Even more conflict was likely for black leaders in this activity than in demanding black instead of white teachers for black schools.

Using examples that reach from the 1830s through the 1890s and come from the metropolitan region north to Albany and Troy and west to Lockport and Buffalo, we can record in this campaign 272 black leaders whose occupations are known. Compared to the blacks who led in asking for black rather than white teachers, the proportion of black pastors is down to 16 percent; in this important area of conflict, pastors were remote from monopolizing leadership. Two other single occupations produced almost as many leaders as pastors; barbers—a new occupational group to come to the front—with 14 percent and journalists with 12.

Now we are ready to compare the total numbers of black leaders in activities of little conflict with those in activities of considerable conflict. To do so, we add black leaders active in additional school matters to each list and then enter the results in columns 1 and 2 of Table 10.1.

The comparison is striking. Those who led in activities involving considerable conflict are of a lower status than those who led in activities of little conflict.

Black pastors, who were a high proportion of black leaders in school affairs involving little conflict, evidently found it more difficult to lead in matters which put them in sharp conflict with other people, whether black or white. On the other hand, black journalists, who were few in matter of little conflict, were numerous in conflict situations. Probably a major factor in this difference is that newspapers tend to thrive on controversy while churches do not.

Like black pastors, black businessmen were less active in school matters when they involved more conflict. Probably some businessmen had a failure of nerve when it came to conflict. Perhaps they feared loss of patronage; they undoubtedly had more to lose than the black workers did. Possibly some black businessmen were already retreating into their world of status-seeking make-believe. It is impressive that the proportion of black workers—both skilled and unskilled—who led in school matters involving *considerable* conflict was larger than the proportion who led in matters involving *little* conflict. Perhaps blacks deliberately chose some types of workers—such as barbers, waiters, and janitors—to lead them in conflict situations because they believed that since they served whites, they knew how to deal with them. The substantial showing of unskilled workers, while small in comparison to their large proportion in the black population, is an indication that at least a significant few blacks at the lower end of the social scale were plucky.

The names of persons we have counted in columns 1 and 2 come largely from such sources as school board records, local newspapers, and black newspapers. We use them here objectively, that is, we accept any names of persons who appear as significantly active in black school matters. We make no attempt to distinguish the relative importance of one such person from another. For example, we give as much weight to the secretary of a black meeting called to ask for a new school building as to someone chosen by the meeting to negotiate about it with a school board. Moreover, we make no effort to judge whether a leader was or was not successful in what he undertook. Fortunately, however, we are able to check these two relatively objective lists against a subjective one, that is, a

TABLE 10.1

Black Leaders in the Nineteenth Century in Black Educational Matters:
Occupational Distribution by Percentages

	Black Chosen			White Chosen
	In Activities of Little Conflict %	In Activities of Considerable Conflict %	Scottron's List %	%
Professionals	52	44	38	35
pastors	35	18	13	29
journalist-editors	3	10	16	1
physicians-dentists	4	4	4	0
lawyers	3	3	2	1
teachers	4	5	0	2
social agency executives	1	2	2	0
Businessmen	20	13	31	10
merchants	9	2	9	5
restaurant operators	4	3	13	1
agents	3	3	4	0
manufacturers	2	0	2	2
Skilled Workers	15	24	24	35
barbers	3	10	7	27
clerks	2	5	2	3
tailors-clothes cleaners	2	3	4	3
printers	0	0	4	0
Unskilled Workers	13	19	7	20
porters	3	2	2	0
whitewashers	2	2	0	4
laborers	2	4	0	1
waiters	0	3	0	9
coachmen	0	3	0	4
janitors	1	3	0	0
cartmen	1	1	4	0
Number of Persons	324	528	45	92

list of blacks who were most important in black school affairs in the judgment of a black who himself was active in those affairs.

This list was made by the black Samuel R. Scottron in 1905. At that time a black New York City newspaper claimed that not much had been done by blacks to improve school opportunities for blacks in the state until the arrival from the South in the late 1870s of two black leaders, editor T. T. Fortune and lawyer T. McCants Stewart. Scottron denied that this was true and gave a list of New York State blacks who had been "ceaseless in our school matters" in the generation before the advent of Fortune and Stewart, and especially in the opening of white schools to blacks.[4] He also gave a list of white leaders, but we will deal with them in later chapters.

Scottron was himself a prosperous inventor and manufacturer, particularly of imitation stone. Born in Philadelphia, he had come to Brooklyn as a child in 1851 and lived there ever since. He attended public schools in Brooklyn and graduated from Cooper Institute with a B.A. degree. In the 1890s he served as a member of the Brooklyn Board of Education, the third black to be so appointed. He compiled his list of leaders in school matters, he said, from his long experience in the field, from examination of surviving copies of black newspapers, and from the recollection of others.

Including Fortune and Stewart, as well as Scottron himself, Scottron's list consists of forty-five leaders. Placed for comparison in the table in column 3 beside the two more objective lists, Scottron's list of leaders is more like the list of leaders in activities of considerable conflict than it is like the list of those in activities of little conflict. Evidently Scottron felt that blacks who were active in conflict were more significant leaders. Notable in Scottron's list is that its proportion of pastors (13%) is less than in either of the other two lists, and that its proportion of journalists (16%) is higher, journalists in fact being Scottron's highest single occupational group. Also notable in his list is that businessmen as a group are much higher than in either of the other two lists, which may be explained in part by Scottron's bias as a businessman.

The first two lists (columns 1 and 2) are of *black-chosen* black leaders in school matters; that is, blacks who by their own action put themselves into a position of leadership, or who were chosen to positions of leadership by being selected by blacks to speak, negotiate, serve as officers of meetings, or the like. Scottron's list is also of *black-chosen* black leaders at least in the sense that they were leaders in the judgment of Scottron who was a black. Fortunately we can check these three lists against a list of *white-chosen* black leaders. It gives us an opportunity to see whether white-chosen leaders were different in occupational distribution from black-chosen leaders.

Included in the names of the white-chosen leaders are blacks chosen by the Troy school board to visit its black school and examine the pupils in their studies; blacks elected (1840s) by the Brooklyn Common Council as trustees for black schools, or appointed (1880s and 1890s) by the Brooklyn mayor to serve on the school board; and blacks chosen by various school boards to participate in special ceremonies at black schools, or to advise them about black schools, or the like. Placed for comparison beside the three lists of black-chosen black leaders in Table 1, the white-chosen black leaders have a lower occupational status than the black-chosen black leaders. Evidently white men of power—who were usually business or professional men themselves—preferred black leaders to be of a lower status than blacks thought was useful when they chose their own leaders. The proportion of pastors is fairly high in comparison with the other lists—evidently both whites and blacks found pastors to be useful as black leaders. The fact that the proportion of businessmen is only moderate does not support the idea, reported to be true in recent decades in the South, that black businessmen were more acceptable to whites as leaders than other blacks were.[5] The proportion of journalists, a class blacks often chose as leaders in activities involving considerable conflict, is very low, suggesting whites found journalists too bold for comfort.

Altogether, according to these four lists, the most outstanding single occupation in black leadership in school matters was pastors. They appear with the highest percentage in three out of the four lists.

In serving black interests, pastors had the advantage, like journalists, that their patrons were likely to be blacks. Many of the pastors also had the advantage that, being related to black denominations which were only loosely organized, they had considerable freedom to lead as they chose, limited only by the need to carry their congregations with them. The position of pastor provided men of suitable talents a comparatively open road on which to rise—a road relatively free from white prejudice and without rigid education or class restrictions.

Informed observers in the nineteenth century and since have often stressed the role of clergy in black leadership in America. As applied to black leadership in school matters in New York State, however, I believe that some of them have overstated the case. If Nell was right in claiming that pastors monopolized leadership among blacks, one would expect pastors to appear as somewhere near 100 percent of the leaders, while in fact the list presented in Table 1 which gives them their highest percentage gives them only 35 percent, and that was in matters of little conflict.

Journalists have the highest percentage in one list and tie for second place in another. Particularly striking is that in activities involving little conflict the proportion of journalists was only 3 percent, but in activities involving considerable conflict it jumped to 10 percent.

Nearly all the journalists in our lists were the editors of black newspapers. As editors, they were more nearly automatically leaders in black protest because of their occupational function than any other black occupational group. Black editors were, in effect, black professional protesters, the forerunner of what was to become by the mid-twentieth century a considerable group.[6] As professional protesters, black editors like Frederick Douglass in Rochester and T. T. Fortune in New York performed the vital function of leaders in fact-finding about inequality in black educational opportunities and in crusading to alter it.

After pastors and journalists, the next most prominent single occupation in the lists of leaders was barbers—they were a close second in the white-chosen list and tied for second in the black-chosen list of those who led in actions of considerable conflict. Barbers were a far larger portion of the black working population than pastors, journalists, lawyers, and physicians combined. In New York City about 1850, although black barbers were not numerous enough to dominate barbering as they did at the time in some cities of the South, barbers did at least constitute 4 percent of the black work force. Even in 1890, when black barbers were being displaced by European immigrants, especially Italians, black barbers were still 2 percent of the black work force in the state.[7]

In contrast to black pastors and journalists, black barbers were usually dependent on whites for patronage. Black barbers sometimes considered that they were more respectable when they served whites rather than blacks; as we have seen, they sometimes even refused to serve blacks. The fact that black barbers usually served whites may help to explain why barbers appear high in the white-chosen list of black leaders. Evidently whites felt that they knew barbers and could work with them as black leaders. But blacks also chose barbers as leaders in fairly high degree and not nearly so much in activities involving little conflict as in activities involving considerable conflict. Apparently many blacks believed that in controversial school matters barbers would negotiate effectively with whites in the interests of blacks.

Because job opportunities were limited among blacks, unusually able blacks sometimes became barbers. While some of them undoubtedly

T. Thomas Fortune was one of the most effective black editors in the nation from the 1880s into the early 1990s. With regard to the South, he was at times an ally of Booker T. Washington, and as such supported separate "industrial" education for blacks. However, for New York State, he fought fiercely for the right of black pupils to attend white schools and of black teachers to teach whites. *Simmons, Men of Mark, 1887.*

wasted their talents as barbers—the black Martin R. Delany wrote of the tragedy of talented blacks being permitted to "expire" in barber shops— other barbers attained considerable status and used it for the benefit of blacks. An example of a barber who did so was William H. Johnson of

Albany, who became a member of the Republican State Committee and the major black lobbyist in Albany for black causes, including equal school rights. Another such barber was William Rich of Troy. Called a man of "decidedly intellectual appearance," he often presided at colored state conventions. As a barber in a prominent Troy hotel, Rich came to know leading whites well enough for a white newspaper to describe him as enjoying the "personal warm friendship" of Governors Marcy, Seward, and Wright.[8] Rich led both in asking Troy's school board for black instead of white teachers for Troy's black public school and in going over the head of the school board to ask the state legislature to require Troy's high school to admit blacks. Nevertheless, the school board repeatedly chose Rich to its committees to examine the black school, and in his old age, the board even named a splendid new black school building after him, an unusual honor for any black in nineteenth century New York State.

Black students played a negligible role as leaders in nineteenth century school issues, in marked contrast to their role in black leadership in the 1960s. All six of the known examples of student leaders were ministerial students. All took action in matters of considerable conflict, four of them protesting against General Theological Seminary's refusal in the 1830s to admit black students as equals.

As for black women, thirty-eight of them are among those counted as leaders in school matters, a large number compared to students, but small compared to men. Scottron did not include any women in his list of leaders, but women were almost evenly divided among the other three lists, being 4 or 5 percent of each.

Significant about women is that their participation in school issues increased as the century advanced. In the 1820s and 1830s black women were active in matters of little conflict such as raising funds for black schools and collecting clothing to assist black children to attend school. In the 1840s—the decade in which the national women's rights movement was born in a convention in Seneca Falls, New York—the first known instance of a black woman's leadership in a matter of considerable conflict occurred when a black laundress asked the Rochester school board to permit black children to enter a white school. However, it was not until the 1880s—the decade in which state law first allowed women to vote in school elections—that women began to play a major role. At that time black Principal Sarah Garnet, a wisp of a woman, appeared in a delegation of blacks not only before the New York City school board but also before the governor in Albany to ask his help in desegregating the New York City schools without letting the black teachers lose their jobs.

In the 1890s, black women, buoyed by the progress of the white women's suffrage movement, were becoming increasingly aware of their potential. In the New York metropolitan region, as we have seen, black women organized an action group of their own, the Women's Loyal Union. On the larger scene they also organized the National Association of Colored Women, for which Sarah Garnet was soon to become superintendent of suffrage work, and Elizabeth C. Carter, who had been principal of the Howard Colored Orphan Asylum's school, was soon to become president.

Suddenly in the 1890s more black women became leaders in school issues than in all the rest of the century put together. Several black women held positions overseeing black schools, as they did not early in the century. In Brooklyn they served on committees that supervised the Howard Asylum school. In Manhattan they served as trustees of the black McDonough Memorial Hospital which had its own school of nursing— among the trustees were the journalist Victoria Earle Mathews, and of course, the kinetic Sarah Garnet. Black women became involved in controversial school matters, too. In Stapleton, on Staten Island, a black mother, who had attended President Hunter's Normal College, refused to send her child to the black public school, charging it was unsanitary and provided ineffective education. In Jamaica, on Long Island, the burly operator of a scavenger business, Elizabeth Cisco, became a major figure in whipping up a black school "war" which led, in a story we shall follow later, to a boycott of the black public school, the arrest of black parents, and finally in 1900, to a state law limiting school segregation.

HOW MUCH BLACK CONTROL?

I N OUR TIME BLACKS have often clamored for a greater share in controlling the schools that teach their children. We easily assume that it is only recently, in the last twenty years or so, that blacks have begun to achieve significant control over these schools. We are likely to be impressed with the claim of black historian Carter G. Woodson that in the period from the Emancipation to the 1930s, in the nation as a whole blacks had "no control over their education."[1]

If this was true for the South, where overwhelmingly most blacks lived at the time, was it true for the North? In particular, were blacks in New York State in the period from about 1830 to 1930 really powerless in regard to the education of their children?

For blacks in nineteenth century New York State, the extent of their control over the schools that taught their children was often an issue. It was common for them to complain that whites concerned with black education did not consult them enough. As early as 1839 the *New York Colored American* so complained, adding that whites should have an intelligent black committee to consult "on all occasions wherein our interests are involved."[2]

New York State blacks often wished to participate in policy-making more than whites allowed. In 1859 a black New York City magazine charged that the city's board of education "feel themselves little if at all responsible to colored voters." In 1872 a colored state convention resolved to "demand the selection of one colored man in every school district in the state for the purpose of protecting the interests of the colored citizens" in the schools.[3] Blacks in Troy in 1858 created, outside of the legal school structure, a committee of blacks "to have an oversight" of the Troy black public school. Similarly, blacks in Albany in the 1860s maintained for at least two years what they called an "executive committee acting for the colored citizens of Albany" which made requests of the board of education.[4]

In a black neighborhood of Brooklyn in 1869, a public meeting of blacks asked that the Brooklyn Board of Education create a "competent colored committee to have the supervision of our colored school"; for the board to do so legally, the mayor would have had to appoint black members to the board, but the board was not willing to ask him to do so. In 1882 Brooklyn blacks directly asked for blacks to be appointed to the board, and this time the mayor—the reform mayor Seth Low—appointed one. From then on to 1898, as long as Brooklyn remained a separate city, blacks were proud that one black was on the Brooklyn board. Said the black *New York Globe* in 1883, the black Brooklyn board member "has justified the expectations of those who most desired to have a colored member." It added why can't New York City have a colored board member too? "Surely our interests demand one."[5] While there were black public schools in at least forty-three different villages, towns, or cities in New York State, it was characteristic of the limited formal role which whites allowed blacks in making school policy in the nineteenth century that Brooklyn was the only place in the state known to have a black on its school board.

Why Brooklyn was exceptional in this respect the author has examined in detail elsewhere. Among the major reasons appear to be, first, that Brooklyn blacks to an unusual degree had developed their own black-run institutions and thus had unusual opportunities to develop organizational skills and black pride; and, second, that Brooklyn, with its quiet, tree-lined streets and its lesser degree of prejudice compared to other parts of the New York metropolitan area, had long attracted the more family-minded, responsible, middle and upper class blacks, whose values whites could tolerate as not threatening their own.[6] In contrast to Brooklyn, New York City waited till 1917 to place the first black on its city-wide board. Other communities in the state waited much longer.

Although in the nineteenth and early twentieth centuries New York State blacks did not find as many ways to share in the control of schools as they wished, nevertheless, they did find ways to do so. Blacks shared with whites in voting for many of the officials who made school policy. In general elections in the state, blacks had the equal right to vote from 1870 when a United States Constitutional Amendment gave blacks that right in all states. In school district meetings, the state superintendent of schools ruled as early as 1836, in a dispute arising in Rensselaer County, that blacks had the equal right to vote providing they met the usual district voter requirement of holding property. There is ample evidence that blacks were aware of this right. As early as 1841, in Williamsburg, Long Island, blacks took a vociferous part in a school district meeting and voted without any question of their right to do so. In 1859, when Rochester editor Frederick Douglass proposed that blacks organize a state drive to open all public schools to blacks, one method he urged blacks to use was to attend local school meetings and demand that school officials admit blacks to all public schools.[7] In Amityville, Long Island, at an annual school meeting in the 1880s, a black parent successfully moved that "funds be appropriated to put the colored school house in decent condition." In Flushing, Long Island, in 1891, only a decade after women had won the legal right to vote in school elections in the state, among the conspicuous voters were three black women, including the principal of the black school.[8]

More directly, blacks shared control over black schools through their black teachers and principals. As we have seen, from about 1832, because blacks pushed for it, the teachers and principals of both the public and non-public black schools became largely black in the New York metropolitan area; they later became fairly often black, too, in the Hudson River counties north to Albany and Troy, less often to the west. The black teachers were often unusually able blacks if for no other reason than because other suitable employment for ambitious and intelligent blacks was severely limited. Moreover, the black teachers were often militant for black rights—as we have seen, 27 percent of the 390 teachers in nineteenth century New York State who are known by name and can be identified as black were active in black protest. That is, they took part in colored state conventions, helped to edit anti-slavery newspapers, circulated petitions for equal suffrage for blacks, protested cases of segregated seating on streetcars, or the like. Such able and outspoken teachers were likely to make an impact on their colleagues, their pupils, and school policy.

Black teachers sometimes took the initiative by making requests of school boards. In Troy a black principal asked for an additional teacher, and he got one. In Flushing, Long Island, a black principal arranged a meeting of black parents which petitioned for a new school building for their school, and by the next year they had it.[9] In New Rochelle between 1857 and 1888, four different black teachers made a total of seven appeals to their board. Four of the seven appeals the board granted; one asking for a janitor, another asking for repairs to the school building, and two more asking for help in disciplining pupils. The other three appeals the board denied; one asking for readmission of a pupil who had been suspended and two asking for an increase in salary. In Roslyn, Long Island, in the years 1900 to 1904, one strong-minded black teacher made six requests of her board, all of which were granted: for drawing books, writing books, a globe, repairs to the water closet, the dismissal of two incorrigible pupils, and an increase in salary. In Brooklyn in 1900 a black teacher who had a temporary appointment to teach in a predominantly white school complained to Brooklyn's one black board member that he had been denied a permanent appointment to the school. The board member at once asked for an investigation of the "alleged unfair treatment." Within a few days the teacher—the highly competent William L. Bulkley who held a Ph.D. degree from Syracuse University—had received his permanent appointment.[10]

In the latter half of the nineteenth century, black teachers sometimes worked with white teachers in such a way as to give them a chance to share in influencing school affairs. In Flushing, when the school superintendent resigned in a dispute with the school board, two black teachers joined white teachers in signing a letter of regret that he had resigned. At a meeting of the Queens County teachers association, a black principal presented a demonstration of her pupils in gymnastics exercises. In Brooklyn at various times the teachers association or the principals association chose the black Principal Charles A. Dorsey as its treasurer, secretary, or vice president. In New York City, the teachers association chose the black Principal Charles L. Reason as chairman of its committee on grammar school work and repeatedly elected him to its board of directors.

Black teachers who were concerned to develop black pride—as some clearly were—faced the problem that the subject of black history was not in the regular curriculum. The general policy of public school districts in the state was that what was taught in the black schools should be the same as what was taught in the white schools. Moreover, the textbooks used were usually the ones adopted by school boards for all the schools of a given school system. This meant that texts might at best show humanitarian sympathy for blacks—for example, among the most commonly used history and geography texts in the New York State schools before the Civil War were those by Peter Parley which described the horrors of the slave trade, the injustice of colonial New York to weak and defenseless slaves, and the unhappy impact of slavery in the South on both blacks and whites. It also meant that history texts were likely to present blacks as passive and ignorant and as having had scarcely any part in the American armed forces, the abolitionist movement, or in contributions to civilization.

In much of the nineteenth century there was little authentic black history available. In the 1840s the black Amos Beman, before he became a teacher on Long Island, asked Noah Webster, the distinguished author of dictionaries and school spellers, to advise him who was the best author on the origins of the African race. Webster wrote in reply: "Of the wooly-haired . . . inhabitants of Africa, there is no history and there can be none. That race has remained in barbarism from the first ages of the world." Few books on black history or culture were in school libraries. An anonymous writer in *Frederick Douglass' Paper* in the 1850s protested that in the library of a colored public school in Brooklyn there was no book on the history of the black people, and he added that the only way for black youths to know the early history of their race on Long Island, was to ask old black men what they knew. In the 1840s an Albany abolitionist paper reported that abolitionist books were not permitted in school libraries in the state. As late as the 1890s, in a list of about 180 history and biography books recommended by the state's Department of Public Instruction for inclusion in school libraries, none was primarily on blacks.[11]

However, even before the Civil War, a few blacks were already writing what may be called black history, propagandistic though it was, and several of these black authors were teachers in New York State. In 1841 J. W. C. Pennington, who had just been teaching in a black school in Newtown, Long Island, and would be again, published his pioneering *Text Book of the Origin and History . . . of the Colored People.* In 1851 William C. Nell, who had recently been teaching the black public school in Rochester, published his *Services of Colored Americans in the Wars of 1776 and 1812,* and later he revised and expanded it. In 1857 James T. Holly, who had recently been teaching in the black public school of Buffalo, published a history of Haiti. Because these authors were teachers in New York State, as well as prominent in other ways among blacks, it is likely that some black teachers and pupils in the state became familiar with their works even if they were not authorized texts. Besides such works, numerous antislavery publications were available by this time, including biographies and autobiographies of blacks, as well as sermons, lectures, and periodicals which included considerable black history mixed with polemics.

After the Civil War, blacks produced still more writing on black history and culture, as well as publications directly intended for use in black schools. In the late 1860s the largely black-controlled African Civilization Society began to publish in Brooklyn a monthly which was intended to be used to teach reading to blacks. Since Junius C. Morel, the principal of a black public school in Brooklyn, was on the staff of this monthly, he as well as other black teachers in the state may have used it to help teach reading.[12] In the 1880s the young black lawyer T. McCants Stewart, who became a member of the Brooklyn school board, wrote a book on his experience as a teacher in Liberia. About the same time Rufus Perry, an influential black Baptist editor who frequently took part in Brooklyn black school affairs, gave an address—which was afterward published and republished—in which he argued that blacks should be proud of their ancestors because they included the ancient Ethiopians and Egyptians. By 1890, Edward A. Johnson, a black teacher in North Carolina, had written what has been called the first history of the Negro for schools; it was adopted for use in many black schools about the nation and was reprinted in New York. On October 4, 1906, when Johnson was about to move to New York to practice law, the *New York Age* explained that Johnson's book was needed because "few white histories mention the Afro-American, and those that do only speak of him as a slave and a menial, and make no mention of anything creditable he has done." In 1910 the popular black journalist John Edward Bruce, who had lived at various times in New York, Albany, and Yonkers, published a volume for youth called *Short Biographical Sketches of Eminent Negro Men and Women.* By this time altogether a considerable number of New York blacks had published works on black history and culture, among them several suitable for use in the schools, and the more recent of these works were becoming more sophisticated.

There is evidence that black teachers found ways, directly or indirectly, to make their pupils aware of black history and culture. At a public exhibition of his school upstate in Geneva in 1849, Principal Henry Highland Garnet arranged for his pupils to present themes they had written, including one on slavery and another on liberty; he also invited the soon-to-be historian William C. Nell to come from nearby Rochester, where he had recently been acting editor of Frederick Douglass' weekly, to speak on how blacks could elevate themselves. In 1886 at a black public school in Brooklyn, pupils gave recitations from Stewart's *Liberia,* and Stewart himself was present to speak. Three years later at similar exercises in the same school, one pupil gave a reading about the black American revolutionist Crispus Attucks, and other pupils presented to a school official a copy of the autobiography of the black teacher and churchman, Daniel Payne. In Flushing, on an Arbor Day in the 1890s, the efficient black principal, Mrs. Mary Shaw, led the pupils of her black public school in planting a tree in honor of the black hero of the Haitian revolution, Toussaint L'Ouverture.[13] Regardless of the course of study or textbooks used, these schools were teaching Afro-American consciousness and pride.

Black principals saw to it that black visitors played a prominent role in their schools. They invited black visitors to appear at opening exercises, graduations, and holiday celebrations. They arranged for black visitors to examine the children orally, in accordance with the custom of the time, and award prizes. They saw to it that black visitors had a chance to meet white school officials and tell them their hopes for the black schools.

At various times between 1854 and 1892, black visitors found their way in considerable numbers through the noisy streets of Manhattan's west side to Charles Reason's black school. They found it first on Broadway near 36th Street, in a heavily black area of shabby tenements, and later on 41st Street. The visitors included Henry Highland Garnet, the crusading minister, who hobbled over from his home nearby; writers on black history like William C. Nell; students who were successfully pursuing higher education like Henry C. Flipper, who came down the Hudson from West Point, natty in his cadet's uniform, to tell the children how he was outfacing the hostility of the white cadets. Black visitors also included two sage college professors, Alexander Crummel of Liberia College in Africa and President Daniel Payne of Wilberforce University in Ohio; and physicians such as the well-established James McCune Smith of New York City and the astonishingly impressive Susan McKinney of Brooklyn, who was the valedictorian of her medical class, served both blacks and whites in her practice, played a church organ on Sunday, and was active for black women's rights.[14] Such visitors inevitably helped to shape the black schools.

According to black newspapers, in the 1880s and early 1890s more than half of the prominent black visitors to the black schools of the New York metropolitan area were clergy, reflecting their importance in the black community. Among the black clergy, the most frequent visitor was the Reverend William T. Dixon, the long-time pastor of a huge black Baptist church in Brooklyn. Dixon was an admirer of his fellow Brooklyn pastor, Henry Ward Beecher, the famous white abolitionist, and when Beecher died, Dixon gave the eulogy for him at a giant black memorial meeting. Dixon was active in protecting the rights of black teachers. While he believed that public schools should be open to all regardless of race, he also believed that blacks should continue to support the traditionally black public schools which blacks taught.

The second and third largest groups among these black visitors at the black schools were businessmen and lawyers. Among businessmen the

Henry O. Flipper was the first black to graduate from West Point Academy, in 1877. *Flipper,* Colored Cadet, *1878.*

most frequent visitor was Philip A. White, the wealthy Manhattan whole-sale druggist who, when he was appointed to the Brooklyn Board of Education, became the first black in the state to serve on any public school board. Since before the Civil War, White had been advocating school de-segregation, and in the 1880s he was a major figure in persuading Brook-lyn to move toward it in such a way as to protect the interests of black teachers. Among lawyers, the most frequent visitor was T. McCants Stewart who followed White as a member of the Brooklyn board. Though only in his thirties, Stewart was already an associate editor of the aggressive black weekly, the *New York Freeman*. He was in demand as a speaker on such themes as black pride and black self-help. A militant for equal rights for blacks, he was suing a Hudson River steamship line for denying him a stateroom on account of his color.

All three of these frequent visitors at the black schools, Dixon, White, and Stewart, were articulate about the problems of blacks in America. By their presence at the black schools, they and other black visitors were encouraging black children to study hard for the benefit of themselves and their race, to be aware of black interests and black history, and to insist on black rights. Whether consciously or unconsciously, they helped to set the tone for the schools and provide examples of respected blacks for the children to emulate.

Not only did black authors, black principals, and black visitors influence the schools but also black parents and black citizens generally. A common way in which they did so was by appealing to officials. In New York City in 1857, a black organization, the Society for the Promotion of Education Among Colored Children, told a state commission which was investigating the city's schools that the buildings used for black schools were neglected, and they painstakingly documented their charge. Two years later, a black magazine claimed that "mainly in consequence" of this well-supported charge, one black school had been moved to a better site, another had been "taken down, to be replaced immediately by a new and elegant structure, replete with all the modern furniture and equipments," and a third was to be remodeled; "yet there are men among the colored people who say, that we cannot do anything in this land!"[15] In 1884, as we shall see in detail, when the New York City Board of Education was threatening to close all its black schools, and blacks tried in vain to persuade the board to protect the jobs of the black teachers, blacks went over the heads of the board by pushing through the state legislature a special law to keep the black schools open and protect the teachers.

Black citizens appealed to school boards or the equivalent. Sometimes they went in person to a board meeting or annual school meeting to face the imposing white merchants, bankers, lawyers, and the like who usually dominated there. As we have seen, in Poughkeepsie, the black Abraham Bolin, himself employed by the board of education as a school janitor, went to a board meeting to remind the board politely that an out-of-town black candidate for teacher at the black school had been waiting in Poughkeepsie for weeks to know if he would be appointed or not. In the Finger Lakes region, in Geneva, blacks attended an annual school meeting to press their campaign to abolish the local black school, arguing that it was expensive and maintained "an invidious distinction between the races." In Newburgh, two blacks, a pastor and a barber, attended a school board meeting to present a petition for the dismissal of the teacher of the black school. After listening to the blacks, the board decided to dismiss the teacher at once.[16]

Black appeals to school boards are recorded in the available minutes of sixteen different boards in the state, in the nineteenth or early twentieth centuries, during the time each board operated separate black schools. Additional evidence from other sources is also available for a few other black appeals to these same boards during the same period. Altogether there is evidence of one hundred eleven appeals to these boards. Of these appeals whose result is known, slightly more than half were successful, suggesting a moderate black contribution to making school policy.

In some places in the state, school boards not only listened to blacks who petitioned them, but also appointed blacks to committees. The Rochester school board in 1841 appointed a committee of three blacks to advise it on black schools; they were a grocer, a barber, and a pastor. In Troy, the school board regularly placed blacks as well as whites on its committee to examine the Troy black school. From 1856 to 1870 it placed on such committees blacks whose occupations ran the gamut of the typical black occupations of the time, from at least 22 pastors and 21 barbers to 8 waiters, 4 coachmen, and 3 whitewashers, all having a chance to influence school policy. In Flushing in 1890 the school board appointed a black teacher along with four white teachers to a committee to advise it on whether to adopt a phonetic system to teach reading.[17] In Brooklyn the school board regularly appointed its own black members to important committees, including the committees which selected the teachers of the black schools.

When blacks couldn't get satisfaction through committees or other conventional methods of influencing school policies, they sometimes took more drastic measures. In the 1840s a black storekeeper in Bath, in western New York, discovered that his children as blacks would be excluded from a new high school. Angered, he refused to pay his school taxes, and despite warnings, he persisted in refusing to pay. In retaliation tax officials seized some of the goods in the store he owned and sold them at public auction. In Roslyn, Long Island, in 1913 blacks organized a march of the black children to the white public school, demanding that they be admitted there; by 1917 the Roslyn black school was closed. In the latter half of the nineteenth century, blacks tried to influence school policy by taking court action in at least thirty-one cases. In twenty-five of these cases black parents tried to force school officials to permit their children to enter white schools. In the other six, black teachers sued school officials to secure what they considered to be their rights, such as retaining their jobs or recovering salary due. In only five of the thirty-one cases were blacks successful. However, as we shall see, a series of suits by blacks to desegregate Jamaica's white public schools, while directly unsuccessful, indirectly led in 1900, with Governor Theodore Roosevelt's help, to a state law to prohibit urban black public schools.

Blacks sometimes tried to influence school policy by the drastic method of deliberately refusing to send their children to school. Black parents boycotted black schools despite the danger of seriously interrupting the education of their children. They also did so despite the danger of angering whites who had economic weapons in their hands with which to retaliate against blacks.

Blacks boycotted black schools as a deliberate means to insist on black teachers for these schools, as in New York City in the 1830s and in Troy and Albany in the 1850s. Blacks kept their children home from school in Lockport in the 1850s as a protest against the location of the black school in the corner of a lumber yard and against the teacher as qualified only to teach primary grades while she had pupils of both primary and grammar grades. Blacks used boycotts to try to force the opening of white schools to blacks as in the 1840s in the western part of the state in Rochester and Buffalo, in the 1890s downstate in Amityville and Jamaica, and in the 1940s in Hillburn in Rockland County. Blacks also in effect boycotted black schools in several places in which, after some struggle, white schools were opened to blacks while black schools still continued to exist. Many black parents in this situation preferred to send their children to white schools, sometimes intending to destroy the black schools and sometimes not. They often chose white schools in such cities as Rochester in the 1850s, Hudson in the 1870s, Buffalo in the 1870s to 1880s, and New York and Brooklyn in the 1870s to 1890s.

In some cases these boycotts involved but a few children in a school; in other cases they involved nearly all the children. A black who promoted a boycott to protest the degrading conditions at the Lockport school, gloried that he found only four children attending. "We believe in fighting for our rights," he wrote, "and if we expect to get them we *must* fight."[18]

Boycotts were an impressive weapon, and both blacks and whites knew it. As the committee on black schools of the New York City Board of Education said in 1878—when both its black and white schools, though maintaining their separate designations, were already open to those of any race—the black people "understand that they . . . could, did they so wish . . . close every colored school within forty-eight hours, at any time they felt disposed so to do, by withdrawing their children from these schools.[19] By 1882 the parents of over eight hundred New York City black children were choosing to send them to white rather than black schools. Blacks often wielded the school boycott weapon to influence basic school policy. Ultimately they wielded this weapon as a major one to destroy the legally-separate black schools.

Altogether, in present day terms blacks didn't win much control over public schools in nineteenth and early twentieth century New York State. In terms of what blacks wanted at the time, they didn't win very much control either. But in the context of the times—when in general whites kept blacks "in their place"—they achieved a great deal. What control blacks achieved became possible largely because of the widespread system of separate black schools. This made possible the common presence of black teachers and black principals in the schools. It tended to justify black requests for action in the interests of blacks. It made the impact of boycotts greater. After all, if the black schools were to survive, as many whites wanted them to, black parents had to be kept reasonably content with them.

Even more impressive than how much blacks achieved in winning a share of control over schools was how much they tried to achieve. Blacks did not develop any organized state-wide campaign toward increasing their share of participation in control over schools. Because of prejudice, and because their proportion in the state's population remained at 3 percent or less all the way from 1830 to 1930, blacks knew that they would not be likely to succeed on any major scale. Nevertheless, black leaders in New York State, more than in most states, were insistent on demanding what they conceived to be black educational rights. Early in the nineteenth century blacks often tried to persuade school officials to create separate black schools, and by mid-century a considerable number of them were already beginning to try to persuade officials to abolish them. They successfully pushed for state laws to limit school segregation, as in 1873, 1900, and 1938. They tried to help choose teachers and principals for the black schools. They tried to influence policy not only through voting, meetings, and petitions, but also through such drastic measures as court action and boycotts. In a few places in the state, they tried to keep up a more or less steady pressure on the white officials who supervised the black schools.

Black control in the black public schools was probably greatest in the New York metropolitan area and in a few other centers such as Troy and Albany where the black population was fairly large and black leaders tended to concentrate. In much of the central western part of the state, black control was usually difficult if for no other reason than that the teachers and principals in the black schools were often white. Even in some of the smaller places in the Hudson Valley and on Long Island where black public schools existed, blacks were too few, too isolated from the main currents of black activism, and too weak in relation to powerful white employers to exert steady pressure in their own interest.

However, some hints of black success in influencing schools are striking, and they are not confined to any one geographical area. For example, in the late 1850s and early 1860s, when the struggle over the continuation of Southern slavery reached terrible intensity in New York State, and one would hardly expect public schools to take sides on the issue, the black public schools sometimes seemed to do so. In Geneva in western New York, when blacks planned one of their usual annual processions to celebrate the abolition of slavery in the British West Indies, they reserved a place in the procession for the "colored district school"; and in Jamaica, Long Island, according to a newspaper announcement, the black public school planned "an anti-slavery exhibition."[20]

Particularly significant is an example of black psychological control over the attitudes of black pupils which occurred in 1858 in Southern-sympathizing New York City. It occurred at John Peterson's black public school which, compared to most black schools, was a large one, having eight regular teachers, all black.

Two Florida officials, the governor and the state school superintendent, visited the school. To exhibit the scholars' achievement, the teachers assembled the children and examined them orally. The Florida superintendent responded that he was profoundly pleased with the quality of their answers and then suggested that the children sing the popular patriotic song, "Hail Columbia."

The school music teacher, a white man who taught music at several schools, both black and white, led the song, beginning with the words, "Hail Columbia! Happy Land!" but not more than a dozen of the scholars sang with him. Afterward the music teacher explained, according to the *New York Tribune,* that in this school "he had never been able to induce teachers and scholars to sing any of the patriotic tunes; they said that it wasn't a free country for black people, and they could not call it a 'happy land.'"[21]

Blacks were not, after all, entirely powerless. Despite Woodson's claim, blacks in New York State in the nineteenth and early twentieth centuries, by one means or another, often by subtle means, already exerted significant control over the schools which blacks attended. Their doing so in the later twentieth century, while different in form and greater in degree, is a continuation of earlier black experience.

DID BLACKS NEED A BLACK COLLEGE?

I N THE EARLY 1800s few blacks studied in higher educational institutions in the United States. Few blacks were adequately prepared for college or had the necessary funds. Moreover, colleges scarcely welcomed blacks.

A brilliant black who found it difficult to enter college was Alexander Crummell. He had studied in New York City in the Manumission Society's schools for blacks. Having become a candidate for the Episcopal ministry, in 1839 he applied to enter the Episcopalians' national seminary, General Theological Seminary in New York City.

But seminary officials refused to accept Crummell. A major reason for their doing so was that Southerners were donating funds to the semiary, and the officials did not wish to offend them. The bishop in charge explained to Crummell that for the present the seminary was forced to give way to the prejudice of society, but that in the course of time prejudice would decline. When Crummell nevertheless persisted in his application, the bishop scolded him for having a disorderly spirit. What the bishop and the other seminary authorities were doing, Crummell exploded in a personal letter, was exalting a seminary, an institution "of no intrinsic worth," at the expense of men who are the "image of God."[1] Some of the seminary professors, sympathizing with Crummell, offered to teach him privately, but he refused to accept their offer as demeaning.

Crummell's experience at General Theological Seminary was similar to that of many blacks who applied to New York State colleges before the Civil War. James McCune Smith, after excelling as a pupil in the Manumission Society schools in New York City, was refused as a medical student at Columbia College. Martin R. Delany was refused at medical colleges in both Albany and Geneva, New York. Andrew Harris was refused at Union College, Schenectady, while an American Indian was admitted there only after he swore that he had no African blood. John M. Langston, a graduate of Oberlin College, was given permission to enter a law school in Ballston Spa only under the humiliating condition, which he refused to accept, that at lectures he would sit apart from white students and not ask questions. Such obstacles to higher education for blacks were not only likely to prevent black youths from entering useful careers but even to dampen the motivation of black pupils in elementary school.

Under such circumstances, abolitionists, both black and white, often dreamed of creating a college for blacks. They did so especially in the Northeast, where the nation's educational institutions were concentrated.

In 1829 the black abolitionist editor Samuel F. Cornish wrote in his New York paper, "I have no doubt, but the monies spent annually for ardent spirits by the colored population of the three states, Pennsylvania, New Jersey, and New York, would richly support a college for the education of our sons." Cornish proposed that an agent be hired to travel and collect money to establish a black "seminary of learning on a large scale."[2] Nothing came of the proposal at the time, but Cornish clung to his dream.

In 1831 a young white abolitionist, Simeon S. Jocelyn, the minister of a black church in New Haven, drew up a plan for a black college to be located near Yale College. Jocelyn presented his plan to the New York abolitionist merchant Arthur Tappan and others, and Tappan promised to contribute generously if sufficient support came from other sources. To help blunt white uneasiness about a black college, as well as to give the students an opportunity to help pay their expenses, the college promoters proposed that their college would be, like a few white colleges, a "manual labor" college; that is, besides giving students the usual liberal arts curriculum, it would give them practical work as in a trade or on a farm. When the promoters presented their plan to the first national convention of colored people, the convention was enthusiastic. At its request, editor Sam Cornish began to solicit funds for the college among blacks.

Unfortunately, at this point Nat Turner led a slave revolt in Virginia, producing a wave of hysterical reaction throughout the nation. Many whites became more afraid than ever that educating blacks would make them dangerous to society. Besides, many whites blamed the Turner revolt incorrectly on abolitionist leaders, including Tappan and others involved in the college proposal. Rioters, evidently mostly Yale students, broke windows in Tappan's house in New Haven and yelled obscenities. A mass meeting of New Haven whites protested that the proposed college would ruin the prosperity of both Yale College and the town. Not one Yale professor defended the college project, and it collapsed.[3]

Yet the idea of a black college persisted. The *New York Journal of Commerce* supported it, saying that since New Haven didn't want the college, "it ought to be placed in some country town, at a considerable distance from any of our cities, and among a people (we presume not difficult to be found) who will give it a welcome reception."[4] The Negro national convention continued for many years to consider the college, as it did in its convention of 1847 held in Troy. At that time the college was still to be essentially a liberal arts institution, with students incidentally expected to do "manual labor."

By that time, however, substantial controversy had developed among blacks about the college proposal, exemplifying the recurring black ambivalence about separatism. At the convention the imposing Frederick Douglass, who had just moved to Rochester, New York, to begin publishing his own newspaper, opposed such a college. He and other Garrisonian abolitionists took the position that separate institutions for blacks, whether colleges or otherwise, contributed to prejudice; it was better to insist on principle that white institutions be open to blacks. The Reverend Henry Highland Garnet, who sometimes fiercely opposed Douglass, agreed with him this time; there were already some white colleges open to blacks, Garnet pointed out. Other delegates added that black students needed to prove themselves in competition with whites. They also said that the expense and energy necessary to establish a separate black college could better be spent in securing access to existing white colleges.

But the majority of the convention—including blacks like Alexander Crummell and James McCune Smith who themselves had been rejected at white colleges—favored establishing a black college. They believed it would raise black aspirations. It would employ black professors and thus for the first time give the brightest black youths a chance to become college professors—as yet no college in the United States had employed a black professor. They argued that the black student in a white college felt depressed because those around him did not regard him as an equal. But the black student in a black college, under black teachers, would not feel depressed and, therefore, black colleges would be the most favorable to his mental growth. The convention appointed a committee to solicit funds for such a college. But at the time nothing came of this plan.[5]

In the early 1850s, the black college idea took a somewhat different form. The college was now to be an "industrial college," one which would emphasize a trades education more than a literary education, much

Editor Frederick Douglass, of Rochester, about 1855. Paradoxically, he fought fiercely to abolish black schools, but advocated the founding of a black college. *New York State Historical Association, from Douglass,* My Bondage, *1855.*

as Hampton and Tuskegee Institutes afterward did. The drive for a black industrial college gained momentum from the expectation that the anti-slavery novelist Harriet Beecher Stowe would contribute substantial funds for it. Frederick Douglass—who suprisingly was the most preeminent black leader in the drive for this college—proposed that it be located in his home city of Rochester; later it was decided to locate it within one hundred miles of Erie, Pennsylvania, which meant that it could be located in Pennsylvania, Ohio, or New York. In any event, if it were to be located in New York State at all, it would be located in the western part of the state where there were fewer blacks and accordingly whites had more favorable attitudes toward them than in the New York City area.

Douglass, despite his general belief that separate institutions for blacks would increase prejudice, believed that a black industrial college was desperately needed. It was needed, he believed, because blacks were losing jobs to white immigrants. It was also needed because, while the usual black schools of the time did not teach trades, black youths could rarely find white craftsmen who were willing to accept them as apprentices. Dr. James McCune Smith also supported an industrial college, as he had a more classical college earlier. Smith supported it, he said, because, despite twenty years of abolitionist effort, "the same terrible destitution of lettered and mechanical and business education" still continues among Northern blacks "especially" in the Midwest and also "in part" in Pennsylvania and New York.[6]

The Negro national convention, held in Rochester in 1853, endorsed the plan for a black industrial college. So also did the Negro New York State Council, held in Syracuse in 1854. In doing so both bodies understood that the college would be open to whites as well as blacks, but expected in fact that few if any whites would attend.

Eventually, however, many black leaders turned against a black industrial college. Some, like the well-known Troy barber William Rich, opposed it on the principle that separate black schools increased prejudice which would otherwise die; anyway, he added, blacks were too poor to support a college of their own. Other black leaders argued that there was room for all the blacks who were ready for higher education in the schools and colleges already open to them. In 1855 the Negro national convention, short of money anyway, voted not to create such a college after all.

Meanwhile black opportunities for higher education in New York State as well as elsewhere in the North were increasing, though only slightly. In New England by the mid-1840s most academies and colleges were said to be open to blacks, and in the Midwest by the 1850s abolitionist-related colleges like Oberlin, Antioch, and Knox were open to a few blacks also. In New York State in the period 1830 to 1860 black students were believed to have openly attended non-abolitionist colleges as follows:

William G. Smith	Columbia College	New York City
William Brown	Columbia College	New York City
Isaiah De Grasse	Geneva (now Hobart) College	Geneva
Henry L. Simpson	Madison (now Colgate) University	Hamilton
Philip A. White	N.Y. College of Pharmacy	New York City
George S. Phillips	N.Y. College of Pharmacy	New York City
David Roselle, Jr.	Union College	Schenectady
John B. Reeve	Union Theological Seminary	New York City

But that these non-abolitionist colleges had admitted one or two black students does not necessarily mean that they freely admitted others, or that they would readily accept blacks of very dark skin and distinctly Negroid features, or that they treated black students as the equals of whites.

However, two colleges in the state did accept backs as the equals of whites. Both these colleges were abolitionist-oriented. Both survived as such about a dozen years, Oneida Institute from 1833 to 1844, and New York Central College from 1849 to 1861. Their existence undoubtedly helped to reduce the pressure for a separate college for blacks in the Northeast.

Both these colleges were located upstate in rural areas where there were few blacks and correspondingly white attitudes toward blacks were relatively favorable: Oneida Institute in Whitesboro, near Utica; and some fifty miles to the southwest, New York Central College in McGrawville, near Cortland. Both were liberal arts colleges. Both colleges were Christian—Oneida tied especially to Presbyterians and New York Central to Baptists—but neither was narrowly sectarian. Like many colleges of the time, both colleges were small. The largest known number of students at any one time at Oneida was about 125, and at New York Central about 225. Moreover, as was common in colleges at the time, many students were at the preparatory level rather than actually at the college level proper.

What proportion of blacks each college had among its students is difficult to estimate;[7] probably it was small. At any rate, these colleges accepted enough blacks to be ridiculed as "nigger schools," and as a result, they both suffered financially.

Among the blacks who studied at these two colleges were representatives of prominent black abolitionist families, including, at Oneida Institute, Bemans from Connecticut and Crummells from New York City; and at Central College, Hogarths from Brooklyn and Purvises from

Oneida Institute, Whitesboro, near Utica. *New York State Historical Association, from Rohman,* Here's Whitesboro: An Informal History, *1949.*

Philadelphia. Among the black students at Oneida Institute who later became prominent were Henry Highland Garnet, of New York City, and Jermain W. Loguen, of Rochester, both of whom became ministers, teachers, and black protest leaders; and at New York Central College, Mary Edmonia Lewis, of near Albany, who became a sculptor, and Benjamin Roseman, Jr., of Troy, who became a surgeon.

    At both colleges many students were poor. During the financial panic of 1837, when President Beriah Green of Oneida Institute declared his students and faculty were in "bitter poverty," collections were taken in nearby churches to aid them.[8] Both colleges required their students to work, as in the college kitchens, or on the college farms, or at various trades; this was partly to help students pay their expenses and partly because the college believed in "manual labor" for health and education. In addition, some black students received financial assistance from white abolitionists or from their home churches.

    Compared to Oneida Institute, New York Central College was more daring: Central College was open to women as well as to men, as few American colleges were; it appointed women faculty members, as few American colleges did. Central College was also, as we have seen, the first college in the United States to appoint black faculty.

    Charles L. Reason of New York City, the first of the three black professors the college appointed, was quietly effective. A black paper claimed that he was the most popular professor at the college.[9] However, the second black professor, William G. Allen, brought the college notoriety. As we have seen, when he announced that he intended to marry one of the white students at the college, he was mobbed in the girl's home town of Fulton, and soon after fled to England with his bride.

Both of the colleges infused a measure of reform-mindedness and protest into their campus life. Their walks and halls buzzed with talk of antislavery, temperance, socialist communities, non-resistance, and the like. Oneida's President Green was himself the presiding officer of the convention which founded the American Antislavery Society, and he later supported the Liberty Party and harbored fugitive slaves. Oneida students printed the state antislavery society paper. When one of Oneida's former students, Alexander Crummell, was denied admission to General Theological Seminary because he was black, Oneida students held an indignation meeting. At Central College visiting speakers over the years included such Afro-American radicals as the advocate of slaves refusing to work, Henry Highland Garnet, and the ride-inner in segregated horse cars meant for whites, J. W. C. Pennington. They also included such Anglo-American radicals as Gerrit Smith, an advocate of drastically reducing the powers of government, and the sweet little old lady in the Quaker bonnet, Lucretia Mott, who insisted on woman's equality, on refusing to buy slave-produced goods, and on denying the divinity of Christ.

Abolitionists publicized the two colleges and tried to raise money for them. Black abolitionist papers did so, like Frederick Douglass' *North Star;* so did white ones, like Garrison's *Liberator.* The Tappan brothers, of New York City, were major contributors to Oneida Institute; Gerrit Smith of Peterboro, New York, was a major contributor to both colleges. In 1851, a state colored convention, over which Frederick Douglass presided, praised New York Central as, like Oberlin, a college "in which colored students find themselves emphatically at home."[10]

Nevertheless, both colleges became financially embarrassed. After the Tappan brothers went bankrupt, Oneida Institute was finally forced to close. In the 1850s, New York Central College was only able to pay its faculty poor salaries. At about the time when the black principals of the black public schools in Troy and Albany were receiving $500 a year, the college was scarcely able to pay its black professor of Latin, George B. Vashon, $200 a year. Yet Vashon was a graduate of Oberlin College, the valedictorian of his class; he had taught in a college in Haiti and practiced law in Syracuse; while teaching at Central College, he was nominated by the abolitionist Liberty Party for state attorney general. The college considered letting him go for lack of money to pay him properly, but Vashon told the trustees that by economy he was able to support his family on his income. "I love New York Central College," he wrote the trustees, and asked to stay on."

By 1859 New York Central College was collapsing for lack of funds, and the white abolitionist Gerrit Smith, one of the wealthiest men in the state, bought its property in the hope of keeping it alive. At this time Gerrit Smith wrote to two black intellectuals, Dr. James McCune Smith and the former Central College professor Charles L. Reason, proposing that New York Central College become a black college and that both of them teach in it.

James McCune Smith replied, however, that while five years before he himself had been advocating "a purely black college," he now knew that such a college would not "meet with cordial support" from either blacks or whites; the college, he said, while primarily intended for blacks, should be open to both blacks and whites. He recommended that the college have both black and white trustees and both black and white professors. Dr. Smith also wrote that he and Reason were not willing to teach there unless the college had an endowment of $50,000 (it had had none before): he offered to try to raise $10,000 of it if Gerrit Smith would contribute the rest.¹²

But the proposal to turn New York Central into a black college did not succeed. Evidently Gerrit Smith—who about this time was terribly shaken by the raid on Harper's Ferry led by his friend John Brown and was sent to an insane asylum briefly thereafter—was not willing to commit the necessary funds. In 1861 New York Central College, like Oneida Institute before it, was allowed to die.

Meanwhile, however, the first black colleges in the United States were in fact being established. They were located in the North because in the South state law usually forbade teaching blacks even to read. But these colleges were not being located in parts of the North most remote from the South, as in New England or New York State. Rather they were being established in locations near to the Mason-Dixon line, where the black population was heavier and the colleges could hope to serve blacks from the South as well as from the North.

In 1849 a white abolitionist and Methodist lay preacher from New York City, Charles Avery, who had become wealthy by investing in cotton manufacturing, gave funds to found a black college, Avery College, near Pittsburgh, Pennsylvania. A non-denominational college, it was intended especially to educate black teachers and preachers. New York State blacks became influential in Avery College, in the 1850s the black Dr. James McCune Smith serving as a trustee, and in the 1860s two blacks, Professor George B. Vashon and Reverend Henry Highland Garnet, serving as presidents. In the 1850s non-abolitionist denominations, predominantly white, also created black colleges, also especially to train preachers and teachers, as the Presbyterians did in southeastern Pennsylvania with Lincoln University, and as the Methodists did in southwestern Ohio with Wilberforce University. The quality of these black "colleges" was undoubtedly inferior to that of the average white college in the Northeast. But many black leaders believed that black colleges had a significant role to play. In 1864 the Negro National Convention, meeting in Syracuse, heartily endorsed such black colleges as these and expressed no disturbance over their standards.

After the Civil War had freed Southern blacks from the harsh restrictions on their education, Northerners felt a new responsibility to educate them.

Northern white philanthropists now led in founding in the South not only black elementary schools but also black colleges to educate black teachers for these elementary schools. Much of this effort was at first channeled through the federal government's Freedman's Bureau, for which the white John W. Alvord, once a student at Oneida Institute, was superintendent of schools. Much of the substance of the drive came from private societies such as the American Missionary Association, which had its headquarters in New York City. This society alone established seven colleges for blacks in the South in the period 1866 to 1869.

After the shock of the death of President Lincoln, many blacks agitated for the creation of a black college in Washington, D.C., as a Lincoln memorial. Among blacks who favored it were Garnet, who was the national president of the organization promoting it; Principal John Peterson; Dr. James McCune Smith; and Robert Hamilton, the publisher of the *New York Weekly Anglo-African.* But Frederick Douglass was doubtful about the proposal. He opposed establishing permanent separate institutions for blacks, he said, returning to his earlier position. "The spirit of the age is against all institutions based upon prejudice. . . . I expect to see the colored people of this country . . . going to the same schools, attending the same churches" as whites. According to Garnet, Douglass' publication of these doubts "smashed our college."[13] Blacks did not succeed in opening their proposed Lincoln memorial college in Washington.

Anyway, it was easier for whites to found black colleges than for blacks to do so. In 1867, whites—particularly Congregationalists—led in opening in Washington a black college, Howard University. Most of its early faculty were whites; its first black professor was George B. Vashon, who formerly had taught at New York Central College.

At the beginning of this period when Northern philanthropists were enthusiastically founding black schools and colleges in the South, the trustees of New York Central College proposed that their college be reopened as a college especially for blacks. They were essentially repeating the proposal Gerrit Smith had made in 1859. The trustees, all apparently white themselves, proposed in a circular in 1866 that the college be revived "on the same principles of impartiality towards all classes of students" with which it opered, but this time the college would be "specially designed" to provide black people "a due proportion of highly educated men and women." They argued that the North ought to take the initiative in educating blacks "and set an example worthy of imitation by the states, hitherto blinded by the existence of slavery in them," to do their duty in this matter. "The Empire State," they said, "ought to be behind no other in the enterprise."[14] One of the New York Central trustees at the time was the corresponding secretary of the American Missionary Association. Despite this connection, the New York Central trustees did not find the response they hoped for. At this time Northern whites who were interested in black education were likely to be concentrating on the South. The college buildings in the peaceful village of McGrawville, far from the centers of black population in the nation and even in the state, remained closed.

The idea of establishing a black college in New York State rose to the surface again in 1870. It did so this time especially among blacks in the Mid-Hudson River region. This was a region where, compared to much of the rest of upstate New York, black population had long been heavy and whites had long been hostile.

In the 1860s probably fewer New York State blacks had attended college than usual (see Table 13 in the Appendix). The Civil War had disrupted the lives of many black youths, some of them becoming soldiers. Besides, with both Oneida Institute and New York Central College dead, it was a question if there were any longer any colleges in the state which fully welcomed black students as equals. There was still no black college in New England, New York, or New Jersey.

In 1870 many schools and colleges in the state had still never admitted a black. Eastman Business College, located in Poughkeepsie on the Hudson River, refused to admit blacks, as its president afterward explained, because its many Southern students would not like it.[15] The recently established Vassar College, also located in Poughkeepsie, did not

Two reactions to the Negro's ambition. At left, the reaction in New York to his ambition for education as a boxer is admiration. At right, the reaction to his ambition for education as a military officer is rejection by white cadets at West Point. A black cadet had charged that white cadets had slit his ears; his opponents charged that he did it himself. The academy dismissed him. *Courtesy of The New-York Historical Society, New York City, from* Frank Leslie's Illustrated Newspaper, *1880.*

admit blacks either; as late as 1900 a Vassar official declared that "the conditions of life here are such" that we "strongly advise" blacks not to enter.[16]

  Down the Hudson from Poughkeepsie at West Point was the fabled United States Military Academy. Though opened in 1802, it had never admitted a black cadet until in May 1870, under the impact of Reconstruction, the Republican administration in Washington directed that it do so. Like many of the first blacks admitted to colleges, the first black cadet, J. W. Smith of South Carolina, was nearly white. But other cadets, anxious to preserve the prestige of their academy as they understood it, taunted Smith for having any African ancestry at all, and even the faculty often seemed hostile. Smith sometimes retaliated—in a famous incident he hit another cadet with a dipper. Smith was in frequent trouble at West Point. President Grant intervened to protect him and other black cadets, and Congress debated their problems. Eventually the issues raised by the blacks' presence seemed to threaten the stability of the academy itself. A Democratic paper in Poughkeepsie declared that Cadet Smith, "with the aid of a few fanatics, has well nigh ruined the discipline of the Academy— [which is] worth more than the entire Negro population." But Frederick Douglass' new Washington newspaper decided that unless the academy was able to stop the persecutions of the blacks, "the sooner Congress abolishes the institution the better. It is now a dishonor to the nation, and men educated therein are . . . likely to prove a curse to the country."[17] It did not seem likely that such noise over the presence of blacks on the castellated campus overlooking the Hudson would encourage other colleges in the state to admit black students.

Meanwhile in early 1870, the Republican administration in Washington succeeded, over Democratic opposition, in securing the ratification of the 15th United States Constitutional Amendment. At last New York State blacks—as well as Southern blacks—were promised the equal right to vote. With this encouragement, New York State blacks felt a new impetus to push for equal opportunity. While clamor against the admission of blacks into West Point rang loudly in their ears, black leaders of the mid-Hudson region pushed to create a black higher educational institution for themselves.

In September 1870, they called an educational convention in Poughkeepsie. Those signing the call included blacks from three Hudson River counties: Dutchess (which included Poughkeepsie), Orange (which included West Point and Newburgh), and Columbia (which included the city of Hudson).

When the convention met, it chose as president the black Isaac Deyo of Poughkeepsie. Being the father of eleven children, he had reason to be concerned about black education. Moreover, he was a leader among blacks. He had attended at least three state or national black conventions. He was active in his local African Methodist Episcopal Zion (AMEZ) Church where the convention was being held. During the election of 1860, he had stood all day at the polls handing out ballots for equal suffrage; and now that equal suffrage had at last been won, he was active as a Republican. Yet it was an ironic commentary on both the educational and occupational opportunities for blacks in the state that the president of this educational convention was himself only a "laborer" and "cartman."

With a touch of bitterness, Deyo asked the convention, have Negroes "not been hewers of wood and drawers of water long enough? Have they not blacked their master's boots and stood behind his chair until their hearts were sick and sore?" The means to elevate blacks above such menial occupations, he said, was education.

The convention voted to establish a school for blacks—they called it at this stage variously an academy, seminary, high school, or college—to be located within two miles of the court-house in Poughkeepsie. The convention appointed a committee, all blacks, to estimate the cost of such an institution.[18]

A month later, in October 1870, a convention of blacks met again in Poughkeepsie, with cartman Isaac Deyo presiding as before. This time they decided to call their proposed institution a college only. Their plans were modest compared to those of Vassar College, which had been established in Poughkeepsie nine years before. On the advice of their committee, they decided that their new college should have fifteen or more acres of ground, while Vassar had two hundred at its founding; and that their new college needed $300,000 for initial costs and endowment, while Vassar had already received gifts of nearly $800,000 from brewer Mathew Vassar alone.

While such black colleges as Avery and Howard had only a few black trustees, and Lincoln University had no black trustees at all, the trustees the convention chose for this new college were all blacks. They came from five Hudson River counties as follows:

Dutchess County

Isaac Deyo	Poughkeepsie	cartman and laborer
Abraham Bolin	Poughkeepsie	gardener and janitor
Charles Cooley	Poughkeepsie	laborer
Samuel P. Jones	Fishkill Landing	laborer

Orange County

| Rev. Jacob Thomas | Newburgh | minister |
| Rev. W. H. Decker | Newburgh | minister |

Columbia County

| Chauncey Van Heusen | Hudson | laborer |

Ulster County

| Hanson Harley | Kingston | barber |

Greene County

| John Goetchess | Catskill | steward[19] |

The fact that these trustees were all black, and often of lowly occupations as well, hardly suggested that they would be able to raise the necessary funds.

Moreover, by February 1871, the promoters had chosen a prickly name for their proposed institution; it was to be called "Toussaint L'Ouverture College" after the leader of the Haitian Revolution. Toussaint had long been a hero to blacks. In the 1850s the Garrisonian black abolitionist, William Wells Brown, who was to become a Toussaint College trustee, had compared two revolutionary heroes, Toussaint and Washington, to the advantage of Toussaint: "Toussaint liberated his countrymen," said Brown, while "Washington enslaved a portion of his."[20] By choosing the name of this black revolutionist for their college, the trustees might be ingratiating themselves with some potential donors among blacks, but hardly with many potential donors among whites. Yet the promoters of the college must have known that black colleges—whether blacks liked it or not—were likely to be heavily dependent on white donors.

In early 1871 the college promoters arranged for a local Republican Assemblyman to introduce a bill into the New York legislature to incorporate the college. In the bill, in listing the names of the trustees, the promoters added new names. It is possible that they were induced to add names by friends who believed that otherwise the college had little chance to come into existence. The name of at least one of the new trustees, the much respected barber William Rich of Troy, who had been president of the colored state convention at least four times, was added by the initiative of a friendly Assemblyman who obtained the consent of the originators of the bill. Among the other new trustees, all black, were the black pastors Jermain W. Loguen of Syracuse and Henry Highland Garnet of New York City; William Wells Brown, author and lecturer of Boston; John M. Langston, dean of the law school of Howard University; Jonathan Wright, a recent Reconstruction appointee as South Carolina Supreme Court justice; and Hiram Revels of Mississippi, the first black to serve in the United States Senate. The greater prestige of these new trustees, and the wider geographical area from which they came, seemed to improve the chances that the proposed college would actually open. Still, the name of the college could be regarded as defiant, and the new trustees, like the original ones, were all blacks. Moreover, the extent of the commitment of the new trustees to the college is uncertain. Except for Garnet, who agreed to attend a meeting of the trustees in Poughkeepsie, no record is available that they accepted their appointment as trustees.[21] It is possible that some of the other new trustees would be less than enthusiastic about a black college. Rich had opposed separate black colleges as early as 1855; and at about the time they were named as trustees, Senator Revels and Dean Langston were advocating mixed rather than separate schools.

The bill of incorporation which the trustees placed before the state legislature provided that the college was designed especially for young men and women of African descent. But as in the plans for the industrial college in the 1850s, and in the plans to revive New York Central College as a black college in 1866, and as was true of many of the new black colleges in the South, the college was not to refuse whites. Still, as everyone knew, a college intended primarily for blacks was likely to have few, if any, white students.

While the bill was pending in the legislature, a Poughkeepsie Republican paper, which was usually sympathetic to black aspirations, appealed for contributions for the proposed college from whites. "It is to be hoped that our people will give this institution a helping hand," the *Daily Eagle* said on February 11, 1871, "as it will go far towards settling the vexed question of the mixture of the races in our schools and colleges." This paper seemed to be supporting the college in part because it would help to keep blacks out of the state's white schools and colleges.

On the other hand, a Poughkeepsie Democratic paper, the *Daily Press,* was hostile both to the establishment of a black college and to admitting blacks to white colleges. On November 14, 1870, the *Press* suggested, with its usual ridicule of blacks, that Poughkeepsie black voters were expecting to contribute to the college the money they received as bribes for voting Republican. "Only one more election," said the *Press,* "and the college will become a fixed fact."

There was no excitement in the Democratic-controlled legislature over passing the bill to incorporate the college. The Senate made minor changes and then adopted the bill unanimously. In April 1871, the Assembly concurred, also unanimously.[22]

However the Poughkeepsie city government didn't push to make the college a reality. Just after the college was incorporated, the go-getter Harvey Eastman—the head of the all-white, four hundred-student Eastman Business College in Poughkeepsie—was inaugurated as Republican mayor of Poughkeepsie. In a speech on the opportunities before the city, he said that he favored inviting more first class schools to Poughkeepsie, "especially a Literary College for young men," but made no mention of the black college proposal.[23] Poughkeepsie, having prestigious white academies and military schools, as well as the white Vassar and Eastman colleges, was already known as "the city of schools"; it didn't seem anxious to be known also as the site of the only black college in the Northeast.

Moreover, the college project was running into stiff opposition from some blacks. This became evident the next month at the New York Annual Conference of the African Methodist Episcopal Zion Church (AMEZ) which happened to meet in 1871 in Poughkeepsie.

The conference represented forty black churches reaching from Northern New Jersey to Long Island and up the Hudson Valley. During its week-long sessions, the conference received generous daily coverage in the local Republican paper, and on Sunday various Poughkeepsie white Protestant churches invited black pastors who were attending the conference to preach as guests in their pulpits.

At the conference, the education committee endorsed the proposed black college. But the blunt Reverend William F. Butler of New York City, a former pastor in Poughkeepsie, objected heartily, and he was one of the most powerful men in the convention. He opposed separate schools. If the black people of the state "stand together," Butler said, "and ask for equal school rights," we will get them. We want "no separate college."

Poughkeepsie gardener and janitor Abraham Bolin, one of the trustees of the proposed college, was present as a lay delegate from the AMEZ church in Poughkeepsie. Though three other of the college trustees were also present, all ministers, Bolin was the only person present who was reported to have spoken up in defense of the college. The arguments against it as a separate black institution are not logical, Bolin said, because the college would be open to both blacks and whites.

But the members of the conference were sure that the college, regardless of intent, would become in effect exclusively black, and the college proposal was drowned by waves of feeling against separate black schools. The conference deleted the section of the education committee report endorsing Toussaint College. In addition, a pastor offered this resolution, which passed: "In this enlightened day, as ministers, we discountenance any scheme or plan that has for its object the establishment of separate schools or colleges for the colored people of this state."[24] Ironical as it was, a separate African church was opposing separate black educational institutions.

Following this overwhelming indication of key black opposition to the separate black college project, openly demonstrated in the city where the college was to be located, the chances for the realization of the project dropped.

In 1872, about a year after the AMEZ conference, when blacks in the Poughkeepsie region met to choose delegates to a state black convention, on the motion of Isaac Deyo they instructed their delegates to bring the claims of Toussaint College before the convention. The delegates they chose were Deyo, Jones, and Bolin, all trustees of the college. At the state convention, held in Troy, three other trustees were also present: Rich, Loguen, and Thomas. Available reports of the convention give no sign of any discussion of Toussaint College. But they do report that Reverend Butler, who had led the AMEZ conference to refuse to endorse the college, also led this convention to take a stand against separate schools for blacks. The convention, eager to capitalize on the gains it believed that blacks were making during Reconstruction, was urging that instead of creating black institutions, blacks should work to open more white institutions to blacks.[25]

Trying to establish a black college under these circumstances was like trying to build a sand castle in front of an advancing tide. While the black leaders in the Poughkeepsie region remained loyal to the college cause, and they continued to have the support of Poughkeepsie's Republican newspaper, they lacked even the perfunctory endorsement of both the black state convention and the major black denomination in the Hudson Valley; they also lacked the support of any significant body of white philanthropists. Without such support, the Toussaint College cause gradually died.

In the 1870s and 1880s, in keeping with the national trend, the number of blacks in the normal schools and colleges in the state showed a marked increase, reducing the need for a black college. After 1900 the increase accelerated.

As we have seen, blacks in the state in the nineteenth century were often successful in launching and helping to sustain schools for blacks on the elementary level, a level on which expenses were minimal and the need for the education of blacks was widely accepted. Blacks were also successful in launching, with some white help, a few schools on the secondary level which was somewhat more expensive and less widely accepted as essential for blacks, but blacks did not succeed in sustaining these schools over a significant period. On the still more expensive level of higher education, a level which many whites doubted was suitable for blacks, blacks were not successful in even launching a black college.

Altogether there were five known specific attempts to establish separate colleges for blacks in or near New York State whose proposed location is known:

1831	New Haven, Conn.
1853–55	Rochester, or within 100 miles of Erie, Pa.
1859	McGrawville
1866	McGrawville
1870–72	Poughkeepsie

It was notable that none of these proposals provided for a location in the New York City area where the largest number of blacks in the state was concentrated. Probably the major reason was the relatively high degree of hostility to blacks in that area at the time, a hostility which by the end of the century had declined.

Long-term reasons for the failure of the attempts to establish a black college in or near New York State were the indifference and poverty of many blacks and the indifference or hostility of many whites. More particular reasons were significant at varying times. The failure of the 1831 attempt to establish a college in New Haven appears to have been in considerable part because of white fear of higher education for blacks, while by the 1840s and 1850s the failure of black college schemes was more nearly due to division among blacks on whether separate institutions would increase prejudice. From this time on, major black leaders in the state, like Garnet, Frederick Douglass, and Dr. James McCune Smith, wavered on the wisdom of creating a black college. Before the Civil War, the concentration of Northern white abolitionists on the struggle to abolish slavery was a factor in the failure to create a black college; after the Civil War, the concentration of Northern white philanthropists on the education of blacks in the South was a factor. In the 1870s belief by both blacks and whites in the practicability of educational integration helped to prevent the creation of Toussaint College, and has contributed ever since to preventing the establishment of a black college.

Perhaps it is a tribute to the efforts of predominantly white Northeastern colleges to improve educational opportunity for blacks that, despite a marked increase in the proportion of blacks in the population of the Northeast in the twentieth century, a separate black college has never yet been established in New England, New York, or New Jersey.

PROTEST UPSTATE

IN THE DECADES BEFORE THE CIVIL WAR, the most sensitive blacks and their friends were likely to feel themselves caught in a dilemma. They regarded black schools as evil. They didn't want to cooperate with them. But if they didn't, and if few whites were willing to let blacks into white schools, how else would most blacks be educated? This dilemma was to trouble blacks in increasing numbers in the decades ahead.

In the 1830s, most New York State abolitionists were still emphasizing the need to educate more blacks in whatever schools they could enter. Many abolitionists, both blacks and whites, as we have seen, were helping to create black schools, raise money for them, or run them. Characteristically, abolitionists both supported black schools and at the same time protested, as they did in their New York State Antislavery Society convention of 1836, that excluding blacks from white schools was unchristian and cruel. It was only gradually that some of the more radical abolitionists came to oppose black schools outright and take action against them. A few began to do so in individual action in the 1830s.

One of these few was the black abolitionist editor, Sam Cornish. He was unusually forthright for his time in his condemnation of black schools. They are "highly calculated to keep up prejudice against color," Cornish wrote in his *New York Colored American* of April 22, 1837; they so shackle the intellect of black youth that the education they offer is, "comparatively, of little advantage."

Because he strongly felt the damage done by black schools, Cornish, acting by himself, tried to enter his own children in white New York City schools. Since he was a Presbyterian minister, he went especially to white Presbyterians, asking them to open their white schools to his children, but they refused. Such refusals so frustrated Cornish that he finally moved his residence from New York City to a small New Jersey town where he expected—mistakenly as it eventually turned out—that his children could attend school with whites. Still he felt forced to cooperate with black schools. At about the same time that he was moving to New Jersey he was also helping to raise funds for the Phoenix Society's black high school.[1]

In the 1840s Garrisonian abolitionists led group campaigns to abolish the few remaining black public schools in Massachusetts, including the schools in Boston.[2] Simultaneously, similar campaigns against black public schools developed in New York State. These campaigns occurred upstate where, much as in Massachusetts, the proportion of blacks was small and of abolitionists, high. As in Massachusetts, both blacks and whites were active in these New York State campaigns, and blacks often employed the method of the school boycott.

The first known campaign in New York State developed in Buffalo. We follow the story of what happened there, noting especially the blacks' limited aims, their methods, and their connections with abolitionists.

By 1841 several black families in Buffalo were refusing to send their children to the black school, insisting that they had a right to send them to the regular white public schools in their own neighborhoods. In particular a mulatto father insisted on sending his three girls to the white public school near his house. By order of the school superintendent, the teachers gave the girls seats but refused to instruct them; later the superintendent even directed the teachers not to give them seats, so that day after day the girls were compelled to stand or leave the school. Both the state superintendent and the Buffalo Common Council backed the Buffalo superintendent, a council committee explaining that "any attempt to force familiar intercourse between the races" only increases prejudice.[3]

In 1846 blacks petitioned the Buffalo Common Council to allow black children to attend school with whites if they wished. Again black children tried to enter the white schools bodily, but this time school officials ejected them. In 1847 again blacks petitioned the Common Council, complaining of the inconvenience in their being restricted to the one black school instead of being allowed to attend the white schools in the neighborhoods where they lived. But the Buffalo Common Council continued to refuse to open its white schools to blacks on the ground that before the black school was created, blacks had indicated they wished to have a separate school.[4]

A white Buffalo newspaper charged that abolitionists were behind Buffalo blacks in their effort to "force" their children into "intimate association" with white children in the schools. Certainly Buffalo blacks, like Boston blacks, were considerably identified with abolitionists. Buffalo, like other upstate cities, was an abolitionist center. In the late 1830s in Buffalo itself there were three antislavery societies, and in the surrounding Erie County there were eighteen more. In the 1840s the abolitionist Liberty Party held two national conventions in Buffalo, and blacks from Buffalo not only attended them but also went elsewhere to attend abolitionist and colored conventions, including one which advised blacks to "use every just effort in getting their children into schools in common with others."[5] One of the Buffalo blacks who refused to send his children to the black school was the fugitive slave, William Wells Brown, who had become a disciple of Garrison. He and other Buffalo blacks read both black and white abolitionist papers. Buffalo blacks had ample opportunity to be informed about the Garrisonians' drive for racially-mixed schools in New England, as well as the Tappanites' support of such racially-mixed colleges as Oberlin and Oneida, and the concern of such black abolitionist editors as Sam Cornish for equal educational opportunity.

By 1855 Buffalo blacks had won at least a partial victory. While officially Buffalo still required all black children to attend the one centrally-located black public school, those who lived in outlying districts, remote from the school, were now allowed, if they wished, to attend the white schools in the districts where they lived. All the outlying schools have some black children attending, reported the superintendent of schools in 1857, "and, so far as I can learn, no evil has resulted from such attendance."[6] From 1854 to 1857 registration at the black school dropped significantly from 216 to 164. Although thereafter it continued to drop, enough blacks continued to attend Buffalo's black school to keep it open for many years yet.

A campaign against school segregation also developed in another upstate abolitionist center, Rochester. In comparison with the Buffalo campaign, the Rochester campaign was more boisterous, more nearly dominated by one black leader, and more directly aimed at abolishing black schools.

The campaign in Rochester began in 1847 after two leading black abolitionists arrived from Massachusetts. They were Frederick Douglass, who came to Rochester to establish his own newspaper, and William C. Nell, an associate of Garrison on the *Liberator,* whom Douglass brought along to assist him. Both Douglass and Nell had been active in the movement to desegregate the Boston public schools.

Douglass repeatedly attacked separate institutions for blacks— whether separate railroad cars, separate churches, or separate schools.

William Wells Brown, fugitive slave and abolitionist orator, boycotted the black public school of Buffalo in 1845, refusing to cooperate with segregation. He moved to Farmington, Ontario County, where his children could attend unsegregated schools. *New York Public Library Picture Collection.*

They were all "the pernicious fruit" of "blasphemous prejudice," he wrote in his *North Star* of March 10, 1848. Douglass, unlike Buffalo blacks, was attacking the black schools directly. He was already developing the bold policies and devastating style which were to help catapult him in the next few years into being the outstanding black spokesman in America.

Meanwhile, though his associate Nell was soon to teach in the Rochester black public school, Douglass in 1848 avoided sending his nine year old daughter to that school. Instead he sought out and found a private white school in Rochester which would accept her. But when Douglass discovered that this private school insisted on teaching her separately from the white children, in a room all by herself, Douglass in a rage withdrew her from the school.

About a year later, the Rochester school board came to believe that black population trends required the establishment of a second black public school if the segregated system was to work. As an alternative that would cut costs, the school board considered dropping the segregation system altogether. But the Democrats on the board—the "pro-slavery Irish faction," as blacks called them—won out, and the board decided, in October 1849, to create the second black school.[7]

To house the new school, the school board contracted with the trustees of the Zion African Methodist Church to rent its basement. Douglass was furious that a black church would thus cooperate in extending school segregation. The church trustees, he said, "sanctioned . . . the spirit of caste, by which we are constantly haunted and tormented." Douglass promised never to send any of his children "to the miserable cellar under Zion church," and in the *North Star* he promoted a boycott of both the old and the new black schools. The publisher of Douglass' paper, the black John Dick, endorsed the boycott, writing that it would be better for colored children to "pick up their education in the gutter" than to attend colored schools. A meeting of black citizens promised to support the boycott. When the new school opened in the Zion Church basement, the *North Star* gloated that both of the black public schools were "almost deserted."[8]

Some whites joined the blacks in asking for the abolition of the black schools. The board of education's committee on colored schools—which included at least one abolitionist, the bookseller Samuel D. Porter—decided that black schools were not only costly but also humiliating to blacks and helped drive them to hostility and crime. The board allowed some blacks to enter white schools. By March 1850, the board noted that twenty-four colored children were already attending five different white public schools, evidently more by favor than by right.[9] However, the board declined to close the colored schools.

Encouraged by the acceptance of blacks at some white schools, blacks continued their boycott of the black schools. At the beginning of the school year in September 1851, the board of education opened the two

Zion African Methodist Church, Rochester, housed a black public school in its basement. *Rochester Public Library.*

black schools as usual. But no pupils at all appeared at the older one. So the board, led especially by its members who were Whigs—the usual political allies of blacks in the state at the time—voted seven to five to close it, a considerable victory for the protesters. School officials then encouraged the black children who lived at a distance from the remaining black school to enter white schools near where they lived. By 1854 the board apparently allowed all black children to attend white schools.[10] Still the board kept open its black school in the Zion Church basement for those who wished to attend it.

In the fall of 1855 the board was hesitant as to whether the small attendance at the remaining black school justified its disproportionately high expense. Nevertheless, the board hired a Massachusetts-born white, Mrs. Lucy Colman, to teach the school. She was already known in Rochester as an abolitionist, and was later to become an outspoken antislavery lecturer. She accepted the black school position, she explained afterward, not only because her husband had recently died and she needed a job to support herself, but also because, opposed as she was to separate schools on principle, she intended to use the opportunity to abolish the school.

During her year as teacher of the school, Mrs. Colman worked quietly to bring the school to an end. She advised black parents to send their more advanced children to the white schools in the districts where they lived, urging them to see that they were "particularly clean" and that their behavior was as "faultless as possible." She also urged the Zion Church trustees to stop renting their basement for the use of the school. The trustees may have followed her advice, if indirectly; at least they raised the rent. By the summer of 1856 the school board, believing that too few children had been attending the school and that the rent for the church basement was becoming too high, decided to abandon its last black school. The superintendent of schools explained that the black children could be accommodated in the regular schools. Prejudice against them would not cause "a very serious obstacle," he said, as in most of the city's schools there were "already more or less colored children, and in some instances they are among the brightest and most intelligent scholars in our schools."[11] The black school closed quietly, without notice in the newspapers, and the children were accepted in the white schools. The first known campaign in the state aimed directly at abolishing local black public schools had at last achieved victory.

The circumstances which led to two other school desegregation campaigns in the state during this period were different from those in Buffalo and Rochester. In both Kinderhook[12] and Albany, the public school authorities had allowed blacks to attend the white public schools for a time, but then in the 1850s changed their minds, requiring blacks to attend black schools again. In both places this reversal of policy aroused blacks.

In Albany in the spring of 1850, when the school board suddenly adopted its new policy of forbidding white schools to accept black pupils, blacks called a meeting to protest. They twice appealed to the school board, but twice the board did not reply. Blacks also appealed to the presumably sympathetic state superintendent of schools, a Whig recently elected with the support of many of the few blacks who were allowed to vote, but he did nothing. According to black abolitionist editor Samuel R. Ward, the state superintendent "saw the black children turned out of school, without moving the outer edge of the nail of his little finger in their behalf." A meeting of Albany blacks decided to test the ouster by appeal to the courts, as Massachusetts blacks had already done unsuccessfully in a similar situation in a well-publicized effort. On behalf of the meeting, two Albany blacks, William P. McIntyre and Francis Van Vranken, both barbers who were active in the colored convention movement, wrote the wealthy white abolitionist Gerrit Smith, of Peterboro, saying that they objected to sending their children to an "inferior" school, "inconveniently located," and asking him to donate funds toward a court test. Gerrit Smith replied that their litigation would probably avail nothing, but "your cause is right." He sent them $25, and suggested that they write again when they needed more.[13]

While evidence is not available that Albany blacks actually took their case to court, they persisted in agitating to open white schools to blacks. In 1851 McIntyre, along with other Albany and Troy blacks, promoted a colored state convention, one of whose stated purposes was to open all the white public schools in the state to blacks. The convention adopted an impressive report on education prepared by three blacks, two of them from Albany, saying that "caste" schools, "while they may not be condemned where better reliances are not to be had, are depressing in their influences, and unfitted to prepare our children to assume an equality of position in the after severe lessons of life."[14] But neither this convention nor continued agitation by Albany blacks had any immediately visible effect on the Albany black school.

While minor, isolated actions occurred against school segregation downstate, it was significant that all four of the major group campaigns against school segregation in the 1830s to 1850s occurred upstate, in Buffalo, Rochester, Kinderhook, and Albany. As already suggested, this may have happened in part because upstate there were proportionately fewer blacks and more abolitionists than downstate. Are there other possible reasons why major group campaigns did not develop downstate?

In New York City in the late 1850s, the black public schools had 2500 pupils, far more than in any other city in the state. The black-run New York Society for Education among Colored Children, which had earlier itself operated black schools, did not ask that the black public schools be abolished. In 1857, when a state commission was investigating the city's schools, the black society presented to the commission a careful statement whose main thrust was a request for the improvement of the black school buildings. At the same time the society incidentally asked that the white public schools be opened to the blacks who cared to attend them. The campaign against separate schools in Massachusetts having by this time succeeded in abolishing all the remaining black schools in that state, the New York society said that, keeping the Massachusetts experience in mind, in New York City "there is no sound reason why colored children should be excluded from any of the common schools supported by taxes levied alike on whites and blacks, and governed by officers elected by the vote of colored as well as white voters."

Two years later, the New York City superintendent of schools, while still recommending that black children attend black schools, claimed that all the public schools of the city "are open, without restrictions" to both black and white children. It is not clear that this open policy came about because of the black education society's request. In stating the open policy, the superintendent gave no explanation for its adoption. At about the same time, the black-edited *Anglo-African Magazine* claimed that the education society's statement had won results by securing better buildings for the black schools, but it made no similar claim that it had won results in opening the white schools to blacks.[15] There is no available evidence of any organized campaign, black or white, for opening the white New York City schools to blacks. In fact, in the next few years, probably largely because there were so many conveniently located black schools in the city and because black pupils sometimes met prejudice in the white schools, comparatively few black parents took advantage of the opportunity to send their children to the white schools.

Similarly, in Brooklyn from at least as early as 1844, local school officials had tolerated a few blacks attending the white schools, but the Brooklyn Board of Education explained later that this was the result of "kindly indulgence" by particular schools, rather than recognition of a right.[16] As in New York City, there is no available evidence that Brooklyn blacks had organized any campaign to secure this "indulgence" or to extend it into a right. Probably as in New York City, the availability of several black schools and the freedom for at least some blacks to enter the white schools helped to inhibit the development of an anti-segregation campaign.

Another probable reason why campaigns against black schools did not develop downstate was that there were more black teachers downstate than upstate, and blacks felt some concern to keep these black teachers employed. Dr. James McCune Smith, the New York City black intellectual, was aware that if black schools were closed, black teachers would lose their jobs. "In our equal school war," he wrote in *Frederick Doug-*

lass' Paper of April 8, 1859, "colored teachers of colored schools should under all circumstances demand our sympathy; it is as natural in them to oppose us, as it was in the weavers forty years ago to raise mobs to put down the power looms." In the 1850s to a small extent, and to a greater extent later in the century, sympathy for the black teachers inhibited some blacks from outright demands for the abolition of black schools.

Altogether, who were the leaders in the struggle against educational segregation in the 1830s through the 1850s? There were sixty-one blacks and forty-two whites who are known to have taken part significantly in such action and whose names and occupations can be identified. Of the black leaders, 80 percent can be identified as abolitionists; of the white leaders, 59 percent. Whites often took the initiative in opening private schools and colleges to blacks. It was usually blacks, however, who took the initiative in trying to open public schools to blacks. While the overwhelming majority of blacks in the state were unskilled workers, it was blacks of higher occupations who led in these actions. The largest single occupational group among the black leaders was barbers, a skilled occupation of considerable status among blacks at the time, and the second largest was journalists. Comparing the occupations of the black and white leaders, the whites were more likely to be in business or the professions (see Tables 14-16 in the Appendix). This probably reflects not only the higher occupational status of whites in the state at large, but also the fact that business and professional whites were in a better position than lower class whites to help blacks in their struggle for equal school rights.

As for the methods which blacks used in their local struggles to desegregate public schools in this period, among the nine places where some information is available, blacks used the unconventional method of boycott in five places, which is a larger number of places in which blacks were to use the boycott than during any subsequent period. Blacks also used another unconventional method, the refusal to pay school taxes, in one place, Bath, in western New York. That blacks depended considerably on unconventional methods in this period probably stemmed to some extent from the fact that they did not yet have the equal right to vote in the state.

As for the degree of black success, none of the four concerted campaigns led directly to unqualified success. Only in Rochester did the campaign lead to the abolition of the black schools, and there it did so only obliquely, quietly, after the major part of the campaign seemed to be over. In Buffalo, the campaign achieved a partial success in that blacks were allowed to attend white schools if they lived at some distance from the black school, but even this partial success came about not clearly as a direct result of the campaign. Among the isolated actions, only the one in

Lockport, in western New York, is believed to have led directly to success. In Lockport, a pattern maker, the black Richard Hancock, repeatedly tried to enter his youthful brother-in-law, the son of a prominent Connecticut black abolitionist, into the white high school. When he finally succeeded, a black pastor boasted that in Lockport "the barrier" that kept black boys out of this school "has been broken down by the indomitable perseverence of Mr. Hancock."[17] Altogether in this period the record of achievement is meager. More significant is the gradual growth of a strong undercurrent of objection among blacks and their white allies to separate education for blacks, and the willingness of a few blacks to take firm, even sacrificial action, if necessary, to desegregate schools.

In the 1850s there were still black activists, including those in good standing among black abolitionists, who defended separate black schools, and for reasons which point up the terrible black predicament about schools. Upstate, as we have seen, a major figure in the colored convention movement, Austin Steward, wrote that there was so much prejudice against blacks in white schools that timid black children had better stay home altogether rather than attend white schools. Similarly, downstate, William J. Wilson, himself a teacher in a Brooklyn black school at the time, wrote in his regular column in *Frederick Douglass' Paper,* that blacks who attended white schools were injured by the prejudice they met there. If blacks are openly attending white schools as blacks, they "are the continual subjects of contempts and ridicule"; if they are nearly white-appearing, and attending under the pretense of being white, they "are ever trembling and shaking for fear of exposure." Wilson admitted that black schools in general were "languishing" and "sickly"; but if blacks had more confidence in them, he said, they would improve. Black institutions—our schools and churches— "have made us all we this day are"; they are the "only monuments of our people." Black schools, Wilson insisted, should no more be closed than black churches.[18]

By the 1850s there had come to be considerable awareness of the issue of separate black schools among black activists and their friends in New York State and in the North at large. In 1854 the black New York State Council adopted a firm statement against separate schools for blacks. In 1855 the colored national convention, meeting in Philadelphia with several school boycott leaders present, including Nell from Boston and Douglass from Rochester, resolved that schools, when "open to every class," are "the greatest leveller of all species of prejudice." In 1859 Susan B. Anthony, who was already well known as an advocate of equal rights for both blacks and women, proposed a resolution at the New York State teachers convention that both males and females and both blacks and whites should be educated together. The resolution was tabled.[19]

At about the same time, Frederick Douglass proposed that blacks organize a state drive to desegregate schools. Perhaps he had learned from his experience in Rochester that to attack the black school directly, as at first he had, raised unnecessary complications, for he did not propose that now. He proposed instead that blacks attend local school meetings to demand that school officials admit blacks into all public schools, and if they refused, to sue them. He also proposed that blacks hold a state educational convention to petition the legislature for a law to admit blacks into public schools with whites; and that the convention "raise funds to keep a lobby in Albany during the next session of the legislature" to press for such a law. "An earnest, well-organized and persistent effort in this direction must succeed," Douglass wrote in his *Douglass' Monthly* of March 1859. "Whatever may be the prejudice against colored men, it must be less against colored children, and we touch a chord of ever-living sympathy in the public heart, when we struggle manfully to give our children a fair chance for a good education." While Douglass also favored the drive, then under way once again, for equal suffrage for blacks in the state, he thought that a drive to open all the schools to blacks equally had more chance to succeed.

In fact, no organized state-wide drive to open white schools developed, and blacks failed again in the 1860 state referendum to win equal suffrage. Thus it continued to be difficult for blacks to work for school desegregation by political means.

In the 1830s to 1850s, the movement against school segregation in New York State remained weak. It centered upstate in areas where abolitionists were strong, blacks were few, and where blacks were likely to be more willing to attack the black schools because their teachers were more likely to be white. Actions in one locality were little coordinated with actions in another. Despite the ideological support of abolitionists and of state and national colored conventions and despite Douglass' proposal for a state-wide campaign, there was as yet no state-wide organization to provide funds, legal aid, or legislative lobbying for such a campaign. There was also as yet no significant body of federal or state law which could provide a clear underpinning to the movement. Despite the abolition of the black public schools in Rochester and the increasing opening of white schools to blacks, as in Buffalo, Brooklyn, and New York City, the impact of the movement on the black public schools in the state at large was hardly noticeable. In the 1850s, 1860s, and early 1870s the legally-separate black public schools of the state were at their peak strength, with the largest numbers of schools and the largest number of pupils they were ever to have.

JANITOR JOHNSON'S LAW

THE AGONY OF THE CIVIL WAR deepened the conviction of many Northern whites that slavery was wrong. But that didn't mean that they were anxious to have their children attend school with blacks. In New York State during the war, whites allowed few blacks to attend the new public high schools that were springing up here and there about the state.

In 1862 Ada Boseman, having graduated from Troy's black elementary school, applied to enter Troy's public high school. She took the usual high school entrance examination and passed with a low score. While a black student had never been in the Troy high school before, the Troy Board of Education, after some dissension, voted to admit Ada.

It was probably easier for the Troy board to admit Ada because she came from an unusually enterprising black family. At about this time, her father, Benjamin Boseman, was sailing his own sloop in the Atlantic coastal trade. At about the same time or soon after, one of Ada's brothers had become a clerk for a Troy broker and another a surgeon in the United States army. No doubt the relatively high status of the Boseman family helped some white pupils to accept Ada when she entered the Troy High School, but it did not prevent some white parents from objecting. Within two weeks of Ada's admission to the high school, the board of education voted not to allow any other Afro-Americans to enter.

In 1863 after the Emancipation Proclamation went into effect, another black girl, Jane E. Williams, tried to enter the Troy High School. Unlike Ada, she was refused permission even to take the high school entrance examination. When her father, the whitewasher Alfred B. Williams, appealed to the board of education, the board replied that state law permitted school officials to create black schools and assign blacks to them; and it developed the idea, apparently a new one, that the teachers of the black school, when asked to do so, were expected to give instruction on the high school level as well as on the usual elementary level.

Mr. Williams, still dissatisfied, took the case to a state court, the first time in the state that any black is known to have taken a case to court in a school segregation matter. When this court refused to order the Troy high school to admit blacks, Williams planned to appeal to a higher state court.[1]

Meanwhile, in sympathy with Williams, an interracial group of Troy citiziens—supported by the prominent white John E. Wool who had just retired as a Union army general—became convinced that Williams' court action would not succeed. They decided to go over the heads of both the Troy Board of Education and the state courts to persuade the state legislature—the body which had created the Troy High School by a special law—to require it to admit blacks and whites equally.[2]

By February 1864, the Troy interracial group had found a local state senator, a Republican, who was willing to introduce such a bill for them. The Senate referred the bill to its education committee whose chairman was a young Republican college professor, Andrew D. White, who was sympathetic to black aspirations. Whitc's committee held hearings on the bill. Representatives of the Troy Board of Education spoke against admitting blacks to their high school. But several other Troy whites spoke in favor, among them a Unitarian pastor and a bookkeeper who was a perennial superintendent of the Sunday school of a black church. Several blacks also spoke in favor, including the barber William Rich, a long-time black activist; and, daringly, Benjamin Boseman, one of whose daughters the board of education had already allowed to enter the high school but could remove at any time, and another of whose daughters was employed as a teacher of the black school by the board he was defying.[2]

White's education committee twice reported in favor of the bill, but the Troy Board of Education was probably correct in insisting that "a very large majority of the citizens of Troy . . . are opposed to the admission of colored children into the high school."[3] The Republican legislature would not enact the bill into law. Williams abandoned his appeal to a higher court, and the interracial drive to open Troy High School to blacks collapsed.

Meantime, however, Senator White was working toward the far more difficult objective of opening all public schools in the state to blacks. Probably the controversy over Troy High School helped to push White in that direction. Andrew D. White was a member of the Senate from the abolitionist center of Syracuse. A wealthy young intellectual of New England ancestry, White considered himself a gentleman of breeding who had obligations to try to improve the lot of the common people. He had recently dared to propose that New York State establish a great new university which would accept students regardless of race or sex. When this university was finally opened in 1868 as Cornell University, White was to be its first president. In the meantime in 1864, as chairman of the Senate's committee on education, White was responsible for drafting a revised state education law, and that gave him a chance to try to write into it a provision prohibiting separate public schools for blacks.

For help in developing arguments against separate schools, White appealed to his friend, fellow-Yankee Samuel J. May, a Unitarian pastor in Syracuse. May had long been an outstanding Garrisonian abolitionist. He is said to have been a major factor in preventing Syracuse from establishing a separate black public school, and was himself a member of the Syracuse school board. May replied to White, in March 1864, that the existence of separate schools for blacks was a "perpetual imputation of . . . inferiority." In most of New England, blacks had been admitted to schools with whites, May wrote, "and everywhere it has led to good results." In New York State, too, there had been favorable results where it had been tried. In New York Central College, of which he himself had been a trustee, several blacks "were good scholars." In Syracuse, he said, "for more than fifteen years, we have had no separate schools for colored. . . . They are to be seen in all our schools. Several have graduated from our high school very respectably."[4]

May's assistance was hardly enough. Like the attempt to open Troy High School to blacks by state law, Senator White's attempt to abolish all New York State's black schools by state law failed. Though at this time black and white youths from New York State were dying side by side on the battlefields of the South, public opinion in the state was still often uneasy about their studying side by side in school. Lower class whites—especially the Irish—often considered blacks to be not only competitors for their own menial jobs but also responsible for the coming of the hated Civil War draft. Just the year before, in 1863, they had slaughtered blacks in the anti-draft riots in New York City, Troy, and elsewhere, as well as in a lynching in Newburgh. Such extreme white hostility to blacks reinforced many whites in their belief that blacks and whites could not usefully attend school together.

Still, as the war moved closer to becoming a war to end slavery, popular consciousness of black rights increased. Public opinion in the state was at least moving toward recognizing that black schools, where they existed, should be equal to white schools. Whites could better rationalize their support of segregation if they could argue that black schools provided equal education. With Senator White's help, the Republican legislature wrote into the education law for the first time a section which, as we have already seen, provided that black schools must be supported equally with white schools and be furnished with equal facilities. For the time, this was a significant step for black education.

With the close of the Civil War and the beginning of Reconstruction, the issue of school rights for blacks swirled more than ever in the air, over both North and South. The abolition of slavery in the South gave blacks throughout the nation renewed faith in their ability to win equality in America. They became increasingly confident that the law was, or could be made to be, on their side. They increasingly agitated for white schools to admit blacks. In 1866 Rhode Island by law abolished its few remaining separate black schools. In 1868 Connecticut did the same. In Ohio, the African Methodist Episcopal Church helped to lead blacks in agitating for the abolition of separate schools, but was not successful. Frederick Douglass' new newspaper in Washington pushed for the abolition of separate black schools nationwide.

Meanwhile school segregation was becoming a national party issue. Republican Senator Charles Sumner of Massachusetts, a long-time anti-segregationist, sponsored a federal civil rights bill which included a provision to prohibit separate public schools everywhere. Most Republicans supported the provision, but most Democrats did not, and the bill failed to pass.

In 1870 one of the Reconstruction amendments to the federal Constitution at last gave blacks in New York State, as elsewhere, the equal right to vote. From this time blacks applied their increased political power to their struggle for equal school rights. They usually applied it through the Republican Party.

In Poughkeepsie, the Democratic *Daily Press* of October 21, 1870, taunted local Republicans by charging that they were planning to let black children sit in school "side by side" with white children on orders from the Republican Administration in Washington. In Geneva, in central New York, a black asked an annual school meeting to abolish the separate colored school, arguing that the North should practice the racial equality it was trying to force on the South; according to a local Democratic paper, the *Gazette* of January 5, 1872, this made the Republicans present at the meeting squirm "like worms on a fishhook."

Anti-draft riots of 1863: Negro boy hung on 8th Avenue. These riots, in which poor whites blamed the hated Civil War draft on blacks, helped to convince whites to keep separate black schools in the state. *Courtesy of The New-York Historical Society, from* New York Illustrated News, *August 1, 1863.*

In several places in the state, blacks who sought to open white schools organized themselves more and were increasingly persistent.

In Lockport, under the lead of the black lumber-yard operator Aaron Mosell and his family, blacks beginning in 1867 repeatedly appeared before the school board asking that all the white schools be opened to blacks. At the same time many black parents refused to send their children to the black school, keeping its attendance down to six or seven pupils. In early 1873, some black parents kept sending their children to white schools even when school officials ordered the teachers to refuse to teach them.[5]

In Buffalo in 1867, black parents withdrew eighteen of their children from the black school, sending them to white schools instead. When the city council decided that the children must leave, the superintendent of schools had the problem of removing them. At one school, when he asked the black Aletha Dallas, the daughter of a church sexton, to leave, she insisted on remaining. According to her, the superintendent then took hold of her brutally and led her out. The black parents decided to make a test case out of Aletha's ouster. With the help of a prominent white lawyer, they carried her case to the state Supreme Court, which in 1868 ruled that Aletha had no right to enter a white school when a black school was provided. However, blacks continued to petition to open Buffalo's white schools to blacks. By 1872 a new superintendent had become convinced that the white schools should be opened to prepare blacks to make better use of their newly-granted equal right to vote. Under the superintendent's urging, the Buffalo common council, in a bipartisan vote, at last decided, as New York City had long before, to open all the white schools to blacks, but still to keep the black school open for those who wished to use it. Thereafter, Buffalo blacks increasingly attended white schools and did so without serious problems.[6]

In Albany black children lived scattered over much of the city. Some of them were obliged to walk two or three miles to the black school, passing white schools which were closed to them. This angered Albany blacks. "Upon this point," reported an Albany Republican newspaper in 1871, "the colored people universally are exceedingly bitter, and demand that their children may have the same privileges as the children of white parents."[7] One of the black parents took legal action to force a white school to admit his children. The parent was William A. Dietz, one of the wealthiest blacks in Albany, where it was claimed that blacks were more prosperous than in any other city in the state. Dietz had been a "body servant" of the white Dudley family. He had gradually gained their respect until he became a business agent for Mrs. Dudley, having the power of attorney to sign checks and deeds for the Dudley estate.

In November 1872, a state Supreme Court judge ruled against Dietz, saying that the Albany school board could properly exclude black children from white schools so long as it provided equal education for blacks. The judge suggested, however, that if the black citizens "as a body" calmly decided that they wished the discontinuance of the black school and the admission of their children to the white schools, "their views . . . will doubtless have great weight with the board." Following the judge's hint, blacks—led especially by the local black Republican leader, barber William H. Johnson—learned from board members that the Republican-controlled board in fact would open all the schools to blacks if blacks made clear that they desired it. In January 1873, Albany blacks held a public meeting to find out what blacks wanted. At the meeting blacks considered asking that the black school be closed, but rejected this proposal. Instead they decided to ask the board simply to open the white schools to blacks.[8] The board did not respond at once.

So far in New York State, from the beginning of the Civil War up to early 1873, there had been accumulating pressure from both blacks and whites to open white public schools to blacks. While the state legislature in 1864 had decided to require "equal" education in black schools, in the legal cases brought by blacks to open white schools to blacks in Troy, Buffalo, and Albany, the state courts had continued to support separate schools. So far in this period, pressure against segregation was not known to have led directly to the abolition of black schools anywhere in the state, but such pressure had helped lead school officials to open white high schools to blacks in two places. In Troy in 1869, at a time when neither of the two teachers of the black elementary school was qualified to teach high school, thus making untenable the school board's claim that the black school could teach high school subjects, the board finally voted to admit all blacks equally into the white high school. At about the same time in Geneva, when blacks were pressuring to close the black elementary school, a school meeting tried to fend them off by at least letting blacks into the white high school.[9] Moreover, in Buffalo in 1872, as we have seen, after a long black campaign, officials at last decided to open all white schools to blacks. Now in addition, in Albany in early 1873, local school officials seemed to be on the verge of abolishing the black school in part because they anticipated the passage of a state civil rights law which would force the closing of all black schools in the state.

The colored state convention which had met in Troy in the spring of 1872 had asked for a state law providing for equal civil rights for blacks, including equal school rights. In the fall of 1872 blacks helped re-elect the Republican President Grant, who was portrayed as more clearly favorable to racially-mixed schools than his opponent was; and they helped elect not only a Republican legislature but also a Republican governor, John A. Dix, the erstwhile Democrat and colonizationist. Blacks believed the time was now ripe to press for a civil rights bill. The Albany black, William H. Johnson, who had been president of the colored state convention, drafted such a bill.

Johnson was a barber who had never been to school. As a young man before the Civil War, he had been a correspondent for Frederick Douglass' newspaper and active in protecting fugitive slaves. Now a tall,

William H. Johnson, an Albany barber, was rewarded for his political speech-making by being chosen at various times as head janitor of the state senate and as a member of the Republican state committee. *Penn, Afro-American Press, 1891.*

impressive man in his forties, Johnson was described by a Troy newsman who saw him at work in the colored state convention, as able to "speak ten minutes or ten days on any question that comes up."[10] In 1872 he attended the Republican national convention which renominated President Grant, and in the campaign that followed, Johnson spoke for the Republicans in many meetings in and out of the state. After the victory, the Republican state Senate rewarded Johnson by appointing him as its head janitor, apparently the highest state office yet awarded to a black—a poignant sign of the continued lowly political status of blacks. However, Johnson found the position convenient for lobbying for his civil rights bill.

By February 1873, Johnson had found a prominent Republican Assemblyman, James Husted of Westchester County, who was willing to introduce the bill. In support of the bill, a mass meeting of New York City blacks decided to send to Albany a delegation including the hot-spoken anti-segregationist pastor, William F. Butler, who was said to have declared that any black who voted Democratic was "degenerate." Blacks in western New York held a meeting which asked their legislators to vote for the bill. Citizens in sections of considerable black population in the Hudson Valley, as in Troy, Albany, Orange County, and Westchester County, sent in petitions for the bill. According to the Republican *New York Times* of March 20, 1873, Democrats were fond of calling Johnson's bill "radical." When it came to a vote, a Democratic senator representing Queens and Suffolk Counties, voted against it, he explained, because he opposed the "amalgamation" of races. But the bill passed. A Long Island Democratic paper reported that it passed under the Republican "party lash." Republicans evidently felt pressure to support the bill because their black supporters favored it and because it was consistent with national party policy. Republicans voted overwhelmingly for it, while most of those opposed were Democrats, especially downstate Democrats.[11]

Whether janitor Johnson's civil rights law as passed in April 1873 was still in the original form in which he had proposed it is not clear. At any rate, as passed it provided that no citizen because of his race or color shall be "excluded from the full and equal enjoyment" of public facilities such as inns, "common carriers," and "common schools." Particularly "commissioners, superintendents, teachers, and other officers of common schools" were forbidden to make any such exclusion.[12] To the blacks who had promoted the law, it meant that blacks could not be kept out of any public school because of their race. What it would mean in practice remained to be seen.

Soon after Governor Dix had signed the bill, between three and four thousand blacks gathered in New York at Fifth Avenue and 8th Street for a celebration parade. They marched, many of them in colorful fraternal regalia, uptown as far as 42nd Street and then back downtown to Cooper Union, where they held a meeting which was so packed that it was uncomfortable. The black principal Charles L. Reason read congratulatory messages from old time abolitionists like Garrison, Frederick Douglass, and Gerrit Smith. The sanguine white Assemblyman Husted said the law had done its full and complete work for blacks, as if this law would bring the problems of blacks in the state to an end forever. Black head-janitor Johnson urged that credit for passage of the law go to Republicans. John M. Langston, the black dean of the Howard University Law School, rejoiced that, because of the new law, "the common schools were at last open to Negro children."[13]

While Johnson's law was still being considered in the legislature, the Albany school board, anticipating passage of the law, had finally decided to open all its schools to blacks. The board also had decided— though blacks had not asked the board to do so—to close its black school.

After the signing of the law, blacks in several other places in the state tried to enter their children in the white public schools. The *Hudson Register* observed that this movement appeared to be "preconcerted" because it was "springing up almost simultaneously in different parts of the state."[14]

In Newburgh, the black D. B. Alsdorf, who ran a private music and dancing school, wrote the local school board to ask that his three children be admitted to a white public school because of the new law.

In response, the board referred the matter to a committee which found itself, as many other school officials were also to find themselves, unable to agree on interpreting the new law. One member of the committee, a Democratic lawyer, said that he believed that the new law required equal benefits regardless of race, but did not direct that such benefits must be given in the same school building. However, the other two members of the committee, both Republicans—one a lawyer and the other the editor of the *Newburgh Daily Journal*—interpreted the new law as requiring the closing of the separate black school because it did not provide equal education. To make the black school equal, "a new, suitable and commodious building on a healthy site, and the employment of an additional teacher would be absolutely necessary," they said. This would be expensive. Anyway, the "evident tendency of the times" and "continued agitation of the question by the colored people" might lead the legislature to "pass an act on the subject, the provisions of which cannot be mistaken or disregarded." The Newburgh board promptly voted six to two to discontinue the black school and admit all children to the schools of the city without regard to race.[15]

The board's action did not seem to upset the people of Newburgh. "We have known the Common Council to create more excitement by a raid on trees," said the *Newburgh Journal* of May 5, 1873. But a Democratic paper in nearby Middletown predicted trouble when any Newburgh black "hoodlum" resisted being "insulted" in school by "some urchin of a lighter hue." In New York City, the Republican *Commercial Advertiser* of May 5 proposed that Newburgh keep a record of the com-

parative progress of white children and "picaninnies" for the "edifica-
tion" of the people who have long disputed the intellectual capacity of
blacks and "have been ready any time these last thirty years to cut each
others' throats on the subject." The Democratic *New York Herald* of
May 6 predicted that in Newburgh "very many white pupils will be found
who will strongly object to personal association in school with colored
children, and the entire educational system may receive a serious check in
consequence." The Republican *Newburgh Journal*—school board member Cyrus B. Martin's paper—countered that for whites and blacks to
study together was not new, even if New York City papers did not know
it. "The country is full of schools where white and black scholars inter-
mingle in the laudable pursuit of knowledge," it said; the nearby city of
Kingston never has had a black school, and yet has no trouble from black
and white associating in the schools.[16]

Within a few days of its decision, the Newburgh school board
had scattered the black children, eighty or ninety of them altogether, in
the previously all-white schools. To avoid trouble, they seated the black
children in each school room separately, apart from the whites. Within a
few months, the *Newburgh Journal* reported that, thanks to the parents,
teachers, and especially the pupils, the entry of the black children into the
white schools had not created "a ripple on the surface of school life."[17]

As in both Albany and Newburgh, so also in at least three other
upstate places—Geneva, Troy, and Schenectady—school boards responded quickly to the new law by deciding both to open the white schools
to blacks, and, whether blacks wanted it or not, to close the black schools.[18]

In other places school boards were slower to act. In Poughkeepsie, according to the Republican *Eagle*, the school board was "in perfect
harmony" with black parents on keeping the black school open. "In all
probability we shall have no civil rights excitement here as in Newburgh,"
the *Eagle* predicted.[19] But at least one black Poughkeepsie family, the
Rhodes, thought otherwise.

Joseph Rhodes operated his own business for dyeing cloth, and
he owned a substantial $3000 worth of real estate. He had long been ac-
tive with other blacks in struggling for black rights, as for the equal right
to vote. He was capable of acting independently too. Because he believed
his children should not attend segregated schools, he had boycotted the
Poughkeepsie black school, sending two of his children for a time to a
small town in the Finger Lakes region where they could attend school
with whites. As Rhodes and his wife saw Newburgh and other cities opening their schools equally to blacks while Poughkeepsie did not, they prepared to take action on their own to force Poughkeepsie to do so, even if

most Poughkeepsie citizens, whether black or white, did not agree with them.

When Poughkeepsie's public schools opened in September 1873, the Rhodes sent their two girls, Josephine, aged fifteen, and Marietta, aged nine, to a white school. A teacher told them she thought they had come to the wrong school. But the children replied that they were where they wanted to be and insisted on staying. The teacher let them stay. In the afternoon when a white child hit Marietta, the teacher asked her to go home early. Marietta went home crying.

By the third day of school, according to the *Poughkeepsie Eagle*, the question of school segregation had become "the chief topic of conversation" in Poughkeepsie. On this morning, the Rhodes children, having been informed that because of the location of their house, they had gone to the wrong white school, went to another one in their proper school zone. The principal of that school, Miss Vail, and her pupils were expecting them. According to the *Eagle*, "nearly all the scholars were at school far ahead of time to note the distinguished arrival." To keep the situation under control, Miss Vail, when she saw the black girls coming down the street, walked some distance to meet them, while a few of the "dare devil" white children called out, "Here come the Modocs."*

The calls didn't last long. "Miss Vail's determined manner . . . overawed the young mischief makers." Inside the school, the teachers soon secured order. In the afternoon, despite rumors that some white parents might refuse to send their children back to the school, all the children were in their places as usual.

A few days later, the Poughkeepsie board chairman told his board that, while in principle he was opposed to racially-mixed schools, he no longer believed that black children could legally be required to attend a black school. He reported that not only the Rhodes children, but also three other black children had recently entered the white schools. He also reported that he had visited the black school and found only twenty children attending, though seventy were on the roll. Under these circumstances, he said, keeping the black school open was "an imposition on the taxpayers."

In response to its chairman, the board voted to adopt his argument that, legally, black children must be accepted in the schools with whites. But since there was some black opinion in favor of keeping the black school open, and since some whites opposed the presence of blacks

---

*Literally, the Modocs were a tribe of California Indians, who in the early 1870s were bitterly fighting United States troops.

in school with whites, the board, acting especially under Democratic influence, planned not to close the black school at once.

A month later a cynical letter writer in the Republican *Eagle* probably explained the position of the Democrats on the board accurately. According to him, when the Democrats talked with the recently-naturalized anti-Negro voters who supported them, especially the Irish, they said, "We did what we could to 'keep out the niggers,' but the law passed by the Republican legislature was too much for us." On the other hand, when these same Democrats talked to the less anti-Negro native-born whites who also supported them, they would say: "We had strong prejudices, especially among the Irish, to contend with, and therefore had to ease matters the best we could, but it is alright now."[20]

In November the board decided not to employ a black teacher for the black school but to keep the white teacher. This decision probably helped reduce the interest of blacks in keeping the black school open. In June 1874, the board quietly allowed the black school to die. At least one other upstate city, Hudson, closed its black school similarly, not at once after Johnson's civil rights law was passed, but later in the 1870s after the white schools had been opened to blacks for some time, and consequently, attendance at the black school had dwindled.

In Buffalo and New York City before Johnson's law was passed, as we have seen, school officials had already opened their white schools to blacks while keeping their black schools open. The passage of the new law in 1873 reinforced these local policies and made them better known, drawing more blacks into the white elementary schools. Still, most school officials in New York City and Buffalo were not convinced—as school officials in Newburgh, Albany, Geneva, Schenectady, and Troy seemed to be convinced—that the new law required them, whether directly or indirectly, to close their black schools.

In New York City, more and more black children kept leaving the six black elementary schools and entering the white schools instead. Doubtless this trend was accelerated both by Johnson's civil rights law and by the tendency of blacks to move ever farther uptown, as into the West Eighties, farther from most of the black schools. In 1877 the city school board reported that enough black children were entering the white schools to reduce attendance noticeably at the black schools; by this time the board had cut the number of black schools from six to four. The next year, the board reported that 250 black children were already attending white schools and admitted that it had long considered closing all the black schools; the board cut the number of black schools still more, to three.[21]

In 1878 a member of the New York board, a German-American dry goods merchant, proposed that all the black schools be abolished. He did so, he said, because the black schools were "contrary to the spirit, if not in direct violation" of the 1873 civil rights law and were more expensive than other schools. In response, the board's committee on black schools interviewed leading blacks and reported—probably accurately as we shall see—that they opposed the abolition of the black schools. The committee noted, however, that since black children could freely enter the white schools, as they believed the civil rights law required that they should, black parents themselves could abolish the black schools whenever they wished simply by choosing to send their children to the white schools. They believed the black schools would gradually fade away as more and more blacks preferred white schools.[22]

In other localities, school boards believed that the new civil rights law did not require them even to open their white schools to blacks, much less to abolish their black schools. They in fact did neither during the 1870s. This was certainly true in Brooklyn. It was also apparently true for several other places which had separate black schools—including Flushing, Jamaica, Roslyn, Amityville, and Stapleton—inasmuch as later when blacks tried to enter the white schools in these places, officials refused to allow it. These places were all downstate, where the black population was heavier and prejudice likely to be greater than upstate.

Still, how could it happen that Brooklyn, which in some respects, as we have seen, was unusually advanced in black rights, seemed unresponsive to the civil rights law? The question of the effect of the law was certainly raised in Brooklyn. In May 1873, soon after passage of the law, a member of the Brooklyn school board, W. P. Libby, the president of a gas light company, made a bold motion to give blacks the right to enter all the white schools and to discontinue the four black schools. His motion was tabled. In August Mr. Libby proposed a much milder motion: that the designation of the black schools as "colored" be dropped, but that the schools continue to exist. This motion was also tabled.

Meanwhile, a group of Brooklyn blacks, saying that the existence of black schools was incompatible with the new civil rights law, supported Mr. Libby in asking the board to drop the designation "colored" from any schools. This group, according to a black newspaper, had the support of all the black churches of Brooklyn. When this group held a mass meeting, it adopted resolutions declaring that separate black schools were not only inferior but also "painfully humiliating."

While much of Brooklyn's black leadership sided with this integrationist group, a segregationist group of blacks was led by one black of some weight, the modest, hard-working Reverend Henry M. Wilson. A black newspaper, reporting his efforts to keep the black schools open, dubbed him a "contented" black who had come to the front in Brooklyn "as the apologizer for the most contemptible prejudice known to the world."[23] Wilson had strong ties to black institutions and believed in them. In the 1840s to 1860s he had been pastor of various small black Presbyterian churches in New York City; in the 1860s he was secretary and editor for the African Civilization Society which insisted on staffing its schools in the South with blacks only; and also in the 1860s he was a founder of the Howard Colored Orphan Asylum in Brooklyn which he helped develop into a black-run institution, as few such institutions in nineteenth century America were.

Wilson's group, in a petition to the board, said they were not ashamed of being "colored" persons, and wished to make "the distinctive name by which we are known to be . . . as deserving of honor and respect as that of any class of our fellow citizens." A means to accomplish that, they said, was not to close the black schools, but to make them as well supplied with quality teachers, buildings, and furnishings as any other schools. Later in another petition this group argued that it was inconsistent for blacks who were proud of black churches to denounce black schools because they were black.

Meantime, the Brooklyn Board of Education, faced with a division among blacks as to what they wanted, made no formal decision to open the white schools to blacks as a right, and in October 1873, decided both to keep the colored schools open and, by a close vote of 18 to 17, to continue to call them "colored." This arrangement was to persist for a decade. The powerful Democratic newspaper, the *Brooklyn Daily Eagle*, supported it, explaining that admitting blacks into the white public schools in considerable numbers might seriously injure the white schools by driving the wealthier white children into private schools.[24] Apparently Brooklyn had decided not to abolish its black schools or open its white schools consistently to blacks largely because blacks themselves were divided on the issue; because a few blacks had long been admitted erratically into white schools anyway, by indulgence rather than by right; and because in this region of comparatively heavy black population many whites continued to abhor the idea of blacks attending school with whites.

In the downstate region, open support of segregated schooling was considerable among both Republicans and Democrats and among both blacks and whites. In the fall of 1873, regardless of the new civil rights law, the village of Amityville built a new building for its public black school, and blacks were so enthusiastic about it that they even talked of enlarging the new building by themselves so it could also house a black high school to prepare blacks for college. In 1874 school officials in Hempstead village were so unafraid of the new law that they created for the first time a black public school, and they soon reported that more blacks were attending it than had previously attended school with whites.[25]

Though black promoters of the 1873 civil rights law had expected that it would mean that all the white public schools must be opened to blacks, some school officials from the beginning had not interpreted it that way. By 1875, when a Brooklyn black tested the law in the state courts, Northerners seemed to be becoming weary of Reconstruction, and even Republicans, assisted by the United States Supreme Court, were increasingly willing to abandon black rights for the sake of restoring harmony with the white South.

The Brooklyn black who tested the law in the courts was the blind Reverend William F. Johnson. As head of the Howard Colored Orphan Asylum, Reverend Johnson himself was responsible for a publicly-funded black school for the orphan children. But as a believer in equal rights, Johnson applied to have his son admitted into a white public school in Brooklyn. When the principal of the school refused to accept the boy, the Brooklyn school board supported the principal. The Reverend Johnson applied to a court for an order requiring the school to admit his son. Eventually, the state Supreme Court ruled that the 1873 state civil rights law, as some school officials had maintained from the beginning, did not specify that separate schools for whites and blacks could not exist, any more than it held that separate schools for girls and boys could not exist. The law merely required equal education, the court held, and Reverend Johnson could not show that his son would not be as well educated in a black as in a white school. The Republican *New York Times* of September 14, 1875, commended the decision as "very clear and apparently sound." As often in the latter part of the nineteenth century, much of the substance of a law intended to assist blacks had been whittled away by the pressure of public opinion and the interpretation of the courts. Opponents of separate schools were discouraged.

They were also discouraged by their becoming increasingly aware of a disturbing side effect from the closing of black schools. When black schools closed, if their teachers were white, some of them were reassigned by school officials to teach in predominantly white schools in the same school district, but if their teachers were black, they were simply let go.

In both Brooklyn and New York City nearly all the teachers in the black public schools were black. But New York City blacks had more reason to worry about the black teachers than Brooklyn blacks did. While

The Reverend William F. Johnson was head of the Howard Colored Orphan Asylum, Brooklyn, from 1870 to 1902. Though blind, he was a persistent black activist and a power to be reckoned with in debate. *New York State Historical Association, from* Review: Brooklyn Howard Colored Orphan Asylum, 1866–1911.

Brooklyn, without a policy of admitting blacks by right into the white schools, saw the number of teachers in its black public schools rise from 10 in 1870 to 15 in 1880, New York, with its more liberal policy of letting blacks by right into white schools, saw the number of teachers in its black schools drop from 44 in 1870 to 27 in 1880. For a people for whom good jobs for the well-educated were few, that represented a serious drop in jobs.

In 1879 when the New York City Board of Education was considering closing yet another of its black schools, blacks mobilized to protect the remaining black teachers. A committee appealed to the board not to act until blacks had time to hold a public meeting on the issue. The board agreed. At the public meeting, with about five hundred blacks present as well as several members of the board, a young black clergyman spoke for keeping the black schools open on principle. But the old war horse, Reverend Henry Highland Garnet, insisted that the black schools should not be kept open on principle. Instead, Garnet proposed resolutions which thanked God that the board, "in accordance with the mandate" of the state civil rights law, had opened the doors of the public schools without regard to race. However, Garnet was concerned about retaining the black teachers—his wife, Sarah Garnet, after all was the principal of one of the city's three remaining black public schools. Garnet's resolutions continued: since blacks had been informed by members of the board that "there is no probability of the admission of colored teachers into mixed schools," we request the board to keep the present colored schools open "as long as the numbers in attendance shall justify their continuance"; and we urge black parents to see to it that the black schools are "kept full." The meeting debated Garnet's resolutions for two hours and eventually adopted them almost unanimously. Soon thereafter the school board voted to abandon its plan to close another black school.[26]

Six years after the passage of the state civil rights law, New York City blacks were concentrating not so much on their satisfaction that more white schools in the state were being opened to blacks as they were on a mundane campaign for black pupils to attend black schools in order to keep black teachers in jobs. This campaign was to concern New York City blacks, and soon Brooklyn blacks too, for many years to come.

Altogether in response to the civil rights law of 1873, available evidence indicates that articulate New York State blacks generally agreed that they wanted the right to enter the white public schools. But they differed on whether they wanted the black public schools to continue to exist. As for the mass of blacks, according to what they said as well as what they did in continuing to send their children to the black schools, most of them—especially those downstate—still seemed to wish to keep the black schools open.

Similarly, white school officials disagreed on what to do in response to the new law. Often by divided votes, school boards decided to close the black schools quickly during 1873 in five places (Newburgh, Ge-

neva, Albany, Troy, and Schenectady). In three other places (Poughkeepsie, Hudson, and Lockport), they kept their black schools open until later
in the 1870s when finally, because their white schools were now open to
blacks, or because of boycotts, or otherwise, so few blacks attended the
black schools they they felt it was no longer feasible to keep them open.
But in at least nineteen other known places, officials still kept black
schools open into the 1880s.

In making these decisions, school officials were following a geographical pattern. Upstate officials were more willing to open white
schools to blacks and abolish black schools than downstate officials were;
in fact, during the 1860s and 1870s all the places where they are known to
have abolished all their black public schools were upstate. Of the places
where officials kept black public schools surviving into the 1880s only one,
Buffalo, was in the central or western part of the state; all the other known
places were in areas where black population had long been concentrated;
in the Hudson region (seven places) or downstate (eleven places).

Comparing action to desegregate schools in the 1860s and 1870s
with such action in the 1830s to 1850s, who led in these actions? The 109
black leaders who can be identified as having led during the 1860s and
1870s represent a substantial increase compared to the previous period,
while the thirty-two white leaders represent a slight drop. The Civil War
and Reconstruction stirred blacks to more hope for assimilation into
American life, and the increasing education of blacks in the state was
working: it was producing more blacks who had the same aspirations as
other Americans, including the aspiration for equal educational opportunity. In fact, of all the decades from the 1830s to the 1940s, the decades of
the 1860s and 1870s were the decades when the largest number of known
leaders, black and white combined, was active for educational desegregation (see Table 16 in Appendix).

While blacks took local action to desegregate schools in the
period of the 1830s to 1850s in only nine known places, during the shorter
period of the 1860s to 1870s they took action in eleven known places.
Most of the methods which they used in the 1860s to 1870s they had used
before, including agitation in meetings or the press, appealing to local officials or school district meetings, sending their children to the white
schools in a direct challenge to the segregation system, and the deliberate
school boycott. However, blacks and their white allies used two methods
which they are not known to have used before: they took cases to court
and they campaigned for state legislation.

Blacks took at least four school segregation cases to court, in Albany, Troy, Buffalo, and Brooklyn. The court actions all failed, the courts

ruling consistently in favor of segregation. Blacks and whites made three attempts to curb school segregation by state legislation, the last of which succeeded in the passage of janitor Johnson's civil rights law of 1873.

By the late 1870s, the drive to close the black schools was slowing down for several reasons. The national climate was shifting toward appeasement of the white South. The 1875 court decision in Brooklyn had reduced the impact of the 1873 civil rights law. Some blacks were becoming less confident of the possibility of their assimilation into American life than they had been in the heyday of abolitionism and Reconstruction and were reawakening to the strategic advantages in some aspects of black separation. Certainly blacks were increasingly unwilling to immolate black teachers on the altar of school integration.

PROTECTION FOR TEACHERS DOWNSTATE

THE 1880s AND 1890s were not a favorable time to press for black rights in New York State or anywhere else in the United States. In the South blacks were losing the right to vote and were being increasingly segregated. In the North many whites were tired of hearing about black rights and were more anxious to become reconciled to the white South. Race prejudice in the North was said to be growing. The *New York Times* warned that for blacks to demand rights would sharpen white prejudice.[1] Nevertheless, militant blacks continued to press against separate schools.

In the years from the 1830s to the 1870s, the movement against separate public schools had centered upstate, and most of the upstate black public schools had been closed. But in the period of the 1880s and 1890s, the movement to desegregate schools began to shift downstate, where most of the remaining black public schools were, and where most blacks now lived.

In the 1880s and 1890s, many black leaders in Brooklyn and New York City hoped to abolish the black public schools. But their hope was increasingly complicated not only by the unfavorable social climate but also by their concern for what would happen to the black teachers.

In New York City in the early 1880s when the board of education talked of closing its three remaining black schools, the aggressive black editor T. T. Fortune proposed that the board itself should be held accountable for jobs for the threatened black teachers. According to Fortune, the board was planning to wipe out one injustice—the placing of black children in separate black schools—and at the same time create another "as repugnant as the first," that is, driving the black teachers out of the schools just because they were black. What the New York board

213

"The school of the future. Teacher Sarah: 'Look at de white trash's impudence!'"
At this time, some New York City blacks were asking that since many of the public schools were becoming racially mixed, black teachers should be allowed to teach in them. *Anti-Defamation League of B'nai B'rith presentation, "The Distorted Image," from* New York Judge, *March 3, 1883.*

ought to do, Fortune said—much as Brooklyn blacks had earlier unsuccessfully proposed to the Brooklyn board—is to abolish the separate black schools and then employ the black teachers, if they had the qualifications, in the predominantly white schools.[2]

In reply to such arguments, one board member said that the black teachers gave their pupils "imperfect tuition" and were "immensely overpaid," and that anyway the schools were run for the benefit of the pupils, not the teachers. In early 1883, the board directed a committee to prepare for the complete abolition of the black schools without continuing to employ the twenty-six remaining black teachers.[3]

In alarm, black leaders called a mass meeting on the issue. The meeting considered Fortune's plan of insisting that the black teachers be allowed to teach in the predominantly white schools. But the meeting became convinced that such a plan was unworkable in the existing climate. The meeting compromised by asking the board to keep the black schools open, but to develop them into regular city schools which whites as well as blacks were encouraged to attend, and to keep the black teachers employed in those schools.[4]

The agitation on behalf of the teachers was at least successful in persuading the board of education to postpone the closing of the two larger of the remaining black schools. But the board did close at once the smallest school, located on Mulberry Street, as originally planned, and without any provision to employ its black teachers elsewhere. These teachers were let go. Some of them became unemployed, joining the increasing numbers of black young women graduating from the city's Normal College who could not find teaching posts.

During the next academic year, 1883-1884, the two remaining black schools were allowed to continue to exist—the one on West 41st Street of which Charles Reason was principal and the one on West 17th Street of which Sarah Garnet was principal. To help justify keeping these schools open, the teachers of these schools tried to recruit more children, both black and white. Teachers canvassed black neighborhoods as far uptown as 99th Street, offering children free elevated-railroad tickets as an inducement for them to attend at a distance from home. In spite of such inducements, black parents increasingly sent their children to the predominantly white schools in their own neighborhoods, as they were freely allowed to do, and few white parents were willing to send their children to black schools.

Meanwhile in the city of Brooklyn in 1882, a black real estate dealer, Simon King, tried to open all the Brooklyn schools to blacks by right, as all the New York City schools long had been. King sent his daughter Theresa to a white school in his neighborhood. When because of her color she was refused, King sued in a Brooklyn court, claiming the right to send his daughter to any school in the district where he lived. On an appeal in 1883, the state's highest court decided against King. The court held, much as in the earlier case of Reverend Johnson, that the civil rights law of 1873 did not prohibit separate schools for blacks provided they offered equal facilities.[5] Disappointed, Brooklyn black leaders were looking for new ways to work toward opening Brooklyn schools legally to all.

In December 1883, when the New York City school board was planning to abolish its two remaining black schools, the Brooklyn board, proceeding in quite a different direction, opened a handsome new brick building for one of its black schools. A speech at the opening ceremony helped to set in motion the Brooklyn board's desegregation policy, a policy which seemed to black teachers less ruthless than the desegregation policy the New York City board was following.

Speaking at the Brooklyn ceremony, Brooklyn's reform mayor, Seth Low, doubtless aware of the black disappointment with the court decision in the King case, delighted some of the audience by saying that he believed that Brooklyn's schools should be open to all regardless of color.[6]

Within a few days, Philip A. White, the black druggist whom Mayor Low had appointed as a member of the Brooklyn board, moved to take advantage of the mayor's statement. White had long been opposed to segregated education. Now at a Brooklyn board meeting, White introduced a resolution directing that the city's white schools must accept black children. This would legalize a practice which Brooklyn had only erratically permitted. The resolution said nothing about the black schools accepting white children, but perhaps it didn't need to, for Brooklyn had often permitted this anyway. White's plan, contrary to the New York City board's plan, would keep the black schools open and keep the black teachers teaching in them as long as enough pupils chose to attend them. White's plan was essentially the compromise plan that the recent black mass meeting had recommended for New York City.

According to White, who was a Republican, the discussion of his desegregation resolution in the Brooklyn board was not partisan. "Many Democrats" favored the resolution, he explained, "while there were Republicans who voted against it." After a long debate, in which White had an opportunity to bring into play the diplomatic skills he had developed in his forty years of operation of one of the largest wholesale and retail drug firms in New York City, the resolution passed by a vote of 21 to 14. Afterward, a Southern-born member of the board, a Democrat, led a campaign to reverse the board's decision but failed.[7]

In the next few years, a few white children attended the three traditionally black schools of Brooklyn—which continued to be officially called "colored"—and black children attended them at first in larger numbers than ever. One reason that so many black parents chose to send their children to the traditionally-black schools was that, according to one school board member, they sometimes met "frozen courtesy" from school officials when they tried to enter their children in the traditionally-white schools. Another was, however, that both many black parents and many school officials thought there was a place for schools which the black community considerably controlled, schools with black principals and black teachers. The *New York Globe* claimed proudly that the quality of Principal Dorsey's school—which was housed in the handsome new brick building whose opening ceremony had sparked the desegregation move—compared favorably with any school in Brooklyn.[8]

From the black point of view, particularly fortunate was the fact that Brooklyn continued to hire new black teachers. From 1883 to 1885 school board member White, who was the chairman of the school board's "local committee" for each of the Brooklyn black schools, was advertising in black newspapers for black teachers for these schools. In 1890 White urged more blacks to take the exams for Brooklyn teaching certificates, saying no blacks holding Brooklyn certificates are now unemployed.[9]

In Brooklyn, unlike New York City, black teachers were not being thrown out because all the schools were now open equally to black pupils. The number of black teachers in Brooklyn, which was fifteen when the white schools were officially desegregated in 1883, even rose slightly thereafter. For black teachers, Brooklyn's policy of continuing to operate the black schools and to warmly support them was manna from heaven in a weary land.

In New York City by the spring of 1884, those blacks concerned about keeping their black teachers in jobs were working for a policy of partial desegregation, much like that which had recently been adopted in Brooklyn, which would keep the two remaining traditionally-black schools open. But these blacks had no black member on the New York board, such as Brooklyn blacks had on their board, to argue their case from the inside. New York City blacks discovered that they could not persuade their board to drop its plan to close the two remaining black schools and fire the teachers. So they conceived of a plan to get around the board. They would ask help from the state legislature, which at this time, under such reform-minded leaders as Governor Grover Cleveland, Democrat, and the youthful Assemblyman Theodore Roosevelt, Republican, was strongly for protecting public employees from arbitrary dismissal. The friends of the New York City black teachers petitioned the state legislature to require that the existing New York City black schools, like other schools, be open to all children without regard to color, but "be continued with their present teachers until said teachers shall be removed for cause." Supporting the petition, black editor Fortune said in his *New York Globe* of April 5, 1884, that it should appeal to the legislature as providing another opportunity to apply "the principles of Civil Service Reform, in preventing the wholesale discharge of tried and capable public servants without adequate cause."

In Albany the bill was promoted especially by two persons, one a white Democratic state senator, Michael C. Murphy of New York City, and the other, Albany's most prominent black Democrat, James C. Mathews. As a lawyer Mathews had helped to close the Albany black school, and consequently, his sister had lost her teaching job there. Maybe Mathews had learned from this experience to be more concerned about black teachers.

Senator Murphy introduced the bill in the Senate and managed to move it quickly along to passage. Murphy and lawyer Mathews worked together on the floor of the Assembly to get it through there also. A Republican Assemblyman from New York City, in explaining why he would vote for the bill, said that it was desired by the black citizens of his city. The Assembly passed the bill, too, in April 1884, with no one voting against it.

Still, black leaders—doubtless fearing the influence of the New York City Board of Education—were worried that Governor Cleveland might not sign the bill. Cleveland, though he came from an old Puritan family which had fought to abolish slavery in New England, was not committed to integrated education.[10]

To bring pressure on the governor, the chairman of the leading black Republican organization in the state, Reverend William B. Derrick, first worked among legislators. Derrick was so magnetic that, according to the *New York Globe*, when he had been pastor of an African Methodist church in Albany, his congregation had been two-thirds white—"not the rude [white] element that generally attends our [black] churches, but respectable persons." Now pastor of his denomination's most prestigious church in New York City, Derrick brought with him to Albany three other New York City blacks who were well informed about what was happening to their city's remaining two black schools. They were the elderly Congregational minister, Charles B. Ray, who had once been editor of the *Colored American* and now had two daughters among the threatened teachers, and the principals of the two schools concerned, Sarah Garnet and Charles L. Reason.

In Albany, lawyer Mathews introduced the delegation to Governor Cleveland. Principal Reason explained that he was opposed to all institutions based upon complexional differences, and that the only reason the bill was necessary was that, while the New York City Board of Education members "are willing to destroy the color line so far as the pupils are concerned," they "do not desire the principle to extend to the teachers." Principal Garnet said she already had some white scholars in her school. Reverend Ray said that the petitions in support of this bill "ought to have some weight with the Governor as they were signed by some of New York's best citizens." Reverend Derrick "made a passionate appeal," as he was well able to do. Soon afterward, Governor Cleveland signed the bill, in May 1884.[11]

The new state law forced the New York City board to keep its two remaining black schools open and, following the Brooklyn model, to regard them as regular city schools open to all races. However, the New York City board by no means behaved like the Brooklyn board. The New York board, irked that blacks had foisted the new law on them against their will, seemed to try to make life difficult for the twenty black teachers in these two schools.

First, the board withheld pay from the black teachers for several months. Second, in what was apparently an attempt to reduce the number of pupils in Reason's school, the board tried to move its location from West 41st Street to a dwelling house on West 42nd Street, which was not only smaller but also located only one block from a white school, so that it had little chance to attract white children. Reason and his teachers sued school officials to prevent them from carrying through with this relocation but did not succeed. Third, the board dismissed at least four black teachers on the grounds that the number of pupils in the two schools had dropped. The dismissed teachers brought suit against the board for reinstatement on the basis of the law which Governor Cleveland had signed. They won their suit and returned to work.[12]

However, neither of the two surviving traditionally-black schools had as many pupils as their teachers thought they needed to keep their jobs safe from further harassment by the board of education. The teachers paid car fare out of their own pockets to encourage black children to come from far uptown to attend these mid-town schools. Over several years the teachers and their friends—including leading black editors and pastors—kept appealing for more blacks to send their children to these schools. Commenting on one such appeal, a columnist in the black *New York Freeman* of March 12, 1887, said, "It is almost characteristic" of black parents "to instill the false impression into their . . . offspring, that the tutor of his own race and color is totally incapable of instructing and advancing him." Enrollment in the surviving traditionally black schools continued to decline. By 1895, after the death of Principal Reason, the two schools were consolidated into one with Mrs. Garnet as principal.

Although black children increasingly attended Manhattan's traditionally white schools, signifying that desegregation for pupils was going forward, in 1895 desegregation for teachers still had not begun. No black teachers were yet known to have been appointed to teach in the traditionally-white public schools of either Brooklyn or New York City. Even blacks who graduated from New York City's own Normal College (Hunter) found it impossible to win such positions.

Susie E. Frazier, a black girl who had graduated from the college in 1887 and was placed on the New York City list of eligibles for appointment, was appointed as a substitute teacher, but year after year she could not secure a regular appointment as a teacher anywhere in the city. In the early 1890s she visited ward trustees and members of the school board to impress upon them the injustice done her by declining to appoint her because of her color, wherever teachers were needed, but to no avail. In 1895 she retained the black attorney T. McCants Stewart to secure a writ to compel officials to appoint her because she was on the eligible list, but she failed in this attempt also. Finally in 1896, after securing political assistance, she was appointed to a position in a traditionally white school. She was immediately successful with her pupils, "and since then," reported the over-enthusiastic white social worker, Mary Ovington, in 1911, "the question of race or color has not been considered in the appointment of teachers in New York."[13] At least Susie Frazier had broken the ice. Though some white teachers objected, in the late 1890s school officials appointed a few other black teachers to the city's traditionally white schools and stood firmly by them. New York City's school administration, which had just become highly centralized, thus better isolating it from popular prejudice, had made a startling reversal from distrust to support of its black teachers, and the support was to last a long time.

In Brooklyn in the early 1890s, before either Brooklyn or New York had appointed any black teachers to predominantly white schools, a notable struggle began to create a school in which not only the pupils but also the teachers would be racially mixed.

Naturally, integrationists ran into trouble when they proposed to create such a school. Though Brooklyn was advanced in the 1880s and

1890s in recognizing black rights, even in Brooklyn achievements came only with strain. The blacks were often divided among themselves on what their interests were and jealous of those among them who attained status and power. The whites were often condescending to blacks, inclined to think they knew more about what black interests were than blacks did, afraid that blacks would misuse power and would lower property values and school standards. In the 1890s even the practice of appointing one black member to the school board could be called into question by such a moderate organ of opinion as the *Brooklyn Daily Eagle*. When an obscure dispute developed between the black member of the board, Scottron, and the now venerable black principal Dorsey, in which Scottron tried to fire Dorsey, on March 6, 1897, the *Eagle* blandly assured its readers that the school board was incapable of injustice to blacks: "Even if no other colored men should find a place in the board of education," the *Eagle* said, "the interests of their children would not suffer."

The circumstances that gave rise to the proposal to create a thoroughly integrated school were partly accidental. When the black Philip White had been a member of the school board, he had suggested the construction of a new brick building for the traditionally black school number 68 on Troy Avenue in the Weeksville section of Brooklyn, a community which, while it still had black residents, was becoming increasingly white. When whites in the neighborhood objected, saying their children needed more new school space than black children did, blacks held a meeting to defend the erection of a new black school and attended a board meeting to insist on keeping the site already assigned for their school.

"The result," as black lawyer T. McCants Stewart explained afterward, "was just what the colored people hoped for." The whites of the neighborhood became convinced that the only way they could secure a new school for their children was to come to an accommodation with the blacks. In a joint meeting of blacks and whites with a committee of the board, the whites proposed that the new building be made larger and that both white and colored children attend it. "The white representatives," explained Stewart afterward, "said that they had no objections to colored teachers," as some of them had themselves attended this very colored school 68 and been taught by colored teachers. The blacks and the committee accepted this compromise, and the board endorsed it too. Thus in 1890 the unusual experiment of a school, racially mixed in both teachers and pupils, was planned.[14]

It was indeed a daring plan. It is doubtful that any plan like it had ever been carried out in any public school in the nation. Although there had been rare, isolated instances of a lone black teaching in a predomi-

Brooklyn's Colored Public School No. 2 (also known as Public School 68) on Troy Avenue near Dean Street. In the early 1890s controversy arose over the proposal that this school merge into a new interracial school. *Long Island Historical Society.*

nantly white public school in Northern states, including New York, this was a much more threatening attempt to mix a considerable proportion of both black teachers and black children into a predominantly white school.

Naturally, as the building for this mixed school neared completion, racial tension mounted. Black lawyer Stewart, who by this time had succeeded White as a member of the Brooklyn board, put up a determined fight to keep the plan for a thoroughly mixed school, but the board retreated. The board decided to place an existing predominantly white school, called Public School 83, upstairs in the new building, but to allow the predominantly black Public School 68, for which the whole building had been intended, to occupy temporarily the first floor until a smaller building could be constructed for it. This was quite a step backward from the integration plan but at least a predominantly white and a predominantly black school were temporarily to occupy the same building.

In September 1892, the two schools moved in. The traditionally black school, composed of about 150 children, mostly black, with their five black teachers, moved into the first floor. The traditionally white school, of about 500 pupils, including less than fifty blacks, with their all-white teachers, moved into the second floor. The *Brooklyn Eagle* at first reported that the joint occupation of the building was producing "no conflict between th' white and colored children." A few months later, however, a committee of the board reported that white parents were keeping large numbers of their children from the school. But black member Stewart claimed that it was only the parents who were prejudiced. As far as the children were concerned, joint occupancy worked "without the slightest friction. I see children, white and colored, arm in arm together up there. They play leap frog, they shoot marbles together. The white and colored boys alike . . . [are] innocent of the feelings of prejudice."

Stewart was using what he considered to be the success of the joint occupancy of the building as grounds to press for revival of the original plan for a thoroughly mixed-race school, in which the two schools, both pupils and teachers, would be merged into one school. Stewart said later that during the two years in which he agitated for this plan, he was supported by a few blacks who "week after week, attended the meetings of the school board, sustaining me in the heat of the battle by speech and petitions."[15]

Stewart's agitation came to a climax at the school board meeting in March 1893. At the meeting, member Stewart, deliberately following the argument which lawyer Charles Sumner had used in a desegregation case in Boston in 1849, claimed that separate education hurt white children as well as black. Debate sometimes waxed hot. At one point Stewart charged that members of the board "have in times past gone about with professions of friendship for the Negro on their lips and a knife in their hands to stab him," while at another point a white board member charged that an argument for mixed schools was but "an agglomeration of sentimental platitudes." There was confusion about what most blacks wanted. One board member claimed that most of the blacks in the district wanted to keep their separate black school, while Stewart claimed they were pushing him for a mixed school. The view that came to prevail in the meeting was expressed by one white board member: to mix the black and

T. McCants Stewart was a member of the Brooklyn Board of Education. Brooklyn was the only place in the state known to have blacks on its board in the 19th century. *Long Island Historical Society.*

white pupils was "manifestly the right thing." The board finally voted 17 to 11 to return to its original plan to create a thoroughly mixed-race school in the new building, calling it Public School 83.[16] At last the notable experiment of a school substantially mixed both in pupils and teachers came into actuality.

The experiment succeeded. Four years later, in 1897, a committee of the board reported that the school had demonstrated that black teachers could successfully teach white children, and by 1899 the school had grown to over 1700 pupils. It survived a long time as a mixed school, serving especially Italian, Jewish, and black children. Many years later one of the black teachers who had taught in the school, beginning about 1898, described her experience. She was assistant principal at the school, she wrote, serving under a white principal, "a gentleman who was an American and a citizen without reproach." Under his direction, she supervised the teachers of the first three grades, whether black or white. She remained at the school till in 1918 she retired from teaching, after having lived "with never a doubt" as to her choice of a vocation and "with no great problems" to confront her.[17]

By the end of the nineteenth century, despite a national climate increasingly hostile to black rights, school officials in Manhattan and Brooklyn had moved far toward desegregation in their schools by a curious combination of inconsistent means—both by direct integration moves and by retaining separate schools as long as blacks seemed to want them, and as long as they served the purpose of employing black teachers who otherwise would be unemployed.

Desegregation was coming later downstate than upstate. Still, in the 1890s, now that desegregation had significantly begun downstate, it was being carried farther there than upstate. There was regularly one black member on the Brooklyn board, while there were none on school boards upstate. Black teachers were beginning to be appointed regularly to teach in white schools both in Manhattan and Brooklyn, as was true nowhere as yet upstate. There was one school in Brooklyn which was deliberately racially mixed with respect to substantial numbers of both teachers and pupils, and it was doubtful if this was true anywhere else in the nation.

Why, once it came, was the desegregation in the downstate metropolitan area more advanced than upstate? A special factor assisting desegregation in Brooklyn was the unusual degree of black influence on public schools, while a special factor in Manhattan was the change from a decentralized to a centralized school administration. General factors probably were the decline of the abolitionist tradition upstate where it had been strong; the increasing concentration of black leadership in the metropolitan area; the increasing availability to metropolitan blacks of quality higher education; and the flooding in of immigrants from Southern and Eastern Europe who did not share the traditional anti-black hostility of the older American stock, including the Irish.

LONG ISLAND'S BLACK SCHOOL WAR

To ILLUSTRATE THE STRUGGLE against separate schools in New York State in the 1880s and 1890s by concentrating on Manhattan and Brooklyn alone would give a false impression. Most of the twenty places in the state which still had black public schools in this period were more rural than urban. Moreover, the impetus that led in 1900 to a new state law against segregation in schools came not from Manhattan or Brooklyn but from more nearly rural Long Island.

In the 1890s a few blacks in the more rural parts of Long Island moved to break their long tradition of separate schools. These blacks did not, like metropolitan blacks, make a point of trying to keep their black schools open for those who wanted to attend them. In small communities this would not be likely to be practical. These blacks also did not, like metropolitan blacks, show concern about what would happen to the black teachers. They were simply trying to secure what they considered to be a better education for their children.

Blacks moved against segregation in the villages of Amityville, Hempstead, Flushing, Roslyn, and Jamaica. In Jamaica, blacks developed a notable anti-segregation campaign.

Among historians, the Jamaica campaign has characteristically been mentioned, if at all, largely in terms of one court case.[1] In fact, the Jamaica campaign deserves to be known for its numerous court cases, for its school boycott, and for the open participation in the campaign of many poor blacks at the risk of their jobs. Anyone who easily assumes that, in the nineteenth century, obscure, small-town blacks supinely accepted the denial of what they understood to be their rights should consider the story of the Jamaica black "school war."

The Jamaica war came to a climax in 1900 in the "Roosevelt" state law to limit school segregation. Historians have claimed that the law was passed on the "initiative" of Governor Theodore Roosevelt, which this author believes to be misleading. They have described the law, even recently, as abolishing all the black public schools in the state,[2] which is certainly wrong. Nevertheless, especially because the law was a landmark in the history of black-white relations in the state, the story of the Jamaica campaign and the state law to which it led deserve to be better understood.

Jamaica in the early 1890s was still a semi-rural village, but it was tied to the metropolitan area by railroad and trolley lines, and it was rapidly being suburbanized. New York City was already eyeing it and the surrounding farm land for annexation. The proportion of blacks in Jamaica was 6 percent, far higher than in either the state as a whole or New York City.

Since slavery days, considerable numbers of blacks had lived in Jamaica and in the surrounding Long Island towns as farm laborers and domestics. In 1854, after a local newspaper had published the complaint that Jamaica blacks were "untaught, except in wickedness, untutored, except in crime," Jamaica whites had led in establishing a separate one-room public school for blacks. Whites had apparently done so more out of a desire to protect themselves from blacks than out of confidence in black mental capacity. A major figure in establishing the school was the attorney Pierpont Potter, who served on the Jamaica school board almost continuously from its beginning in 1853 till his death in 1886. As a defender of slavery in the South, he tried to prove that blacks and whites were not equal in ability by pointing out that Africa was "the same unredeemed savage wilderness that she was 4000 years ago, except what the white man has done."[3]

In the late 1880s the Jamaica black school was still only a one-room school. Its teacher was Eveline Williams, a young black woman who had recently graduated from Albany State Normal School. The Jamaica correspondent of a New York City black paper believed that the seventy-five pupils she taught were too many even for the "energetic" teacher that she was and campaigned for the school to be divided into two rooms with two teachers.[4] But the board of education, developing a reputation for stubbornness in regard to blacks, refused. Miss Williams was still the only teacher in the school in 1895 when a group of black parents decided to act against school segregation.

In doing so, the Jamaica parents had before them the example of blacks who had just succeeded in closing the black school in another Long

Island village, Amityville. Like Jamaica, Amityville had long had a one room black public school which local school officials required all black children to attend. When the Amityville school board proposed that a new school be built for white children, some blacks were persuaded to vote for it, they claimed afterward, on the promise that blacks would be allowed to attend the new school too. However, in early 1895 when the new school opened and Charles D. Brewster, a black laborer, sent his son to this school, he was refused admittance because of his color. Brewster and other blacks then became angry and refused to send their children any longer to the black school. They charged that the black school did not offer equal education as state law required. In the summer of 1895, Brewster startled a district school meeting by proposing that the black school be abolished. The meeting, already well aware of the high cost of the separate school, endorsed his proposal. However, when white voters not present at the meeting heard about it, they petitioned for the calling of another meeting, and when that meeting was held, it asked that the black school be kept open after all. But the school board, amid confusion and controversy, closed the black school and kept it closed.[5]

When the black victory in Amityville was becoming clear, several black parents in Jamaica decided to try sending their children to a white public school. Jamaica school officials refused to admit the children, directing them to the black school instead, and the children went home crying. As one of the parents, Samuel Cisco, said bitterly afterward, "I and my father and mother have paid taxes in Jamaica for eighty years." Yet my children are "denied a place in the school near my home, while Irishmen, Italians, and Dutchmen who have been here only three months, can go there, although covered with dirt."[6] Some of the black parents then refused to send their children to the black school and petitioned a court for a writ to compel the board of education to admit their children to the white schools.

For blacks to appeal to the courts in an effort to desegregate schools was not new in New York State. As we have seen, they had done so as early as 1863 in Troy and soon after also in Buffalo, Albany, and Brooklyn. But for small-town blacks to appeal to the courts was new.

The Jamaica black parents—including a pastor, gardener, janitor, notary, and porter—were acting on the advice of Alfred C. Cowan, a black Brooklyn lawyer. Cowan had studied law at New York University and was now president of the state Colored Republican Association. Through him, the black parents argued in court that they wished to send their children to the white schools because only thus could they secure the equal education the state law required. The black school was inferior, they said. Its one teacher was expected to teach the work of seven grades, and its location was too remote for some of the black children to reach. However, Jamaica school officials replied in court that the black school provided equal facilities; and soon they warned black parents that if they did not send their children to school as the state compulsory education law required, they would be arrested.[7]

Thus was established the pattern for Jamaica's "school war," as the struggle over the black school was popularly called. Over a period of five years, black parents boycotted the black school and made legal moves to try to force school officials to open the white schools to blacks; while white school officials resisted the opening of the white schools to blacks and moved to arrest black parents for not sending their children to school.

To avoid the penalties of the compulsory education law, some of the black parents had their children taught at home. Other parents sent their children to school in Brooklyn or elsewhere where they could enter school with whites. Those who sent their children to other schools claimed that they could see a marked improvement in their children's progress, further proving the inferiority of Jamaica's black school.

Nevertheless, Jamaica school officials brought about the arrest of black parents for deliberately refusing to send their children to school, as officials are not known to have done in school desegregation struggles anywhere else in nineteenth-century New York State. Officials caused the arrest of at least seven different Jamaica blacks whose names are known. One of those arrested—Annie Robinson, a grandmother whose husband was a waiter—was arrested twice. Three others were arrested three times each. These were Stephen White, an illiterate stableman, and Mr. and Mrs. Samuel B. Cisco, who operated a prosperous scavenger business and were the parents of six children. Several of these blacks were declared guilty and fined. Samuel Cisco refused to pay one of his fines, hoping, like Thoreau, to be sent to jail to witness more effectively against unjust law, but someone else paid it for him.[8]

The precise effect of the boycott on attendance at the black school is difficult to judge. It is impossible to separate completely those blacks who deliberately boycotted the black school as a protest from those who failed to send their children for other reasons. There had long been a pattern throughout the state for blacks to attend school less regularly than whites. Even before the boycott is known to have begun, the Jamaica superintendent complained that the principal trouble with attendance in his schools was from the black pupils.[9]

However, effect from the boycott is evident. In the spring of 1896, a meeting of over one hundred blacks all agreed not to send their children to the black school. In the fall of 1896, the number of pupils still attending the school was reported at various times to be ten, ten to twelve, or only four; and the *Brooklyn Daily Eagle* of November 9 said that "between eighty and ninety colored children of school age are now roaming the streets." In 1899 school officials reported that the "bitter feeling" of blacks in Jamaica still continued, attendance at the school was "very small," and "over sixty children of Negro birth were not in school at all"; they decided that "any attempt to enforce the compulsory education law was futile." In early 1900, when at least Mrs. Cisco, a robust Virginia-born woman, was still deliberately refusing to send her children to the black school as a protest against segregation, thirty-seven children were attending, which was said to be about half of the number of black children enrolled in the district.[10] The boycott evidently had some impact during the whole five years of the Jamaica school war.

At the same time that blacks were boycotting the black school, they also brought altogether twenty different court actions against school officials. Samuel Cisco, who emerged as a leader in these blacks actions, explained that the superintendent of schools has carried "the war . . . into Africa and we now propose to carry it into Caucasia." Mrs. Cisco even committed the "outrage" of having the superintendent of schools arrested.[11]

Nineteen different Jamaica blacks whose names are known participated in bringing these legal actions. A few additional blacks wrote open letters in support of the black school cause, or were officers of meetings held to further the cause, or spoke at such meetings, or were arrested for refusing to send their children to the black school, making a total of twenty-five different local blacks whose names are known as leaders in the Jamaica school fight. Of these twenty-five whose occupations can be identified, two were professionals, both pastors; two were in business, Mr. and Mrs. Cisco; one was a skilled worker, a notary; and twelve were unskilled workers such as laborers, coachmen, servants, and janitors. It was impressive that by far most of those who were conspicuous for participation in such drastic activity as boycotting schools and bringing legal actions were unskilled workers who were likely to be poor and vulnerable to economic reprisal.

Information is available to compare the methods blacks employed in Jamaica with the methods they employed against school segregation in local actions in eight other New York communities in the 1880s and 1890s—Buffalo, Stapleton, New York, Brooklyn, Flushing, Hempstead, Roslyn, and Amityville. While all the major methods Jamaica blacks employed were also employed in at least one other place, blacks in Jamaica employed more different methods than blacks are known to have employed in any other place. What was notable about the Jamaica methods was not their uniqueness but their variety; and not so much the methods themselves as the blacks' open, noisy use of them, regardless of threats of arrest and loss of jobs. The Jamaica campaign was also notable for the persistence of the boycott, and because it enlisted more black parents than were known to have enlisted in such a boycott in any other place in the state during this period. It was notable, too, not so much because of the method of taking cases to court, as that the cases were largely brought by working class blacks, and that there were so many cases. In fact, by far most of the court cases brought by blacks to desegregate schools in nineteenth century New York State were brought by Jamaica blacks.

A court decision which went in favor of the blacks was made by a Republican county judge of old Dutch stock, Garret J. Garretson. As president of the Newtown Board of Education twelve years before, Garretson had led in the abolition of the black school there, stressing it would be a measure of economy. Now he dismissed an indictment of a parent for not sending his child to the Jamaica black school; Garretson accepted the argument of counsel that because the general state education law made public schools free to all children without regard to color, black children were entitled to attend any of them in their proper distiict. However, since contrary decisions in support of separate education still stood in the state's highest court, Garretson's ruling did not have the effect of opening the white schools to blacks.[12]

A Jamaica Democratic paper predicted that because the Republican Garretson had decided in favor of the blacks, many Jamaica voters would vote against him in his campaign to become a state Supreme Court justice. But in fact, Jamaica gave Garretson the highest vote it gave to any of the eight candidates, as Queen County as a whole did also, and Garretson won.

This vote suggests that there was some sympathy among Queens County whites for the blacks in their school fight, and another similar vote suggests so too: The Canadian-born George Wallace, who had a law office in Jamaica, served conspicuously as the Ciscos' lawyer in 1896 and 1897. In a public statement he declared he personally was in sympathy with the Ciscos in their school fight and opposed "any discrimination whatever on account of color in public institutions" because it robs blacks of ambition. Yet afterward in 1898 when he ran as a Republican candidate for Assemblyman from Queens, Wallace was elected.

However, still another vote suggests that many Jamaica voters opposed the blacks in their school fight. When Jamaica's truant officer, who had arrested blacks for not sending their children to school, was running for another local office, a meeting of the school boycotters resolved to ask their supporters to punish him by voting aginst him. Nevertheless, he was elected. A Jamaica Democratic newspaper interpreted his victory to mean that "the people are in favor of the colored children attending their own school."[13]

Newspaper comment on the school war sometimes but not always followed partisan lines. Among Republican papers, the *New York Tribune* and the *Rockville Center South Side Observer* presented the views of Jamaica blacks sympathetically; and the *Brooklyn Times* declared flatly that Jamaica should abolish her colored school "as an anachronism." Among Democratic papers, the *New York Times* declared that Jamaica's whites supported their school board and insisted that, "Nobody, apparently, believes that the colored school is inferior to the white school except the Negroes themselves." But the *Brooklyn Daily Eagle*, also Democratic, defended the opening of the white schools in Brooklyn to blacks as working well and gave friendly coverage to the activities of the Jamaica black protesters.[14]

The one Republican newspaper published in Jamaica, the *Standard*, regretted that the board of education was prosecuting so many blacks for not sending their children to school, recommending instead that the board carry one case as a test case through the courts to settle the matter "once and for all." Of the two Democratic papers published in Jamaica, one, the *Long Island Farmer*, at first was sympathetic to the blacks, saying the black school was not in reality equal to the local white schools; but later this paper became more hostile to the black boycotters, saying whites would respect them more if they obeyed the law by returning their children to the black school. The other Democratic paper published in Jamaica, the *Long Island Democrat*, consistently opposed the black cause. It warned black parents who were engaged in the school fight that they might lose their jobs.[15]

Despite the sharp divisions of opinion reflected in the newspapers, the black protest movement in Jamaica won enough support to help produce some incidental gains for blacks. In one legal action, George Wallace, as counsel for Mr. Cisco, had objected to a panel of jurors on the ground that it had no Negroes; later in the course of the school war, for the first time ever in Jamaica, a black was drawn for jury duty. Early in 1896, the board of education, in its defense of its actions in court, was maneuvered into promising that if black children passed the proper exams they would be admitted into the high school; by 1898 a black was attending the high school for the first time. Furthermore, the school authorities, responding to criticism of their administration of the black school, finally increased the number of its teachers; though the number of pupils attending at the time scarcely seemed to justify such an increase, by 1896 the number of teachers had grown to two, and by 1899 to three.

It is possible that awareness of the Jamaica school war helped to bring about the closing of small black schools elsewhere in the state. The one-room school at Stapleton, Staten Island, closed about 1897 after blacks had criticized it as an inferior school, and after the building burned —it was suspected that someone intentionally set it on fire. The one-room black school in Haverstraw, on the Hudson River, closed about the same time, one reason given by a local white commentator soon afterward being belief that it did not give the black children equal advantages.[16]

It is also possible that Jamaica's school controversy helped to encourage blacks elsewhere on Long Island to try to open white schools to blacks. In Roslyn, a black pastor whose daughter had completed all the courses of study offered by the local black elementary school, tried in 1897 to enter her in the Roslyn high school, but the school board would only allow her to be instructed there by herself, after regular school hours. In Hempstead it is possible that the Jamaica school war had some effect in 1898 in inducing the board of education to open its upper white grades to black pupils; a black pastor attended an annual school meeting and spoke in support of such a move. The Hempstead board even considered that if this particular desegregation step was successful, it might abolish its black school altogether.[17] But there is no available evidence that a black protest movement developed to push the Hempstead board further, and in fact the board moved so slowly that in early 1900 it had still not abolished its black school. In all four of these small communities, if white school officials and black parents read area newspapers, they scarcely could escape being aware of the Jamaica school war. Besides, blacks who led the Jamaica war also led Jamaica's black churches, black political clubs, and black social organizations, thus having numerous paths of communication to blacks in neighboring towns. But there is no evidence available that Jamaica blacks spread their school war into any of these four communities.

Nor is there evidence that Jamaica blacks spread their school war into nearby Flushing village. Flushing was larger than the villages of Jamaica, Hempstead, or Roslyn. Moreover, Flushing had a larger proportion of blacks than Jamaica and had more recognized black leaders as well. This provides all the more occasion to ask, why didn't Flushing blacks, in sympathy with Jamaica blacks, also develop a protest movement against their separate black school?

A basic reason may well have been that Flushing had a longer tradition of support for black education than Jamaica had. One factor in developing such a tradition was that Flushing had an influential Quaker element in its early population. Beginning in 1814 the Quaker-led Flushing Female Association ran a racially-mixed charity school. After 1855, when this school had evolved into a separate black public school, the Association continued to provide a building for it; and even in the early 1890s the Association was paying for a free evening school for blacks. Other factors in Flushing's tradition of encouragement to black education were that Flushing had an unusually high proportion of professionals in its population, as Jamaica did not; that Flushing's public schools, of a high standard, had prepared pupils for admission to top colleges like Columbia, Cornell, and Yale, as Jamaica's never had; and that as early as 1881, the Flushing school board, under Republican leadership, had already permitted blacks to enter its high school, while the Jamaica board, even though it had established a high school in 1892, had not yet done so in 1895 when the school war began.

Probably another reason why Flushing did not develop a protest movement against the black school was that the Flushing black school, unlike the one in Jamaica, had in the 1880s and early 1890s a dynamic black principal, Mrs. John W. A. Shaw. She and her husband had previously taught blacks in the South for the American Missionary Association. Mr. Shaw had been the editor of a black newspaper in New York City; at other times he became the chairman of the State Colored Democratic Association and a Queens deputy tax commissioner. Mrs. Shaw was active in the community, as in helping to establish the Flushing Free Library. At her school she had the distinction at times of having white as well as black teachers under her. She held graduation exercises which were attended by as many as five hundred people. At one such gala event the superintendent of schools paid high tribute to Mrs. Shaw's management of the school, the scholars exhibited their competence in recitations and singing, and a reporter was so overcome by the success of the occasion that he concluded that all those present "must have felt satisfied that the so-called race problem is solved." The quality of Mrs. Shaw's school was further suggested by the fact that the first three blacks to enter the Flushing High School were all from her school, and all themselves became teachers. Meanwhile in Jamaica no black child was ever known even to have graduated from the black school, much less to have become a teacher. As lawyer George Wallace wrote, it was hard to believe that in Jamaica black children were not graduating from the black school because they were all too dull, while in Flushing black children were graduating "with the highest honors."[18]

Mrs. Mary Shaw, principal of the black public school of Flushing, Long Island, from about 1879 to 1892. *Courtesy of The Queens Borough Public Library.*

Probably neither Jamaica, Roslyn, Hempstead, nor Amityville had the black leaders of the stature of Mr. and Mrs. Shaw. And certainly not of the national stature of the eloquent Reverend William B. Derrick, who in 1896, while living in Flushing, became an African Methodist Episcopal bishop. As we have seen, before Derrick came to Flushing, he had led in trying to desegregate the New York City schools without the black teachers losing their jobs in the process. While living in Flushing, Derrick owned his own romantically-gabled house (his detractors considered him too nimble in handling money), edited a black church paper, and became a member of the Republican State Committee. About 1891 the prestigious Derrick tried to enter his son in a Flushing white public school, but the board of education, though controlled by Republicans, refused.[19] Derrick, however, did not lead a movement in protest, either then or later after the Jamaica school war broke out. A weighty figure with experience elsewhere in battling for school desegregation, Derrick made a stab for desegregation in Flushing, but did not lead Flushing blacks into a battle for it, while nearby Jamaica, without any known black leaders of statewide reputation, developed a school war. This suggests that the difference between the two localities, both in the quality of schools and in the whole social context, was more important than black leadership in determining where a black desegregation movement would arise.

While Jamaica's black protest movement did not kindle similar movements in other nearby small communities having black schools, it did lead to a state law to limit school segregation. That is a story in itself.

ELIZABETH CISCO WINS

WHEN CONSOLIDATION OF Queens, Kings, and Richmond Counties into the city of New York was being planned, the question arose as to whether segregated black schools could legally be continued in the new Greater New York. In early 1897 lawyer George Wallace, representing Elizabeth Cisco of Jamaica, said that he expected that under the Greater New York charter, black children would have to be admitted to all public schools. But by the time the state legislature had adopted the charter, in May 1897, the forces which desired to preserve segregation had done their work well. They had succeeded in putting into the charter a provision that the newly enlarged city could operate separate schools for blacks.[1]

The member of the commission especially responsible for drafting the charter's provisions on schools was Seth Low, the President of Columbia University. A humanitarian reformer, Low nevertheless was somewhat ambivalent about racial segregation. As we have seen, as mayor of Brooklyn in 1882, Low had helped to initiate the opening of the white public schools of Brooklyn to blacks in such a way as to preserve the black schools for those who wished to attend them. Later in 1914, when Low was chairman of the trustees of Tuskegee Institute, he was to write that he was "a firm believer not only in the necessity for, but also in the advantage of, separate schools for Negroes, because such schools afford an opportunity for educated colored men and women to have careers as teachers, and because they tend, or should tend, to develop the self-respect of the race." In revising the city charter, Low was probably influenced not only by such views of his own, but also he and other members of the commission were probably influenced by the wishes of local officials in Jamaica and Flushing. The commission had promised to try to protect the interests of the different localities which were to become part of the greater city. As a Flushing paper noted with pleasure, Low in his charter work consulted "those familiar with school affairs in all parts of the Greater New York."[2]

Once consolidation was effected in January 1898, Jamaica and Flushing became part of New York City. The local school boards of Jamaica and Flushing disappeared, being replaced by a new school board for the whole of the new Borough of Queens. To represent Jamaica interests, one of the members of the former segregation-hugging Jamaica board was placed on the new Queens board. The new board, with the authority of the charter behind it, voted unanimously to continue the Jamaica and Flushing black schools as separate black schools. The new board also voted unanimously to continue the Jamaica's school board's resistance in the courts to Mrs. Cisco's effort to enter her children in Jamaica white schools. The new Queens Borough Superintendent of Schools notified the Jamaica blacks that they must send their children to the black school. The board was even reported to be planning to enlarge the Jamaica black school building to permit it to house a black high school, so that even on that level blacks would not attend school with whites.[3]

In 1899 and early 1900 the state's higher courts decided against Mrs. Cisco. They refused to compel school officials to admit her children to the Jamaica white schools. By this time Mrs. Cisco's case had become well known. A public meeting of blacks in Manhattan raised over $150 to help pay Mrs. Cisco's legal expenses. A Jamaica paper called the Cisco case "of much interest to the people of this state." The New York Tribune called it "somewhat famous." A Flushing paper said later that it "caused a great deal of animosity throughout Long Island."[4]

One judge, in giving his decision against Mrs. Cisco, hinted that he would like to admit her children into the white schools, but he felt bound by judicial precedent to decide against her. However, he suggested that she and her supporters could find a remedy by appealing to the legislature. Once Mrs. Cisco had lost her appeals all the way to the highest state court, this possible remedy attracted Mrs. Cisco, her lawyer George Wallace, and their allies.

In early 1900, it seemed to them that they might succeed in appealing to the legislature because both of its houses were under the control of Republicans, the supposed friends of the blacks; the governor, Theodore Roosevelt, was Republican as well. In 1873, when similarly Republicans had controlled the state, the state Senate's head janitor, the black William H. Johnson, and his friends had pushed through the legislature a civil rights bill which they believed would open all the state's public schools

Mrs. Elizabeth Cisco, of Jamaica, Long Island, was a businesswoman, school boycotter, initiator of court suits, and promoter of the 1900 state anti-segregation law. *New York State Historical Association, from William H. Johnson,* Autobiography, *1900.*

to blacks. As we have seen, under the impact of this law, some white schools had been opened to blacks, and some black schools had been abolished, but eventually court interpretations had emasculated the law as an instrument for these purposes. Now anti-segregationists wished to try again.

According to lawyer Wallace, he prepared a draft of a bill to out-law separate black public schools in Greater New York City. When Wallace showed it to Governor Roosevelt, however, Roosevelt insisted it should apply to the whole state. With the support of Republican leaders, the bill was so amended. The three blacks most prominently promoting the bill were the rugged Mrs. Elizabeth Cisco, who, since her husband's death in 1897, still carried on the family scavenger business in Jamaica; M. R. Poole, a long time New York City saloon keeper; and the now veteran Albany black political leader, William H. Johnson, who had returned to his usual occupation of barbering. According to Johnson, Poole was entitled to as much credit as anyone for drafting the new bill. Poole had been a leader in Manhattan black Republican clubs and had been rewarded by becoming one of the blacks employed in the state capitol building—Poole was now, as Johnson had been earlier, head janitor of the Senate. In Albany, according to Johnson, Poole "fathered the bill and looked after it during its conduct through the legislature." But Poole, in Johnson's judgment, was unwise. He was defiantly partisan. He frequently and openly said that "he would rather see the bill defeated than to ask any Democrat to vote for it."[5]

There was little publicity about the proposed law. Several Flushing whites, who afterward wanted the law repealed, complained that in Flushing "there was no intimation that such a law was under discussion" until after it was signed. Newspapers in other Long Island towns, however, mentioned the bill while it was being considered in Albany—a Democratic paper in Jamaica did so at least three times, each time prosaically, without expressing an opinion about it.[6]

According to Johnson, for a time the passage of the bill was in doubt. Many New York black leaders deserted the cause when it needed help, he said, but afterward were anxious to claim credit. However, all the blacks employed at the capitol worked for the bill: "Every colored man possessing any influence whatsoever, from head-janitor down to and including the unassuming porter, was unsparing in aggressive support of the measure." Evidently blacks scarcely held any higher state positions in Albany in 1900 than they had held when head-janitor Johnson promoted the civil rights bill of 1873.

Whites also were active in supporting the bill. Republican Senator Nathaniel Elsberg, of Manhattan, introduced it and pushed it eloquently as a means of attaining equal rights for all. Just before both the Senate and House were to vote on the bill, Governor Theodore Roosevelt sent them a special message saying that the "public interest" required the passage of the bill.[7]

Roosevelt's recent experience fighting with black troops in the Spanish American War in Cuba—partially favorable—may have helped to develop his belief in equal opportunity for blacks. At about the time Roosevelt endorsed the bill, he explained privately that he believed America's political salvation depended on treating each man on his merits as a man. This did not mean, he said, that blacks had equal abilities with whites; he believed they did not. But it did mean for him that he strove to secure equal rights for blacks and whites, including equal school rights. In fact, he said, he sent his own children to school with blacks.[8]

With the support of the governor, the bill sailed through the legislature. In both houses the Queens County representatives voted for it, even though most of them were Democrats. In the Senate, the Democratic majority leader, Thomas Francis Grady, of Manhattan, said the bill would raise an issue that should be left alone and charged that the motive behind the bill was an attempt by Republicans to woo back the New York City black vote which they had been losing. But only five senators voted against the bill; all Democrats and all from Manhattan. In the lower house, no one voted against it.

As passed, the law provided that "no person shall be refused admission into or be excluded from any public school in the state of New York on account of race or color." On its surface, this wording seemed to make it impossible for school officials to keep blacks out of white schools or to operate black schools. But the wording of the new law, like that of the parallel 1873 state civil rights law, was tricky. The new law provided for the repeal of the section of the education law which permitted black schools in cities and incorporated villages. But perhaps inadvertently the law did *not* provide for the repeal of another section of the education law which permitted black schools in "union school districts, or any school district organized under a special act," provided the inhabitants at a meeting decided to have such schools.[9] Thus the law continued to allow certain rural school districts to operate black schools.

If continuing to allow rural school districts to operate black schools was a concession which supporters of the measure deliberately made to reduce opposition to it, available comment on the law at the time and after has failed to mention it. From the first, such comment has even failed to mention that the law still permitted rural districts to operate black schools. Probably supporters of the law didn't even know that it did so.

Inaccurate descriptions of the law seemed to be the rule. When the bill was introduced, for example, the Jamaica *Long Island Farmer* of March 13, 1900, described it incorrectly as a bill amending the general school law by "eliminating the provision authorizing local school authorities to establish separate schools for colored children." After the Assembly had passed the law, the *Brooklyn Daily Eagle* of April 2 incorrectly claimed that the law would take "away from boards of education all over the state the right to establish . . . separate schools for Negro children." Similarly, ever since then, descriptions of the law have characteristically neglected to mention that it failed to eliminate a provision of law which permitted black schools in rural regions.

When the news reached Jamaica that Governor Roosevelt had signed the law, according to the *Brooklyn Eagle* of April 20, 1900, blacks heard it "with many expressions of satisfaction," while some whites grumbled. In Albany, supporters of the new law, led by the black barber Johnson, arranged a celebration meeting. The meeting adopted resolutions thanking Senator Elsberg and Governor Roosevelt for their help in enacting the law. The New York Secretary of State spoke, giving praise to barber Johnson, but adding that the people had forgotten "that little woman," Elizabeth Cisco of Jamaica, "to whom the most credit is due." Johnson then asked Mrs. Cisco to stand, and as the audience became aware of her generous two-hundred-pound proportions, they laughed and gave her an ovation. To honor her, the meeting adopted a resolution, the wording of which suggested pathetic faith in what the law would accomplish: "to no one person, living or dead, is the state of New York under greater obligations for the complete obliteration of racial discrimination."[10] The Ciscos, who together had been arrested six times in five years for not sending their children to school, at least achieved a moment of triumph—the husband only after his death.

With the passage of the law, Queens school officials opened all their schools to children of all races, thus in effect abolishing the black separate schools of both Jamaica and Flushing. In addition, in Hempstead, which was not organized in a union free school district, the school board decided with "regret" that the new law left them "no alternative" but to abolish their separate black school. Thus were ended three legally separate black schools which Secretary Palmer of the New York City Board of Education believed in 1905 to have been "the last colored schools maintained in the state." But Palmer was wrong. Like Palmer, the eminent social worker Mary White Ovington wrote in 1911 that the 1900 law had "closed the question of compulsory segregation in the state. . . . Public education was thus democratized for the New York Negroes, their persistent efforts bringing at the end complete success." She, too, was wrong, but other writers have perpetuated her and Palmer's errors.[11]

Since the 1860s, when the number of known places in the state which had legally separate black public schools had risen to thirty-five, there had been a steady tendency for the number to drop. In the 1870s it had dropped to thirty-one, by the 1880s to twenty, by the 1890s to fifteen (see Table 5 in Appendix). By the end of 1899, only six known places still had legally segregated black public schools.

After the passage of the 1900 law led to the disappearance of the three separate black public schools in Jamaica, Flushing, and Hempstead, at least three other separate black public schools still continued to exist. They were in Roslyn on Long Island and in Hillburn and Goshen in the mid-Huston region, all in rural areas where union free school districts were possible. In these three places school authorities continued to require blacks to attend black public schools.

In addition, there also continued to exist *de facto* black schools. In Manhattan and Brooklyn there were public schools which had once been legally separate black schools, but which were still largely black taught and black attended. In Rossville, on Staten Island, the borough school board opened in 1899, and continued to run for several years, a public school intended primarily for blacks: it was located in a black church, and the board sought black teachers for it.[12] Still other kinds of black schools continued to exist or were soon to be created, some run by blacks, some by whites, such as black orphan asylum schools, black parochial schools, black schools for nurses, black industrial schools, black private schools, and black kindergartens. Though for the moment the number of separate schools was declining, they had by no means disappeared. School segregation in New York State was proving to have, like the proverbial cat, many lives.

New York State was moving gradually against school segregation —compared to her New England neighbors she was moving slowly; compared to New Jersey and Pennsylvania she was moving rapidly. During the latter half of the nineteenth century and the first decade the twentieth century, a long-term factor encouraging New York State to move against segregation, offsetting the national climate of hostility toward equal rights for blacks, was that the proportion of blacks in the state remained steadily low. New York State whites did not yet feel, as they were later to feel, inundated by waves of incoming blacks. Another factor encouraging the state to move toward desegregating schools at about the turn of the century probably was the flood of Eastern and Southern European immigrants coming into the state. Some observers believed that such immigrants were weakening the white community's traditional belief, rooted more in American than European experience, that blacks should be kept apart. For instance, according to a former black member of the Brooklyn school board, Samuel R. Scottron, writing in the *New York Age*, July 13, 1905, European immigrants in the state "were indifferent, all except the Irish, to American color prejudice, and . . . did not care a fig whether a

New York Colored Orphan Asylum, Riverdale, the Bronx, which operated its own school. This building was occupied from 1907 to 1946. *New York State Historical Association, from Riverdale Children's Association,* 120th Anniversary, *1956.*

black or white child sat beside their children in the school room."
     Another immediate factor encouraging desegregation was action by blacks. Scottron stressed that Brooklyn was making progress toward desegregation because Brooklyn black leaders—who were often substantial professionals or businessmen like Scottron himself—moved "slowly, noiselessly," in behind-the-scenes negotiations, usually avoiding doing "the many silly things that are ofttimes done in such cases."[13] But in small-town Jamaica, where blacks found their opponents much more stubborn than in Brooklyn, a number of blacks, mostly of the working class, moved noisily to do what Scottron undoubtedly considered to be "many silly things." When, especially through the persistence of Mrs. Cisco, these methods finally aroused considerable black and white support elsewhere, they led the state legislature to take a significant step to curb, but not yet abolish, legal school segregation.

BLACK SCHOOLS REVIVE

IN THE TWENTIETH CENTURY, beginning especially during World War I, Southern blacks poured into New York State. Ironically, their doing so threatened the continued existence of the racial tolerance which helped to draw them there.

It was questionable if the trend toward desegregation of schools could survive a prolonged Southern-black invasion. Many New York State whites felt threatened by the often uncouth, little educated blacks from the South and tried to separate themselves from them. A result was that in the largest cities, segregated housing spread, and with it, *de facto* segregated schools appeared.

In the first two or three decades of the new century, black rights in America were at their lowest ebb since the Civil War, encouraging the forces making for more segregation. But blacks, in association with white reformist allies, were becoming better organized to insist on their rights. They created the National Association for the Advancement of the Colored People in 1909 and the National Urban League in 1911, both with headquarters in New York City. Moreover, the cataclysms of two world wars and the growth of revolutionary ideologies like communism and fascism led many Americans to rethink the relation of race to democracy. Gradually, as black population increased, blacks developed more political clout—for the first time in New York State blacks were elected to the state legislature (1917) and to Congress (1944). Disillusioned with Republican promises, blacks from the New Deal period usually allied themselves with Democrats, helping to solidify the shift in the center of the desegregation movement downstate, away from the upstate region where abolitionists and Republicans had been strong. From the 1930s the state government became increasingly committed to preventing racial discrimination. Still, educational segregation, while curtailed in its more obvious forms, was fed by hostility toward the hordes of incoming Southern blacks. There were still not only whites but also large numbers of blacks who saw advantages to separate institutions for blacks, as evidenced by the fervent mass support for Marcus Garvey's black nationalist movement.

The waves of incoming blacks raised the proportion of blacks in the population of the state from 1 percent in 1900 to 6 percent by 1950, and in New York City from 2 percent to 10. As early as 1913 there were two public schools in Harlem whose pupils were predominantly black; by the 1930s there were fourteen.

In the 1910s and 1920s many urban blacks still found unsegregated schools and sympathetic teachers. Particularly in the 1920s, when some of Harlem's housing for blacks was still not overcrowded and Harlem's literary renaissance was promising major black contributions to American culture, many Harlem teachers, black and white, still had faith in their black pupils' capacity to learn. The gifted Adam Clayton Powell, Jr., the light-colored son of one of Harlem's prestigious black pastors, recalled that in these years he and other black boys used to fight Irish boys on their way to school, but in class it sometimes paid to be black. "What you did seemed to shine a little brighter," he said.[1]

But already about this time some of the city's teachers were finding black pupils difficult, in a pattern that was to become more pronounced. Many of the black children, having begun their schooling in inadequate rural schools in the South, were already disadvantaged when they arrived in New York. Since black families were usually poor, housing was often crowded, and mothers were often forced to work. The children, pushed into the street, early became familiar with violence, gambling, prostitution, and narcotics. They were often poorly prepared with their homework or were truant from school. They learned to have little hope that school would lead to satisfying jobs. They achieved less in school than whites did; they dropped out earlier. It disturbed the black editor W. E. B. DuBois that in proportion to population far fewer blacks graduated from high school in New York City where, legally, schools were racially mixed than in Washington and Baltimore where, legally, schools were separate.[2]

The problems of black pupils encouraged talk among both blacks and whites that racially-mixed schools could not do justice to either whites or blacks. But in 1911 one of the upper-class white founders of the NAACP, Mary White Overton, who chose to live for a time in the city's worst black slum in the West Sixties on Columbus Hill, insisted that on the whole the public schools of the city were impartial to blacks—while some teachers showed prejudice against blacks, she said, others gave them special kindness.[3] On September 18, 1913, the black *New York Age* advised black parents that they had derived so much advantage from racially-mixed schools that to ward off more segregation they should lecture their children to avoid clashes with white children. In March 1923, the NAACP's *Crisis,* while admitting that black children in the racially-mixed schools of the North sometimes did not get proper attention and could be systematically discouraged, emphatically denied that the remedy was a return to segregation. In fact, it cited New York City as "pointing the way" in which "constructive effort" can "overcome the present evils" which black children face in "mixed schools." Under black leadership, a promising experiment to improve vocational guidance for black pupils was being tried.

Early in the great depression in 1932, when there were already more black children in New York City than in any other city in the world, a spokesman for the Children's Aid Society felt able to say that New York City's black neighborhoods still had school buildings and teaching staff of the same quality as the rest of the city. But he feared that if these black neighborhoods continued to grow, "we must not be too sure that our civic virtue is so invulnerable as to guarantee the continuance of this fair treatment." As the depression lengthened, a mayor's committee reported that the city was not building as many new public schools in Harlem as in the rest of the city, its schools were more congested, and teachers assigned to Harlem felt they were being punished.[4] Blacks and their allies were charging that, regardless of ability, black pupils were being shunted to industrial rather than academic education, and a state commission agreed that such charges were true for several places in the state, and especially New York City.[5] By the 1940s there were reported to be at least fifteen predominantly black public schools in Manhattan, as well as eight in the South Bronx, and ten in Brooklyn. While many blacks accepted virtually all-black schools as normal in black neighborhoods, other blacks did not. All-black schools are a "humiliation" for blacks, cried the black *Amsterdam News* of February 10, 1945.

In the increasingly segregated schools, black children reacted variously. In Brooklyn's Bedford-Stuyvesant ghetto, Floyd Patterson, a Southern-born black boy who was to become a world boxing champion, was never at ease. According to his recollection afterward, he was ashamed that his clothes didn't fit. He didn't know how to make friends. He was afraid to talk because he expected everyone to laugh at him. He could scarcely read or write and felt too inadequate to try. His parents kept telling him to go to school to keep out of trouble, never telling him to go to school to learn to cope with the world. His teachers, he explained later, had too many pupils to be able to help those who didn't learn quickly. Anyway, Patterson couldn't conceive of teachers wanting to help him. He became a habitual truant.[6]

At about the same time, James Baldwin, another shy black boy, one who had strangely protruding eyes, had problems of another kind. During the years when "Pop Eye" Baldwin was attending school, his step-father, a man with a twisted psyche, sadistically denied him the parental love he craved. Moreover, because the family was desperately poor, his mother was forced to work as a domestic by day and was too tired at night to care adequately for her many children. Young Baldwin, lonely and afraid, was developing a supressed capacity for rage.

However, Baldwin's teachers helped him. When Baldwin was attending Frederick Douglass Junior High School, a de facto segregated school in Harlem, his teachers were trying to persuade him that he had a talent for writing. One of his black teachers, the already well-known poet Countee Cullen, introduced him to black literature. Another of his black teachers, a Harvard graduate, individually took Baldwin downtown to show him the treasures of the great central New York Public Library. Still another teacher, a Midwestern white, took Baldwin to his first play and gave him tickets to the World's Fair of 1939 which he otherwise could not have attended; she became a major factor in saving his life from waste. According to the black psychologist Kenneth Clark, who also attended Douglass School in the 1930s, Harlem teachers had not yet cultivated the belief that they could not teach Harlem pupils because they were culturally deprived; many of the teachers expected the best of their pupils and pulled it out of them. Baldwin went on to a predominantly white high school in the upper Bronx where he continued to be encouraged by his teachers, and his most intimate friends were Jewish boys who were dedicated to intellectual and literary pursuits like himself. It was not so much his schooling that created Baldwin's capacity for rage and directed it against whites as his step-father's vindictiveness, his family's poverty, and his head-long crash into white hostility after he left school.[7]

The trend toward more segregation in the cities showed itself not only in the public schools but also in Catholic schools. By the 1920s, as the numbers of blacks in the state grew, Catholics reported having five separate schools for blacks, and by the 1940s twelve, among them parochial schools in Buffalo, Albany, Brooklyn, and Manhattan.

In the 1930s when Lawrence Lucas, a sensitive black boy who was later to become a Catholic priest, was six years old, his family at-

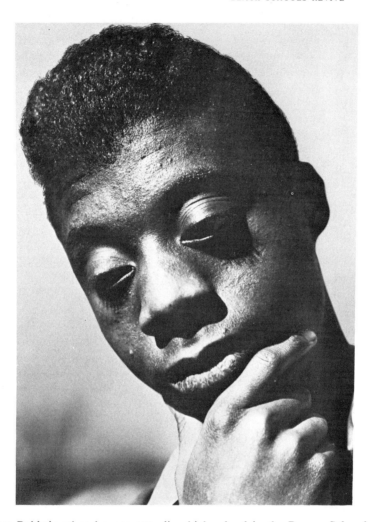

James Baldwin when he was attending high school in the Bronx. *Schomburg Center, New York Public Library.*

tended a Catholic church in a part of Harlem which was shifting from Irish to black. The Irish in the church had paid to build it; they felt the church was theirs. They told blacks to sit in the back of the church and would not even allow them to attend the parish school. The effect of this on Lucas, he said later, was to make him wish to be white. For a time he attended a public school. Later when he was old enough to walk the necessary eleven blocks, he attended the black parochial school of a black Catholic church on West 138th Street. He didn't feel "blatant racism" in this school, he recalled later, but he found that the other black pupils, like himself, craved to be white. He learned that the white sisters in charge— who would not even consider admitting blacks into their Blessed Sacrament order although it was founded for the benefit of non-whites—reinforced the children's yearning to be white. He felt that it was easier for the sisters to identify with the whiter than the darker pupils; if a pupil looked almost white, the sisters were more likely to choose that pupil to become a monitor. Lucas became convinced that white priests and nuns were in charge because whites were "smart," but that the lay teachers, janitors, and cleaning women were blacks because blacks were "dumb."

By 1945, as whites continued to flee from Harlem, one Catholic high school, at 124th Street and Lenox Avenue, still refused to admit blacks. But by this time leaders of the Catholic interracial movement had been reminding archdiocesan officials that Communists were taking advantage of Catholic school discrimination to discredit Catholics, and most of the Irish-controlled parishes of Harlem had abandoned their desperate struggle to keep their parish schools pure white.[8] There were probably six Catholic schools in Harlem which, once opened to black pupils, had become predominantly black.

Not only did the number of black elementary schools—both public and Catholic—increase, but there was a significant development of one form of professional school for blacks, in nursing education. Lincoln Hospital, which white philanthropists had founded in Manhattan before the Civil War as a home for elderly blacks, was for many years virtually the only hospital in the city which accepted black patients. In the mid-1890s as Lincoln Hospital planned to move to new buildings in the Bronx, it still refused to permit black physicians to practice in its building. Black physicians hotly protested this discrimination, and under the circumstances, objected to the hospital's plan to found a nursing school for blacks. In 1898 these black physicians themselves founded the small McDonough hospital and nursing school on West 41st Street, convenient to where many blacks lived; it was supported by such black leaders as Bishop William B. Derrick and Principal Sarah Garnet. But in the same year, Lincoln Hospital went ahead to found its own nursing school for blacks. The black-run McDonough hospital and nursing school was too small and poor to compete with the white-run Lincoln hospital and school and survived only about three years. The white-run Lincoln nursing school received the blessing of Booker T. Washington and funds from the

Lincoln Hospital School for Nurses, the Bronx, graduating class of 1904. At the time, most white schools for nurses were closed to blacks, and this was the only black school for professional nurses in the state. *Lincoln Hospital,* Annual Report, *1903–1904.*

Rockefellers. By the 1920s it had over 140 students, and had attained a high standard.[9]

By the 1920s the profession of nursing had become a prestigious one for black women, one of the few professions, like teaching, which was open to them in any significant degree. By this time New York had opened its city-owned hospitals to black patients, but blacks complained that the overwhelmingly white staff of these hospitals discriminated against black patients, and that their nursing schools were closed to blacks. Such complaints led blacks to mount an organized drive— supported by black politicians, the black press, and the NAACP—for the creation of another school of nursing which would be open to blacks, this one at the city-owned Harlem Hospital. When this school opened in 1923, city officials sometimes claimed that it was open to all, but largely because of its location, it became a black school, no matter how often city officials or blacks might decry the fact. When the first black nurses began to work in Harlem Hospital, white nurses sometimes walked off their posts, and black nurses were forced into a segregated dining room. By the 1930s tempers had calmed, and the hospital staff, including the instructors of the school of nursing, had become mixed.[10]

Besides black nursing schools, black Catholic schools, and black public schools, there were also in the state in the first half of the twentieth century a plethora of other types of black schools, serving a great variety of needs. White churches, settlement houses, and children's agencies ran nurseries, after-school classes, and adult literacy programs. The interracial Urban League ran black kindergartens, one on Dean Street in Brooklyn, another in Harlem. The white-controlled Children's Aid Society ran a black industrial school in the Columbus Hill ghetto of Manhattan, as well as a boys club in Harlem which taught trades, and a summer camp upstate near New Paltz on the Wallkill River. New York City itself ran industrial schools primarily for blacks and also special evening classes for blacks in tuberculosis prevention. Because the proportion of black delinquent boys in New York City was rising alarmingly, the Episcopal City Mission Society created a school for them, the Wiltwyck School, up the Hudson at Esopus, a school in which Eleanor Roosevelt came to take a special interest. In the 1940s when a Brooklyn court sent the truant Floyd Patterson to Wiltwyck School, Floyd was amazed to find that the windows were not barred, the boys were dressed in clothes which fitted them, the classes had only seven or eight pupils, and his counsellors and teachers really cared. At last he learned how to read and write and make friends.

Blacks ran black schools too. Black teachers in Brooklyn and Manhattan ran their own private academic schools, music schools, art schools, beauty schools, auto schools, and day nurseries. Father Divine ran fifteen "Kingdom" schools which offered vocational training. A black synagogue in Harlem organized a black Hebrew school. Blacks in Yonkers ran a boarding school. A black welfare league in White Plains offered classes in child care, cooking, and sewing, as well as providing a nursery to care for the children of working mothers. Blacks in Binghamton ran two industrial schools which gave instruction in furniture repair, carpentry, cooking, and the like. Hugh Mulzac, a West Indian mulatto who had served as chief officer of a ship of Marcus Garvey's Black Star Line, founded in Harlem a nautical school for blacks aspiring to become ships'

Typing class at the Harlem YWCA Trade School, 1943. *YWCA Archives, New York.*

officers. He secured over fifty students, most of them aflame with Garvey's black nationalism. In 1922, when the Black Star Line collapsed—according to Mulzac it collapsed because the management was incompetent and more concerned with propaganda than business—the students lost confidence that they would find jobs, and the school collapsed too.

Black staff from Tuskegee organized a military summer school for blacks in Ulster County. Black orphan asylums ran regular day schools for their children in the Bronx, Brooklyn, and in Westchester and Suffolk Counties. In Harlem, the Adam Clayton Powells' Abyssinian Baptist Church—called the world's largest Protestant church—administered weekday classes ranging from business to dressmaking; lectures ranging from birth control to communism; and a drama school led by Richard B. Harrison who played "De Lawd" in *Green Pastures.* Beginning when World War I opened new employment opportunities for black women, the Harlem YWCA developed an impressive trade school; by the 1930s and 1940s it was drawing over two thousand women a year from across the nation. The staff of the school—including Lillian Alexander, the civil rights activist, and Ann Petry, the future novelist of the broken dreams of Harlem—not only trained black women for jobs already open to blacks, but also for jobs scarcely open to them, such as typing and operating power garment machines, and then went out to do battle with business and unions to persuade them to accept their graduates.

In the 1930s the New Deal, in its efforts to relieve the unemployed, developed innovative ways to lead blacks into greater participation in their own education, and in doing so, sometimes furthered segregation. The WPA drew black adults into neighborhood educational planning. It provided predominantly black public schools with extra staff for guidance, recreation, medical and psychiatric testing, and group therapy, most of the staff being black. The WPA's exciting Harlem Art Center, directed by the black sculptor Augusta Savage, drew as many as 1400 students at a time, of all ages, to *de facto* segregated classes; among their teachers were Elton Fax, Selma Burke, and Norman Lewis, who were to become among the best known black artists in the nation. The WPA also taught more than six thousand adult Harlemites at a time in adult classes, the most popular being classes to improve reading or business skills.[11]

For the Civilian Conservation Corps, the New Deal deliberately created separate black and white camps in New York State, as in most of the nation. Not only did no significant black protest develop in the state against the segregated character of these CCC camps, but the black camps were so popular that blacks kept asking for more of them. Black camps were opened in at least twenty-one different rural locations in the state, scattered from Suffolk County on eastern Long Island to Jefferson County on the St. Lawrence River in the north and Chautauqua County on Lake Erie in the west. These camps were in effect black schools. The enrollees, who were usually disadvantaged young men from the cities, were expected to learn new skills from their work, as in swinging axes, planting trees, driving trucks, and constructing trails or roads. In addition, each black camp had a college-trained black educational adviser who helped develop a voluntary education program. The advisers found that the usual enrollee could be "passive" about whatever smacked of schooling, as one of the advisers explained, because in the past schooling had "never got him anything." However, most black enrollees took part in some aspect of the voluntary education program. At a forestry camp near Norwich, in Chenango County, the men flocked to an evening class in black history. At a flood control camp in Wawayanda, Orange County, which was called the largest black CCC camp in the nation, groups of men vied with each other in drama tournaments. Many camps offered ba-

WPA art class, New York, 1941. *F. D. Roosevelt Library, Hyde Park.*

sic education classes, vocational classes, visiting speakers, and a library; some camps mimeographed their own camp newspaper. Regardless of the segregated nature of the camps, the black enrollees often gained better food, health, and work habits, new skills, new educational interests, and new confidence both in themselves and in America.[12]

From time to time there were revealing impulses toward still more educational segregation in the state. Such impulses came mostly, but not exclusively, from whites. In Flushing, Long Island, in 1911, when a white gymnasium teacher asked a black boy to dance with a white girl, some white parents threatened to try to repeal the 1900 law limiting school segregation. The *New York Times* predicted that in one way or another Flushing would succeed in restoring segregation to its public schools, but nothing obvious came of the incident. About 1915 several white social workers in New York City proposed the creation of a school to train black girls in domestic service; however, a study for the New York Public Education Association opposed it on the ground that it would help to confine black girls to domestic service instead of opening varied employments to them.[13] In 1923 a black Brooklyn lawyer tried to push through the state legislature a proposal to establish in Putnam County a state agricultural and mechanical school for blacks, such as New Jersey and Pennsylvania already had. A mass meeting of Brooklyn blacks denounced the plan, and the *New York Amsterdam News* of April 18 warned that it "would undoubtedly open the flood-gates of separate schools throughout the state." The plan died in committee. In Rockville Center, Long Island, in 1930 a village health officer proposed that schools be segregated to keep slum-dwelling blacks from spreading their diseases to whites. The NAACP bristled; and the school board promised it would do nothing illegal. In 1930 in New Rochelle—where the black population had more than doubled in twenty years—the school board redrew the school zoning lines into a crazy shape so that most blacks were kept out of white schools and instead were herded into one school which became increasingly black. While the local and national NAACP protested, the New Rochelle board found ways to continue this policy through the 1940s without running into serious legal challenge. In Hempstead, Long Island, in 1941 blacks charged that some black children were being shunted to schools which other blacks already attended rather than being allowed to attend school in the neighborhoods where they lived; when the local NAACP investigated, the school board revised its policy.[14] In New York City in the 1930s and 1940s, blacks complained—sometimes on good evidence—that white school officers were keeping blacks out of some high schools and pushing them instead into others like Wadleigh High School which was becoming nearly all-black. The impulses to segregation were often curbed but by no means entirely prevented.

Altogether in New York State, in the period from 1900 to 1945, there were substantial numbers of blacks in black schools—including both intentionally segregated and *de facto* segregated schools. Adding together the largest known enrollment in each black school at any time and rough estimates for other known schools, we find that there were perhaps 350 pupils in legally separate black public schools, 245 in black nursing schools, 1200 in black orphan asylum schools, 6300 in black private and charity schools, 6000 in black industrial schools, 4200 in black Catholic schools, 9000 in black WPA schools, 4600 in black CCC camps, as well as 36,000 in *de facto* segregated black public schools. In total, this meant

Wadleigh High School for Girls on 114th Street at Seventh Avenue, Manhattan, when it opened around 1900. At that time, there were virtually no blacks in this school. By 1930 it had become about 40 percent black and by 1945, 90 percent. Blacks charged that this "humiliation" occurred not just because the school was located on the edge of an expanding Harlem, but primarily because school officials, through their zoning and guidance policies, deliberately steered blacks to this school. *Courtesy of The New-York Historical Society, New York City.*

that far more blacks were in black schools in the state than ever before. Particularly in the lower part of the state, where growth in the black population had been phenomenal, black schools not only had survived but were flourishing.

These black schools sometimes performed significant functions for blacks. Some of them, like the public schools, WPA schools, and the evening classes offered by innumerable church and social agencies, helped blacks to secure a basic education and to orient themselves to their new urban world. Other black schools, like the trade schools, nursing schools, and CCC camps, helped blacks to thrust into new occupations. The teachers of the black schools included able and dedicated men and women, black and white. While even the best teachers could be frustrated by meager facilities, inadequate motivation on the part of the pupils, and the low expectations of society at large, on the whole the quality of education which the black schools offered was good by the standards of the time. However, the experience of Lucas reminds us that no matter how well intentioned the teachers were, segregated black schools in the twentieth century, as in previous centuries, were capable of wounding their pupils, while the experience of Patterson and Baldwin suggests that the continuing struggle to improve black education could not be separated from other struggles, such as those to defuse racial hostility, improve parental attitudes, and to reduce poverty, for both blacks and whites.

RESISTANCE PERSISTS

$\mathbb{D}$ESPITE THE RENEWED GROWTH of separate black schools, during the period from 1900 to 1945 most blacks attended school with whites.

One of the blacks who did so was George Schuyler, the future journalist. According to his recollection afterward, for a long time as a child attending mixed schools in Syracuse, George scarcely felt any race prejudice. When a pugnacious Italian boy finally called him "nigger," George fought him over it. Afterward his family calmed him down by assuring him that blacks were as God made them, and that there were great men among blacks as well as whites. As George grew older, sometimes he struggled against the impact of books which ignored black achievement, newspapers which played up black crime, and his discovery that in Syracuse scarcely anyone of his color exercised authority as a policeman, fireman, teacher, or the like. But he was not overwhelmed by such discrimination. He did not feel inferior. He did so well in school that one teacher asked him to help correct geography papers. He liked school.[1]

There were significant signs in the state in the first half of the twentieth century that the long drive against school segregation, begun as early as the 1830s, was continuing, helping to increase the number of black pupils like George Schuyler who attended school with whites.

One of these signs was that, after the 1900 law had abolished the three legally separate black public schools in Jamaica, Flushing, and Hempstead, the only other such schools remaining in the state, all in rural regions, gradually disappeared. The first to go was the black school in Roslyn, Long Island. Over a period of several years Roslyn blacks petitioned the school board for the abolition of the black school, organized a march of black children from the black school to the white school to demand admission, and appealed to state education officials for help. Under this pressure, in 1917 the Roslyn school board finally closed its black school.[2] The second black public school to disappear was in Goshen, in Orange County, in the mid-Hudson region. Unlike Roslyn blacks, Goshen blacks, as far as available evidence indicates, did not protest against the existence of their separate one-room school. In fact, they were happy with the experience of their children in this school, taught sometimes by a black, sometimes by a white. The Goshen school board decided to abolish the school in 1933, during the great depression, largely because it regarded the maintenance of such a small separate school as unduly expensive.[3] Only one separate black public school operated by a regular school district remained in the state, in Hillburn, Rockland County, near the New Jersey border.

For some time, few people had noticed that New York State law permitted separate public schools for blacks in rural districts, or that such schools still existed. The existing schools were small and inconspicuous. In 1907, the usually well-informed black New York City principal, William L. Bulkley, boasted erroneously that "There is no such thing as a caste public school in the whole Empire State." When the Roslyn black school was under attack, a Roslyn paper mistakenly called it "the only separate colored school" in the state. In 1923 a prominent black Republican of Brooklyn declared that "the State of New York has the most liberal educational system in the world, a system which draws no color line." However, at least as early as 1930, during the flurry over the proposal to segregate schools in Rockville Center, a black lawyer in the national office of the NAACP, William T. Andrews, became aware that a state law permitted rural black public schools, but at the time he did not assist segregationists by publicizing the existence of such a law. The next year, 1931, when the local Hillburn NAACP complained to the NAACP national office about the existence of the Hillburn black public school, Andrews, familiar with the wording of the law in question, charged that the Hillburn black school was illegal because the Hillburn school district was organized as a common school district rather than as a union free school district, as the law permitting black schools required. When Hillburn school officials came to believe Andrews was correct, they hastily arranged—with the consent of the school voters, including considerable numbers of blacks—to reorganize their school district into a union free school district in order to legalize their black school. At this time many of the Hillburn black males were employed, if anywhere, in an iron works whose superintendent was president of the local school board and a chief architect of its segregation policy. An NAACP representative visiting

Hillburn reported that the blacks, weakened financially by the depression, feared economic reprisals if they moved against their black school.[4] For the time being, the Hillburn black school survived.

By 1937, black lawyer Andrews was himself a member of the State Assembly, a Democrat representing part of Harlem. In that year the state created a racially-mixed commission to study the condition of the black population, and Andrews was one of its members. In early 1938 the commission reported that blacks in the state were subject to dangerous conditions of discrimination. The commission recommended remedial legislation, including the amendment of the education law to prohibit "discrimination against Negroes in their admission to schools and colleges of all kinds." While most of the commission recommendations were not acted upon, Assemblyman Andrews did introduce a bill to repeal the section of the state education law which permitted union free school districts to establish separate schools for blacks. The Andrews bill was supported by the New York Civil Liberties Committee, the National Lawyers Guild, and various New York City parent-teacher associations. There is no available evidence that anyone supporting the bill publicly mentioned that if adopted it would make the black public school of Hillburn illegal. In fact, both a teachers' committee and the State Education Department, in supporting the bill, mistakenly claimed that no separate black public schools existed in the state. There was no visible opposition to the bill. It passed both houses with no votes against it. When Governor Lehman— himself a member of the NAACP national board—signed it, he closed the last known loophole in the state's laws against school districts operating black public schools.[5]

With the passage of this 1938 law, the Hillburn black school apparently became illegal. However, it continued to exist unchallenged until 1943. At that time some Hillburn blacks, more secure in their jobs because the iron works was busy with war production, decided to move against their segregated school. Acting on the advice of Thurgood Marshall, a black lawyer in the NAACP's national office in New York, they tried to enter their children in the local white school which, compared to the black school, had a larger, more modern building, with more adequate heating, library, and playground, but fewer students. When the Hillburn board, as expected, refused to permit the black children to enter the white school, the blacks decided both to take legal action and to boycott the black school. The school board, still headed by the same segregationist as in the 1930s, tried to protect itself against legal challenge by hastily adopting a new school zoning plan which allowed a few blacks into the local white school, but put most blacks into a school district for the black school, keeping it all-black. Meanwhile the NAACP ran a temporary, private, unaccredited school in a black church so that the boycotting children would not be deprived of schooling. In Harlem, a meeting of upward of 2500 persons heard both the cool attorney Thurgood Marshall and the flamboyant pastor Adam Clayton Powell, Jr. denounce Hillburn's segregation and urge them to donate funds to the school for boycotters. In the Hillburn region, various white citizens, including playwright Maxwell Anderson, issued statements supporting the boycott.

By this time the Hillburn school board, like the Jamaica school board in the 1890s, had brought charges in court against the black parents for not sending their children to an accredited school. The court declared twenty-two parents guilty, but suspended their fines on condition that they soon send their children to an accredited school. The parents then again tried to enter their children in the white school, but again local school officials refused to admit them, directing them to the black school instead. Finally in October 1943, the State Commissioner of Education ruled that school zoning for the purpose of racial segregation was illegal, that the black school must be closed, and all the black children must be accepted into the white school. The decision "has ended the last vestige of segregation in the public schools of the State of New York," Thurgood Marshall exulted; "The Hillburn case demonstrates . . . that Negro citizens with a just cause can often rally the support of other interested citizens and can secure justice through the proper legal channels."[6] While *de facto* segregation was continuing to grow, the state's last legally segregated public school in a regular school district had finally been closed.

Just as the gradual disappearance of legally-separate black public schools illustrated the persistence of the anti-segregation drive, so also did the gradual disappearance of the privately-run black orphan asylum schools.

One of the black orphan asylums, founded by blacks just after the Civil War, long existed in Brooklyn as the Howard Colored Orphan Asylum. By 1917 it had moved farther out on Long Island to Kings Park, with the hope that it would develop into a big "industrial school" on the model of Booker T. Washington's Tuskegee Institute. The orphanage was about to begin a financial campaign when in the unusually cold winter of 1917–1918 catastrophe struck. Lack of funds and wartime shortage of coal combined to permit the water pipes to freeze and burst. Some of the children, getting up in the morning, ran around on the wet, cold floor in their bare feet, becoming frostbitten. Two of them had their feet amputated. Under the impact of this disaster, the Howard orphanage closed, and it was never able to marshal enough support to reopen. The dream to transform the orphanage into a Northern Tuskegee was dead.

Musicians at the New York Colored Orphan Asylum, Riverdale, the Bronx, in 1939. The asylum ran its own black school from soon after the asylum's founding in 1836 until 1942. *New York Public Library Picture Collection.*

Another of the black orphan asylums had been founded by Quakers in Manhattan before the Civil War, at a time when existing orphanages refused to accept black children. By the early 1900s, this orphanage was relocated in Riverdale, in the Bronx, on an imposing site overlooking the Hudson River. It developed into an institution with handsome buildings and a well-organized school. The black W. E. B. Du-Bois criticized this orphanage for having no blacks on its board and for the tendency of the whites on the staff not to identify closely with the children. However, the orphanage was alert to improved methods of child care; and by 1939 it began to place blacks on its board. By 1942 there was a declining need for separate children's homes for blacks because most such institutions in the state now accepted black as well as white children; and in that year, under pressure from an inter-racial citizens committee, New York City's Board of Estimate ruled that agencies such as orphan asylums which received city funds could no longer discriminate on the basis of color. The asylum opened its doors to white as well as black children, ceasing to operate a separate black school.[7]

There was also a trend away from segregation in schools above the elementary level. Nevertheless, in some places and some types of schools, this trend was excruciatingly slow. In the early 1900s a black applied by mail to a New York City automobile school, and was accepted, but when he showed up and his color became apparent, he was refused. In the 1920s, at the University of Rochester's medical school, when a Southern black applied, he was told flatly that Negroes and Japanese would not be accepted. In Syracuse in the 1940s, a business school refused to accept black girls because it said it would not be able to find jobs for them when they had completed their study.

Girls' schools were often hesitant to admit blacks. In the early 1930s Skidmore College, at Saratoga Springs, accepted black students only as non-residents. It was only in 1934 that Vassar College, which up to that time had never consciously admitted a black, announced that it was ready to do so. In Buffalo the first black to graduate from a school of nursing did so only in 1940. Upstate normal schools were reluctant to admit blacks. In the 1930s Brockport State Normal advised a high school honors graduate, because she was black, not to try to become a teacher and denied her admission. Boarding schools often refused to accept blacks. Even Quakers, despite their long history of concern for blacks, did not admit a black to their boarding school in Poughkeepsie until 1930. The pastor of a black Catholic Church in Brooklyn in 1939 deplored that when he asked five or six Catholic boarding schools to admit a black boy, they refused, one expressing the belief that all such boarding schools barred blacks. Catholic colleges lagged behind most colleges in admitting blacks. In the 1930s and 1940s when the growing Catholic interracial movement was agitating to open Catholic schools and colleges to blacks, faculty would reply that the students wouldn't stand for it, and students would reply that the faculty wouldn't. It was only in 1938 that, over vociferous opposition, the nearly century-old Manhattanville College, a Catholic institution on a cliff overlooking Harlem, admitted its first black student.

Even when blacks were admitted to traditionally white schools or colleges, they were often not treated as equals—whether by faculty, students, or townspeople. Upstate at Colgate University in the 1920s, when a white student discovered that his roommate, Adam Clayton Powell, Jr., was partly black, he refused to room with him any longer. At Columbia University in the 1920s a group of white students tried to oust a black from a dormitory, saying that Southern students did not want him there; they even tried to frighten the black student by burning a cross on the campus, but he persisted in staying. In Rochester in the 1930s a black applicant to the city-owned normal school was only admitted after she swore under oath that if she graduated she would not attempt to secure employment in the Rochester school system. At Albany State Teachers College in the 1930s a young black woman found that because of her color the college was reluctant to permit her to do practice teaching, like the other students, in the college's model school; the college wanted her to do practice teaching in a black school instead. However, the possibility that the Albany Interracial Council, of which her husband was the organizer, might take up the issue, helped the college to overcome its reluctance. In the early 1940s, when a black New Paltz State Normal student was leaving a local restaurant, the proprietor, to indicate his contempt for blacks, picked up a glass the student had been using and smashed it. In New Rochelle in a high school vocational program in the 1940s, black students found that they were not permitted to participate in field work arranged in local retail stores, and the NAACP charged that such discrimination was common in vocational programs throughout the state.

Still, by about 1940 more black students may have been attending New York University than any other predominantly white college in the nation, and so many black teachers were doing graduate study at Columbia's Teachers College that it was called the national "fountain head of Negro education."[8] Altogether the number of blacks attending normal schools and colleges in New York State had made striking gains, the number of such students whom the author has been able to record by name jumping from 67 in the first decade of the 1900s to 425 by the 1920s and to 2912 by the 1940s (see Table 13 in the Appendix).

By the close of World War II, the proportion of black youths who were attending high school in the state had increased until it approximated that of whites. But it was commonly charged that high tuition fees often kept blacks out of colleges, and, besides, that private colleges, particularly medical and law schools, employed racial and religious quotas. State investigators verified the charges. After long agitation, especially by an alliance of blacks and Jews, the state decided in 1948 to provide more equal opportunity by establishing a state university system with low tuition charges and also by prohibiting racial and religious discrimination in all colleges, New York being the first state to adopt such a prohibition.

Nevertheless, in the 1940s blacks still had a long way to go in higher education. Of college age youths in the state, only 4 percent of blacks were attending college, while of all youths, 32 percent were. Blacks had especially far to go in such fields of study as engineering, business, medicine, and public administration. Meanwhile, although a few New York State blacks such as W. E. B. DuBois believed that there was a need for a new black college in the North,[9] a black college had still never been established in the state. Evidently, the predominantly white colleges in the state were meeting the needs of black students well enough so that pressures to found a black college continued to be contained.

As in the attendance of black students in college, so also in the appointment of black teachers on all levels of education, the trend in the state in the period 1900 to 1945 was away from segregation. In New York City available evidence suggests that the numbers of black public school teachers rose strikingly from about 40 in 1900 to 200 in 1920 and to 700 in 1940. Moreover, in the 1920s, when Philadelphia, Baltimore, and Washington still had legally separate black schools and confined their black teachers to these black schools, New York City, with black encouragement, was scattering its black teachers among all its schools so that they taught more white than black children. The black *Amsterdam News,* of December 22, 1934, claimed that "the mixed school system of New York City is the only one among the larger cities of the country which accepts the Negro teacher and pupil on a basis of equality and fair play." About the same time, a study for the American Historical Association reported that in New York City the black teachers, being more highly selected, were "better trained and more intelligent" than the white teachers, and that the black and white teachers mingled freely with each other at social gatherings and were occasionally guests at each other's houses.[10]

In the rest of the state the trend away from segregation in the appointment of teachers was slower. In Buffalo, where the black public school had closed in 1881, by the first decade of the 1900s there may have been at different times a total of five different black teachers in the mixed public schools; by the 1920s, perhaps twelve; by the year 1946 alone, nineteen, but it was charged that discrimination was holding back their permanent appointment. In New Rochelle, the first black teacher believed to have been appointed there since 1889, when the separate black public school was abolished, was appointed after NAACP prodding in 1938; this was enough of an event for Eleanor Roosevelt to call it a big step forward in race relations. In Mt. Vernon when the first black teacher was appointed in 1939, the reason for the delay until then was said to be local fear that appointing black teachers would lead to depreciation of real estate values. In 1939 there was still no black teacher in the public schools of Syracuse and only one in Rochester. A state commission charged that the lack of black teachers hurt black pupils by giving them the impression

Countee Cullen, teacher and lyric poet. A Phi Beta Kappa graduate of New York University, he exemplified the high quality of many of the blacks who taught in New York City's public schools in the 1930s and 1940s. *New York Public Library Picture Collection.*

that blacks do not have the capacity to hold positions of authority. In 1945 when the state prohibited racial discrimination in all kinds of employment—helping to make the state, according to the *Amsterdam News,* "the most progressive" in the nation—the state NAACP planned to submit the names of black candidates for teaching positions to superintendents over the state and expected more black teachers to be appointed.[11] In many places in the state, however, the first black teachers were not appointed until the 1950s or 1960s.

Similarly, a slow trend developed to appoint blacks to teach the increasingly higher levels of education in the state. In the 1890s, when the trend to appoint blacks to teach in predominantly white schools began in Manhattan and Brooklyn, blacks were appointed to teach only in elementary schools. By 1919 the first known black to teach in a public high school in the state was appointed to teach in a predominantly white high school in Queens. By the 1930s there were some thirty blacks teaching in nearly all-white high schools in New York City. Also by the 1930s a few blacks were teaching part-time in recognized colleges in the state, notably James Weldon Johnson, the NAACP secretary, songwriter, and poet, who for several years taught black literature as a visiting professor at New York University. By the early 1940s, more blacks were teaching in college, and for the first time since the abolitionist era, some of them were doing so with regular, full-time appointments, among them sociologist Marion Cuthbert at Brooklyn College and psychologist Kenneth B. Clark at City College. It was significant that these appointments of blacks to college faculties came especially downstate, whereas in the abolitionist era such appointments had come especially upstate. In 1942 when city councilman Adam Clayton Powell, Jr. blasted the city colleges for discriminating against blacks in appointing faculty, the presidents of the colleges warmly denied it, but the number of blacks appointed thereafter increased. By October 1947, *Ebony* claimed that there were sixty-two blacks teaching in predominantly-white American colleges, a pitifully small number as yet, but over one-third of them were in New York State.

In the administration of public schools, the trend away from segregation proceeded only at a crawl. In the nineteenth century there had been many black principals scattered through the state in black separate schools, but in the late nineteenth and early twentieth centuries, as the legally separate black schools faded away, hardly any blacks were appointed as principals in the racially-mixed public schools. Blacks had to wait for the development of a well-trained body of black teachers experienced in teaching in mixed schools, and even then in many cities they also had to wait for considerable black political power to develop. The first and only black principal appointed to a predominantly white public school in the state in the early twentieth century was Dr. William L. Bulkley, who served predominantly Jewish and Italian schools in lower Manhattan from 1909 to 1923. The next black principal known to have been appointed to a legally mixed school in the state was Gertrude Ayer, who was appointed in 1934 to a predominantly black school in Harlem. Afterward, James Baldwin recalled how important it was to him as a child when he attended Mrs. Ayer's school that its principal was black; she was living proof to him that blacks could rise to positions of eminence![12] Although Albany, Rochester, and Buffalo had once had black principals in their black public schools, it was not until long after 1945 that they again appointed black principals.

In the nineteenth century as we have seen, blacks rarely became public school board members in the state, Brooklyn providing a remarkable exception in the 1880s and 1890s. In the twentieth century, blacks were painfully slow to acquire such positions. There were no blacks on the city-wide New York City school board from its founding in 1842 until the physician Eugene P. Roberts was appointed in 1917. Following his short term, although there were a few blacks on the city's local boards from time to time, there was again a long period, despite black protest, when apparently there were none on the city-wide board. (While early in the century the board had often consisted of more than forty-five members, from the 1920s into the 1940s there were only seven members, making it more difficult to justify appointing a black.) The next black appointed may not have been until 1948. Outside of New York City, an early example of a black to be popularly elected to a school board—despite the Ku Klux Klan burning a cross to prevent it—was a Baptist pastor in 1932 in Greenburgh, in Westchester County, where the school population was said to be half black. Another early black to be chosen to a board was in New Rochelle, after the NAACP had long agitated for it, in 1946. Many places in the state with considerable black population are believed to have chosen their first black board members only in the 1960s—including Hempstead, Newburgh, Buffalo, Beacon, Poughkeepsie, Elmira, and Rochester.

Outside of public schools, in marked contrast to the usual nineteenth and early twentieth century practice, blacks made substantial gains in administrative positions in educational institutions. By the 1930s two black women were on the national board of the New York City-based YWCA. By about 1945, blacks were beginning to be appointed to the boards of both Lincoln and Harlem Hospital schools of nursing. At the upstate Wiltwyck school, the black judge Jane Bolin—the granddaughter of the janitor Abraham Bolin who had asked for black teachers at the

Gertrude Johnson Ayer was an innovative guidance counselor in the Manhattan public schools in the 1920s and a principal from the 1930s to the 1950s. Crisis, *March 1923.*

Poughkeepsie black school—was a trustee. The once all-white board of the Riverdale orphan asylum now had eleven blacks on its thirty-three man board.

In many schools, parents, teachers, and pupils became increasingly active in trying to create an atmosphere which would encourage rather than discourage black pupils. Early in the century black principal Bulkley protested to the publisher of a geography text that in presenting pictures of the various races of man, he was unfair to choose an African savage to represent the black race while he chose President McKinley to represent the Caucasian race. When the publisher in reply asked for a better photograph to represent blacks, Bulkley supplied one—a photograph of one of New York's beloved black pastors—which thereafter appeared in the book.[13]

By the socially-conscious 1930s, the Brooklyn black YMCA was holding annual black history bees. The Riverdale orphan asylum school had incorporated black history into its regular curriculum. While the black historian Carter G. Woodson claimed that many of the texts used in New York City's schools were "charged and surcharged" with bias,[14] at least as part of Negro History Week—which Woodson himself had launched in 1926—in Harlem, pupils were seeing dramatic presentations of the role of the black in the development of the American nation; in New Rochelle, the high school library was acquiring more books on black life; and in Buffalo, libraries were displaying books and art by blacks.

By the early 1940s, anti-Nazi war strategy, combined with hostile white reactions to war-time waves of black migration into Northern cities, was forcing more serious effort to create a positive attitude toward blacks in the schools. New York City school officials inaugurated a controversial human relations program, including voluntary in-service training for teachers on tolerance, the promotion of interracial forums, and the withdrawal of texts which were prejudiced against any group. City school officials also initiated an experimental effort to rescue a deteriorating part of Queens—the "asphalt jungle" of South Jamaica—by bringing together Irish, Jews, blacks, and Puerto Ricans in a common community council; the council successfully fought for more community service in the schools and elsewhere, and classroom discipline improved. The city school board not only tolerated teachers who openly protested signs of racial discrimination in schools or elsewhere, as it long had, but also brought to trial a white teacher who was accused of teaching "un-Americanism and intolerance."[15] Fordham University in the Bronx, Hunter College in Manhattan, and St. John's University in Brooklyn offered courses on black culture. The Catholic archdiocese of New York introduced into its seventy parochial schools an experimental program which taught that true Christians could not hold group prejudices. The Albany Institute of History and Art prepared an exhibit of the works of black artists and began to circulate it elsewhere in the state. New York's State Education Department was among the four state education departments in the nation said to have well-established programs of inter-cultural education, limited and vague though its program was. At least significant precedent had been established for conditioning school atmosphere to help minorities respect their heritage and develop their potential.

By about 1945, as post-war economic dislocation raised racial unrest to new highs, it was clear that this effort, extensive though it already was, was by no means enough to solve the pervasive racial problems of the ever more segregated urban schools. They were in fact being increasingly threatened with racial tension. The *New York Herald-Tribune,* reacting to a minor incident of racial violence in an East Harlem school, was calling for special police measures to reduce racial violence in schools. The white chairman of a committee for better city schools was charging that school officials gave little support to programs to reduce prejudice. The black judge, Jane Bolin, was calling for the removal of "frustrated, intolerant" teachers from the schools. A teachers union was pushing for intercultural education to be part of the work of every grade. The black *New York Age* claimed that for years black and white liberals had been calling for a "real inter-cultural education" but that little had yet been done. The Albany Interracial Council asked the Albany Board of Education to include black history in its school curriculum, but the board tabled the request. A state commission reported that most public school systems in the state had not yet even explored the field of education against prejudice and recommended that the entire educational system from elementary to adult levels be redesigned for its "supreme task of helping to make the American creed work."[16]

PERSPECTIVE

FROM THE COLONIAL PERIOD to 1945 the context of black education in New York State was transformed. As blacks became more Christianized and Americanized, whites had less reason to view them as strangers. Legally, blacks moved from slavery to equal citizenship. Economically, most blacks remained underprivileged, but especially in the twentieth century, the opportunity was slowly being opened for a more significant portion of them to enter the middle class.

In the eighteenth century the question of whether slaves should be educated was still in doubt, but by the first half of the nineteenth century elementary schooling for blacks was becoming accepted as desirable. Both blacks and whites helped to create separate schools for blacks—charity schools, private schools, public schools, and the like—as the most practical way to get more blacks into school. Meanwhile, blacks developed considerable control over black schools. Most of the teachers in black schools became black, and these black teachers acquired remarkable freedom to protest against racial discrimination.

However, by the middle of the nineteenth century, when black public schools had become common in the state, significant numbers of progressive blacks and their white allies were turning against separate education as humiliating to blacks and were beginning to campaign to open white schools to them. By the 1890s, after the proportion of blacks in the state had long remained steadily low, separate education seemed to be on the way out—ironically this occurred in a period when in the South separate education was being established more firmly than ever. In 1900 New York State outlawed separate black public schools in cities, and in 1938, in rural areas too.

Meanwhile in the twentieth century, a drastic increase in the proportion of blacks in the cities of the state brought a revival of separate black schools, especially in the form of *de facto* segregation. Up to 1945 this trend was held somewhat in check by such means as appeals by both blacks and whites to democratic ideals and the increasingly effective organizational and political power of blacks.

Through the centuries, did the education of New York State blacks accomplish what its promoters hoped? Three of their early hopes were substantially accomplished, and the importance of these accomplishments in drawing blacks toward full participation in American life can hardly be overstated.

In colonial days the primary purpose of the promoters of the education of blacks was to Christianize them. The achievement of this goal, significantly begun in the eighteenth century, was largely accomplished in the early nineteenth century with the rise of a strong black-led church.

Another major goal of the early promoters of black education was for blacks to atend school in the same proportion as whites. In the eighteenth century, only a tiny fraction of all black children of school age attended any school, a far smaller proportion than for whites. By the mid-nineteenth century, when most blacks who were attending school were attending legally separate black public schools, about one quarter of black children were attending school. At the end of the nineteenth century, when most black children who were attending school were attending racially-mixed schools and the state's compulsory school law was beginning to be enforced, some 40 percent of black children were attending school, still about 13 percent less than of all children. After that, blacks rapidly caught up to whites. By 1940, while the irregular attendance of blacks continued to be a problem, the percentage of blacks attending school at all was only 1 percent less than of all children.[1]

A third major goal of the early promoters of black education was teaching blacks simply to read and write. While in slavery days the overwhelming majority of blacks in the state were illiterate, by 1850 most black adults had attained elementary literacy; by 1880 according to census reports, the proportion of illiterates among blacks was down to 21 percent, and by 1930 to only 2.5 percent—at that time, because of the large number of white illiterates who had recently immigrated into the state from Europe, the illiteracy rate for blacks was actually lower than for Caucasians.[2]

Whether other hopes of the promoters of black education were realized or not can be less easily measured. Various promoters of black education hoped that it would help whites to look more favorably on the

abolition of slavery, on giving blacks the equal right to vote, and on reducing racial segregation. New York State did move toward all these
goals. It did abolish slavery in the state by 1827 and became increasingly
hostile to slavery in the South as well. In referendums, the voters of the
state did give increasing support to equal suffrage for blacks. In the
period from the 1870s to at least the 1910s, the state clearly moved away
from segregation. The improvement in the education of blacks probably
did contribute in some degree to all of these movements, but there is no
precise way to measure to what degree it did so.

Many promoters of black education hoped that it would help
open more equal job opportunities for blacks. The power of education in
this respect proved sharply limited. For example, from about 1800 to
1860 when black education, though largely separate, was clearly strength-
ening, nevertheless job opportunities for blacks narrowed. At the time
many other forces were working against greater job opportunity for
blacks, including competition from hordes of unskilled immigrants arriving from Europe. At least from the 1910s, the increasingly higher levels of
education open to blacks in predominantly white institutions helped blacks
to move slowly and unevenly from menial jobs toward clerical, industrial,
and professional positions. But in judging what brought this trend about,
it would be difficult to separate educational factors from other factors
such as the restriction of immigration, the impact of World Wars I and II
in creating jobs, and the increase in black organizational clout. Anyway,
regardless of improved education, the basic pattern, established in colonial times, of restricting most blacks to inferior jobs, persisted.[3]

From the eighteenth to the twentieth centuries, the teachers of
blacks altered dramatically in their background and purposes, reflecting
the vast cultural transformation in the state and nation at large. In the
eighteenth century, the Reverend Richard Charlton was typical of many
such teachers in that he was male, white, and born and educated in college
in the British Isles. He taught slaves catechism, psalm singing, and reading in part-time Anglican church schools. His major concern was the conversion of blacks and the religious knowledge they attained.

By comparison, in the nineteenth century, most teachers in the
black schools had become black. Representative of many such teachers
were a black couple, the bitter one-legged Reverend Henry Highland Garnet, who had escaped from slavery in the South as a child, and the wife of
his later years, the slight, tactful Sarah, who came from a comfortable
middle-class Brooklyn family. They both had been educated in New York
State: Sarah, until late in her career, only had the advantage of having
trained for teaching as a monitor in John Peterson's school and having

studied in the New York Saturday Colored Normal School; Henry had studied in an abolitionist-supported, interracial college. Both, as they taught black public schools, were demanding of their pupils academically, and being active protesters against discrimination, were alert to the social contexts in which their pupils lived. They awakened their pupils to the frustrations and responsibilities of blacks in an unjust world.

By the twentieth century, many teachers of blacks were well educated, upper-class black women, like the light-complexioned Mrs. Gertrude Ayer who taught in a *de facto* segregated school. The daughter of a black New York City physician, she was educated at some of the city's best colleges. She was conscious of the relation of black education to the organization of society as a whole. She was active as a socialist, contributing articles to A. Philip Randolph's *Messenger*; and as a vocational counselor, she led in a drive to open more industrial opportunties to black girls. Also in the twentieth century, considerable numbers of black teachers were beginning to teach in racially-mixed schools, as the poet James Weldon Johnson did. After coming from Florida to New York, Johnson helped edit a black protest newspaper, and as executive secretary of the NAACP, kept pounding at segregation. When Mrs. Ayer was appointed principal of a Harlem school with a racially mixed staff and when Johnson was appointed a teacher of literature at the predominantly white New York University, they both exemplified not only the state's continued acceptance of black protesters as teachers but also the slowly increasing acceptance of teachers on merit regardless of race.

How black pupils responded to their education also changed significantly from the eighteenth to the twentieth centuries. In the eighteenth century, Jupiter Hammon's education, under the control of his Anglican slave masters, was rural, elementary, religious. It helped develop Hammon into an honest, acquiescent slave who grieved over the degraded morals of blacks, who believed that the Bible was almost the only book worth reading, and who was independent enough to plead—contrary to the official Anglican missionary position—that slavery should be abolished.

By comparison, in the early nineteenth century, the education which the Quaker-led New York Manumission Society offered as a charity to the youthful James McCune Smith was less religious, more urban, more academic, and encouraged higher aspirations for blacks. While it could not open doors for Smith to a medical school in America, it did so in Britain. On his return to New York City to practice medicine, he became, beyond his teachers, a ceaseless campaigner for equal rights for blacks.

In the twentieth century, the education of blacks was still more secular and urban; it more easily opened doors to higher education, but it conveyed a mixed message. In the predominantly white public schools of Syracuse, the easy-going black pupil George Schuyler was aware that school books neglected black achievement. In a black parochial school in Harlem the intense Lawrence Lucas was impressed that the white teachers favored the lighter-skinned pupils; he quickly learned that whites were "smart" and blacks were "dumb." The black and white teachers of the shy, tormented James Baldwin, first in a predominantly black public school in Harlem and later in a predominantly white public school in the Bronx, found ways to give him mind-expanding experiences outside of his parched family life, to introduce him to black authors and black history, and to build his confidence as a writer. Their schooling helped all three of these blacks to prepare for leadership positions—Schuyler as a journalist, Lucas as a priest, and Baldwin as a novelist—which they used from time to time, each in his own way, to rage at whites.

Through the centuries, some blacks and some whites have made strong claims of achievement by black pupils. In the eighteenth century, after he had been teaching religion to blacks for seventeen years, an Anglican pastor proudly recalled that not one black whom he had admitted to Holy Communion had disgraced his profession of faith. About 1830 the officials of the Manumission Society insisted that, although several thousand pupils had been taught in their African schools by that time, no pupil who had passed all the way through their course of instruction had been convicted of a crime. In the 1850s the Brooklyn superintendent of schools decided that the nine hundred children in his black schools "compare favorably" with the children in "corresponding classes in the other schools." In the 1910s and 1920s, according to the recollections of some of the pupils who attended Goshen's black public school, their teacher pushed the pupils so hard that when they were ready to transfer to the fifth grade in a predominantly white school, some of the pupils were in fact two grades ahead of the whites in their studies.[4]

Despite such claims, there was general agreement among most blacks and whites that, while blacks had made significant educational progress, their achievement was not equal to that of whites. Among major reasons they gave for the difference were poor black attendance at school, black feelings of inferiority, and the hopelessness of black children about their own future. In 1819 at a public exhibition at Charles Andrews' school in Manhattan, a boy who was about to graduate spoke of his prospects for employment: "Shall I be a mechanic? No one will employ me; white boys won't work with me. Shall I be a merchant? No one will have me in his office; white clerks won't associate with me. Drudgery and servitude, then, are my prospective portion. Can you be surprised at my discouragement?" Such discouragement persisted, undoubtedly with profound impact on the academic performance of sensitive and intelligent children. In the early twentieth century, black principal Bulkley explained that when black children are small, they show "the same interest, the same faithfulness, the same receptivity, noticeable in other race varieties." But "once arrived at that place where they begin to learn . . . that on every hand avenues of employment are shut tight, discouragement begins, further study ceases, books become distasteful, and they leave school to work at any menial employment that offers itself."[5]

Still another factor which some friends of black education believed was retarding black pupils was educational segregation. From at least as early as the 1830s, campaigns against such segregation developed in the state. In the period of the 1830s to 1850s a black who led such a campaign was the editor Frederick Douglass. He was an abolitionist, was active in the colored convention movement, and lived upstate, all of which were characteristic of the black desegregation leaders of the time. His impressive physical presence, combined with his outspoken style and bold use of the boycott, helped him to develop in Rochester the first clearly successful campaign to desegregate schools in any locality in the state.

The period when, per decade, the largest number of leaders, black and white combined, were active against separate schools was in the 1860s and 1870s (see Table 16 in the Appendix) when the Civil War and Reconstruction were stirring hope of achieving equal rights for blacks. In this period one of the leaders, William H. Johnson, was a barber, a typical occupation for black desegregation leaders of the period. Like Douglass, he lived upstate as black leaders still usually did, and, like Douglass, he had been active as an abolitionist. But Johnson was recognized as a black political leader by a major political party, as Douglass scarcely had been in the previous period. Thus, Johnson symbolized the new political role which blacks played in the state in alliance with the Republican Party after they acquired the equal right to vote. Johnson was able to use his political position as the state Senate's head janitor to lead in enacting a civil rights law which black leaders believed, too trustingly, would open all the public schools of the state to blacks. Johnson's law at least helped to reduce the number of different places in the state known to have black public schools from 35 at its height in the 1860s to 31 in the 1870s, and to 20 in the 1880s.

In the period of the 1880s to 1890s, the center of leadership in the struggle to desegregate schools for the first time shifted downstate, where most of the remaining black public schools were. In this period, black women for the first time became significant in the desegregation movement, while black barbers and other skilled workers sharply declined as blacks lost such occupations to recent European immigrants. Exemplifying big city black leadership in this period was the smooth Philip A. White, the wholesale druggist who became a member of the Brooklyn school board. Cautious in his style, as seemed appropriate at a time when the national climate was swinging back toward more hostility to black rights, Philip White was concerned, as black leaders in the previous periods had barely begun to be, about preserving the jobs of the black teachers. He maneuvered quietly to open the white schools to blacks, and at the same time, to keep the black schools in existence, to improve their quality, and to teach race pride. Despite Philip White, many other blacks as well as whites struggled valiantly to close black schools, and by the 1890s the number of cities or towns in the state having black public schools had dropped still lower, to fifteen.

In the period from 1900 to 1945, when leadership against school segregation continued to be concentrated downstate, for the first time the number of white leaders whom the author has been able to record as active against segregation came nearly up to number of black leaders. White leaders included sons of Jewish immigrants like Joel Springarn, a caustic professor of literature at Columbia, who became a major figure in the NAACP. They included the crusading Fordham law graduate, George K. Hunton, a grandson of Irish immigrants, who ironically depended heavily on Jewish funds to drag Catholic opinion toward racial tolerance. They included representatives of older Protestant families like Eleanor Roosevelt, whose miserable childhood gave her an empathy with the underprivileged which she kept all her life.

It was also in the period 1900 to 1945 that for the first time the black as well as the white leaders were largely professional in their occupations—85 percent of the black leaders were so, reflecting the increasing number of blacks who had achieved a higher education. An example of such black leaders was the Harlem lawyer, William T. Andrews, a graduate of Columbia University. He was at first active against segregation as a member of the legal staff of the NAACP, an organization which symbolized the newly strong organizational position of blacks in alliance with liberal whites. He later was active as a Democratic member of the state legislature, a body to which blacks were first elected during this period. Andrews led in pushing through the legislature in 1938 the law which closed the last loophole in the state's laws against school districts operating separate black public schools; under the impact of the law, the last such school in the state closed in 1943. Andrews' use of political

Eleanor Roosevelt visiting a school pageant, Harlem, 1943. *F. D. Roosevelt Library, Hyde Park.*

means to work against segregation was representative of this period when blacks in the largest number of different localities in the state made appeals to white city or state officials to help them against school segregation, and when such officials were becoming increasingly committed to thwarting school segregation, whether in the openly legal form or in the new *de facto* form, whether in public or private education.

Altogether, the long record of the education of blacks in New York State reminds us that conflicts of race, class, and culture may change in form but are likely to persist, and that in this uncertain world, what seems to be a blessing in one period—such as separate schools for blacks—may turn into the bane of the next. Underlying the narrative is the inherent conflict between the advantages of separate black schools, including the opportunity they give for blacks to participate in determining what education for blacks should be, and the disadvantages of separate black schools, including their tendency to isolate blacks from the major streams of life where the greatest opportunities are likely to be. This story is marked by the irony that, when the long struggle to abolish black schools seemed about to triumph, it was interrupted by an onrush of Southern blacks who were drawn to New York State in part because of its relative freedom from the very segregation which their arrival helped to re-introduce.

At best this agonizing narrative, stretching over more than three centuries, reveals not only the severe limits as to what education by itself can achieve, but also significant improvement in the education of blacks— halting and limited improvement to be sure, but nevertheless improvement, and thus can give us hope.

APPENDIX

TABLE 1

Black Population of New York State and New York City

	Number of Blacks in New York State	Percent of Blacks in New York State's Population	Percent of Blacks in New York City's Population
1750	10,592	14%	16%
1790	25,978	8	10
1800	31,320	5	11
1810	40,350	4	10
1820	39,367	3	9
1830	44,945	2	7
1840	50,031	2	5
1850	49,069	2	3
1860	49,005	1	2
1870	52,081	1	1
1880	65,104	1	2
1890	70,092	1	2
1900	99,232	1	2
1910	134,191	2	2
1920	198,483	2	3
1930	412,814	3	5
1940	571,221	4	6
1950	918,191	6	9
1960	1,417,511	8	14
1970	2,164,560	12	21

SOURCE: Compiled from U.S. Census records; E. B. O'Callaghan, ed., *Documents Relating to the Colonial History of the State of New York* (Albany, 1855)6:133; Edgar J. McManus, *A History of Negro Slavery in New York* (Syracuse: Syracuse University Press, 1966), pp. 197–98; New York City Commission on Human Rights, *Negroes in the City of New York* (New York, 1961?), pp. 6–7.

TABLE 2

Black Population of Regions of New York State

	Percent of Blacks in the Downstate Population	Percent of Blacks in the Upstate Population
1800	13	4
1850	3	1
1900	2	1
1950	9	2

SOURCE: Compiled from U.S. Census records.

In this table, as in the book generally, "downstate" means Long Island plus Richmond, New York, and Bronx Counties. All the rest of the state is "upstate."

TABLE 3

Black Population of Selected Counties

	Percent of Blacks in DOWNSTATE counties				Percent of Blacks in UPSTATE counties			
	New York	Kings	Queens	Suffolk	Dutchess	Albany	Monroe	Erie
1737	16	24	14	14	8	15	—	—
1800	11	32	18	10	5	6	—	—
1850	3	3	9	6	3	1	1	1
1900	2	2	2	4	3	1	0	0
1950	20	8	3	5	4	3	2	4
1970	25	25	13	5	6	5	7	9

SOURCE: Compiled from U.S. Census records and O'Callaghan, *Documents,* p. 133.

TABLE 4

The Earliest Known Black School in Each Place in New York State up to 1945, Arranged Chronologically

Date	Place	Present County	Type of School
1704	New York City	New York	Church
1714	Albany	Albany	Church
1728	Rye	Westchester	Church
1735	Southampton	Suffolk	Church
1735	Richmond (town)	Staten Island	Church
1766	Phillipsburg (Yonkers)	Westchester	Church
1773	Schenectady	Schenectady	Church
1815	Brooklyn	Kings	Private
1815	Flatbush	Kings	Sunday
1815	Utica	Oneida	Sunday
1816	Geneva	Ontario	Sunday
1817	"Guinea," Westbury	Nassau (orig. Queens)	Sunday
1817	Kingston	Ulster	Sunday
1818	Rochester	Monroe	Sunday
1818	Stone Ridge	Ulster	Sunday
1819?	Flushing	Queens	Sunday
1821	Troy	Rensselaer	Private
1822	Jamaica	Queens	Sunday
1828	Hudson	Columbia	Charity
1828	Kinderhook	Columbia	Sunday
1829	Poughkeepsie	Dutchess	Private?
1830	Newtown	Queens	Private
1832	Catskill	Greene	Charity
1834	Peterboro	Oneida	Abolitionist
1835	Amityville (Huntington South)	Suffolk	Abolitionist & Sunday
1835	Huntington	Nassau (Queens)	Abolitionist
1835	Jerusalem (Town of Hempstead)	Nassau (Queens)	Abolitionist
1835	Newburgh	Orange	Public
1837	Buffalo	Erie	Private?
1839	Harrison	Westchester	Private?
1840	Lockport	Niagara	Public
1841	Canandaigua	Ontario	Public?
1841	Ithaca	Tompkins	Public?
1841	Syracuse	Onondaga	Private
1841	Williamsburg	Kings	Charity

(continued)

TABLE 4 (*continued*)

The Earliest Known Black School in Each Place in New York State up to 1945, Arranged Chronologically

Date	Place	Present County	Type of School
1842?	Binghamton	Broome	Public
1842	New Rochelle	Westchester	Public
1843	Bath	Steuben	Public
1845	White Plains	Westchester	Public
1846	Auburn	Cayuga	Public
1847	Lakeville (Town of Hempstead)	Nassau (Queens)	Private?
1848	Elmira	Chemung	Public
1848	Lansingburg	Rensselaer	Public
1855	Greenport	Suffolk	Sunday
1855	Stapleton (Middletown)	Staten Island	Public
1858	Goshen	Orange	Public
1859	Fishkill Landing (Beacon)	Dutchess	Public
1859	Haverstraw	Rockland	Public
1859	Sag Harbor	Suffolk	Sunday
1860	Nyack	Rockland	Sunday
1860	Oyster Bay	Nassau (Queens)	Sunday
1862	Schoharie	Schoharie	Public
1863	Manhasset	Nassau (Queens)	Private?
1865	Middletown	Orange	Public
1868	Flatlands	Kings	Public
1868	Roslyn (North Hempstead)	Nassau (Queens)	Public
1874	Hempstead (Village)	Nassau (Queens)	Public
1880?	Hillburn	Rockland	Private
1898	Bronx	Bronx	Nursing
1906	St. James	Suffolk	Orphan Asylum (farm)
1906	Stony Hollow (near Kingston)	Ulster	Private (military)
1910	Kings Park	Suffolk	Orphan Asylum
1910	Verbank	Dutchess	Orphan Asylum (farm)
1931	Wading River (Port Jefferson)	Suffolk	Orphan Asylum
1934	Wawayanda (near Middletown)	Orange	CCC Camp
1934	Yaphank	Suffolk	CCC Camp
1935	Blauvelt	Rockland	CCC Camp
1935	Norwich	Chenango	CCC Camp

(*continued*)

TABLE 4 (*continued*)

The Earliest Known Black School in Each Place in New York State up to 1945, Arranged Chronologically

Date	Place	Present County	Type of School
1936	Gardiner (New Paltz)	Ulster	Charity (summer camp)
1936	Pulaski	Oswego	CCC Camp
1936	Salamanca	Cattaraugus	CCC Camp
1936	Tioga Center	Tioga	CCC Camp
1937	Birdsall	Allegany	CCC Camp
1937	Camden	Oneida	CCC Camp
1937	Candor	Tioga	CCC Camp
1937	Corning	Steuben	CCC Camp
1937	Esopus (West Park)	Ulster	Charity
1937	Leicester	Livingston	CCC Camp
1937	Panama	Chautauqua	CCC Camp
1937	Williamstown	Oswego	CCC Camp
1938	Cherry Plain	Rensselaer	CCC Camp
1938	Fishers Landing	Jefferson	CCC Camp
1939	Beavers Dams	Schuyler	CCC Camp
1939	Machias	Cattaraugus	CCC Camp
1939	Van Etten	Chemung	CCC Camp
1941	Almond	Allegany	CCC Camp
1941	Big Flats	Chemung	CCC Camp

Total number of different places listed as having black schools: 87. Total number of present-day counties listed: 38. Present-day counties listed as having the largest number of different places with schools:

	No. of Places
Nassau (orig. in Queens)	8
Suffolk	8
Ulster	5
Westchester	5
Kings	4
Orange	4
Rockland	4

Note that if the count were by counties as then constituted rather than by present-day counties, Queens would have the largest number of different places having schools.

Tables 4 through 12 and 14 through 16 are compiled from such sources as state and federal reports; black, abolitionist, and local newspapers; local histories; school, charity society, and church records; census manuscripts; black convention reports; minutes of public hearings; and city directories. Probably many of the schools listed were in fact established earlier, and many other schools existed, but adequate evidence is lacking.

TABLE 5

Black Public Schools in Regular School Districts, by County, Place, and Decade

County	Place	1810s	1820s	1830s	1840s	1850s	1860s	1870s	1880s	1890s	1900s	1910s	1920s	1930s	1940s
Albany	Albany				X	X	X	X							
Broome	Binghamton				X	X	X	X							
Cayuga	Auburn				X	X	X								
Chemung	Elmira				X	X	X								
Columbia	Hudson				X	X	X	X							
	Kinderhook				X	X	X	X	X						
Dutchess	Poughkeepsie				X	X	X	X							
	Fishkill Landing**					X	X	X	X	X					
Erie	Buffalo			X	X	X	X	X	X						
Greene	Catskill				X	X	X	X	X	X					
Kings	Flatbush							X	X	X					
	Flatlands						X	X							
	Brooklyn	X	X	X	X	X	X	X	X	(X)*	(X)				
	Williamsburg				X	X									
Monroe	Rochester			X	X	X									
New York	Manhattan				X	X	X	X	X	(X)	(X)				
Niagara	Lockport				X	X	X	X							
Oneida	Utica				X										
Ontario	Canandaigua					X	X								
	Geneva				X	X	X	X							
Orange	Newburgh			X	X	X	X	X	X	X	X	X	X		
	Middletown						X								
	Goshen					X	X	X	X	X	X	X	X	X	

County	Place														
(Queens)	Flushing							X	X	X					
	Hempstead‡	X	X	X	X	X	X	X	X	X					
	Jamaica				X	X	X	X	X	X	X				
	Newtown				X	X	X	X	X	X					
	Jerusalem§				X	X	X								
	Lakeville‖						X	X							
	Roslyn				X	X	X	X	X	X	X	X			
Rensselaer	Lansingburg				X	X	X	X							
	Troy				X	X	X	X	X						
Richmond	Middletown#				X	X	X	X	X	X					
Rockland	Haverstraw				X	X	X	X	X	X					
	Hillburn							X	X	X	X	X	X	X	X
Schenectady	Schenectady				X	X	X	X							
Schoharie	Schoharie				X	X	X	X	X	X	X				
Steuben	Bath				X	X	X	X							
Suffolk	Amityville				X	X	X	X	X	X					
	Huntington					X									
Westchester	Harrison				X	X	X	X							
	New Rochelle				X	X	X	X	X	X					
	White Plains				X	X	X								
	Total Nos. of Places Having Such Schools	1	1	4	26	34	35	31	20	15	8	3	2	2	1

NOTE: There were additional counties which the New York State Superintendent of Schools, *Annual Reports*, list in the nineteenth century as having expended funds for black public schools for more than one year, including Allegany, Chautauqua, Delaware, Jefferson, Montgomery, Onondaga, Oswego, Otsego, St. Lawrence, Saratoga, Tioga, Ulster, Wayne, and Yates. But because the reports are not reliable, and because I have not located hard evidence for the existence of black public schools in these counties, I have not counted them here.

*The symbol (X) means that in this place at least one black school, while formally desegregated, survived into this decade as predominantly black in its teachers and pupils.

**Now Beacon.
§Now Wantagh.
†Including the later Nassau County.
‖Now Lake Success.
‡Hempstead Village.
#Stapleton.

TABLE 6

Teachers in Black Schools, by Sex and Race

Total Number of Teachers Whose Names Are Known	Sex			Race		
	Of This Total, the Number Whose Sex is Known	Percent Female	Percent Male	Of This Total, the Number Whose Race is Known	Percent Black	Percent White
1,234	1,222	68%	32%	966	67%	33%

Tables 6 through 12 consist only of teachers whose names are known and who taught in black schools in the state up to 1945. The schools included are those believed to have been intended wholly or primarily for blacks. They include Sunday schools only through 1869, as after that time such schools became more religious and less academic. In the twentieth century they do not include regular school district public schools which were *de facto* segregated.

TABLE 7

Teachers in Black Schools, by Decades of Teaching, Race, and Sex

Decade	Number of Teachers Whose Names Are Known	Percent of Those Whose Race is Known Who Are Black	Percent of Those Whose Sex is Known Who Are Female
1700s	1	0	0
1710s	2	0	0
1720s	5	0	0
1730s	5	0	0
1740s	4	0	0
1750s	3	0	0
1760s	4	0	25
1770s	7	0	14
1780s	3	0	0
1790s	5	20	40
1800s	3	33	33
1810s	28	15	29
1820s	33	46	38
1830s	81	67	42
1840s	123	67	54
1850s	208	73	61
1860s	242	70	67
1870s	165	63	87
1880s	154	71	87
1890s	151	76	87
1900s	86	67	85
1910s	129	82	74
1920s	73	81	81
1930s	128	91	63
1940s	94	95	65

TABLE 8

Teachers in Black Schools, by Birthplace

Century		South	N.Y. State	Rest of North	West Indies	British Isles	Other Foreign	Total Whose Birthplace Is Known
18th	Number	0	2	2	0	8	1	13
	Percent	0	15%	15%	0	62%	8%	100%
19th	Number	35	210	64	3	14		330
	Percent	11%	64%	19%	1%	4%	1%	100%
20th	Number	33	35	21	8	0	1	98
	Percent	34%	36%	21%	8%	0	1%	100%

TABLE 9

Teachers in Black Schools, by Highest Level of Educational Preparation

Highest Level of Educational Preparation	Of the *Black* Teachers Whose Highest Level of Preparation Is Known, the Number and Percent Who Attained Each Level is:		Of the *White* Teachers Whose Highest Level of Preparation Is Known, the Number and Percent Who Attained Each Level is:	
	number	percent	number	percent
Grammar	46	14	8	13
High school	33	10	9	15
Part-time normal	64	20	2	3
Full-time normal	47	14	17	27
College	137	42	26	42
Totals	327	100	62	100

TABLE 10

Teachers in Black Schools, by Regions Where They Taught

Century	Manhattan	Rest of Downstate	Hudson Region	Rest of Upstate
		(1) Number of teachers in each region:		
18th	16	2	6	0
19th	417	211	148	996
20th	240	111	41	23
	(2) Percent of teachers in each region whose race is known who were blacks:			
18th	6%	0%	0%	—
19th	66%	78%	51%	29%
20th	85%	84%	90%	100%

The "Hudson Region," as used in this table and in the book generally, means those counties in the state which border on the Hudson River from Westchester north to Rensselaer and Albany, plus Schenectady and Schoharie.

TABLE 11

Teachers in Black Schools, by School Organization

	Numbers of Teachers in:	
Century	Schools Organized Primarily by Blacks	Schools Organized Primarily by Whites
18th	0	24
19th	142	703
20th	203	203

TABLE 12

Teachers in Black Schools, by School Type

Century	Abolitionist	Charity	Church	Nursing	Orphan Asylum	Private	Public	Sunday School
	(1) Number of Teachers in Each Type of School:							
18th	5	0	19	0	0	0	0	—
19th	35	81	2	3	189	48	427	134
20th	0	80	11	17	98	129	72	—
	(2) Percent of Teachers in Each Type of School Whose Race is Known Who Were Blacks:							
18th	20%	—	0%	—	—	—	—	—
19th	67%	84%	*	*	40%	86%	69%	45%
20th	—	57%	70%	62%	85%	99%	89%	—

The symbol * as used in this table means that numbers are so small that percentages would be misleading.

TABLE 13

Blacks Known by Name who Attended Normal Schools or Colleges in New York State

Decade	Number of Black Students Known by Name	Normal Schools or Colleges Having the Largest Number of Such Students, Ranked in Order
1820s	1	*
1830s	13	Oneida Institute Columbia College
1840s	5	N.Y. College of Pharmacy
1850s	8	N.Y. Central College
1860s	5	*
1870s	61	N.Y.C. Normal (Hunter) College U.S. Military Academy at West Point Colgate (Madison) University Long Island College Hospital Medical School
1880s	59	N.Y.C. Normal (Hunter) College N.Y. City College U.S. Military Academy at West Point tie: Albany State Normal School and N.Y. University

1890s	44	N.Y. University
		Cornell University
		tie: N.Y. Homeopathic (Flower) Hospital
		    Medical School and Long Island College
		    Hospital Medical School

1900s	67	Columbia University Cornell University N.Y. City College tie: Union Theological Seminary and Syracuse Univ.
1910s	248	Columbia University N.Y. City College Teachers College N.Y. University tie: Hunter College and Syracuse University

(*continued*)

TABLE 13 (*continued*)

Blacks Known by Name who Attended Normal Schools or Colleges in New York State

Decade	Number of Black Students Known by Name	Normal Schools or Colleges Having the Largest Number of Such Students, Ranked in Order
1920s	425	Teachers College Columbia University N.Y. City College N.Y. University Cornell University Pratt Institute Syracuse University
1930s	1253	Teachers College Columbia University N.Y. University Cornell University Hunter College N.Y. City College Union Theological Seminary
1940s	2912	Teachers College Columbia University N.Y. Univeristy Hunter College Union Theological Seminary U.S. Military Academy at West Point Cornell University

SOURCE: This table has been compiled from such sources as contemporary periodicals, biographical directories, school board records, and college records. The table is undoubtedly affected by some colleges having been more willing and able than others to supply information (among the colleges which were particularly helpful were Colgate, West Point, Teachers College, Hunter, Hamilton, Brooklyn, and Albany State). The table is undoubtedly affected also by the greater adequacy of sources for some decades than others.

The table lists each student as attending only the college he attended earliest and only in the decade he first attended. Note that if Teachers College, which is listed separately, were included as part of Columbia University (which it joined in 1898), the predominance of Columbia in the table would be even greater than it is. The list excludes part-time normal schools, commercial colleges, nursing schools, and the like, but includes two year colleges, law schools, and the like. For the 1940s the literal count was made only through 1945, the date this study properly ends, but the figure has been extended through the decade by extrapolation.

*This symbol means that numbers are too small to be significant.

TABLE 14

Blacks who Led in Desegregating Education, by Occupation

	1830s–50s		1860s–70s		1880s–90s		1900s–1945	
	No.	%	No.	%	No.	%	No.	%
Professionals	**30**	**49%**	**36**	**33%**	**49**	**48%**	**133**	**85%**
clergy	8		17		20		24	
editors-journalists	13		6		13		26	
executives of social agencies	0		2		2		19	
government officials	0		0		0		8	
lawyers	0		2		6		15	
physicians-dentists	2		5		0		21	
social workers	0		0		0		4	
students	4		2		0		7	
teachers	2		2		8		4	
Businessmen	**2**	**3%**	**13**	**12%**	**19**	**19%**	**11**	**7%**
agents (real est., ins., employment)	0		5		2		4	
hotel or boarding house proprietors	0		2		2		0	
manufacturers	0		0		1		2	
merchants	2		1		5		0	
restaurateurs-caterers	0		2		1		1	
scavenger businessmen	0		0		8		3	
Skilled Workers	**25**	**41%**	**33**	**30%**	**3**	**3%**	**10**	**7%**
barbers	19		18		0		2	
cashiers-clerks	0		5		1		4	
notaries	0		0		2		0	
tailors-clothes cleaners	3		4		0		0	

(*continued*)

TABLE 14 (*continued*)

Blacks who Led in Desegregating Education, by Occupation

	1830s–50s		1860s–70s		1880s–90s		1900s–1945	
	No.	%	No.	%	No.	%	No.	%
Unskilled Workers	**4**	**7%**	**27**	**25%**	**31**	**30%**	**2**	**1%**
boatmen	0		2		0		0	
cartmen	2		0		0		0	
coachmen-drivers- chauffeurs	0		3		7		2	
gardeners	0		0		3		0	
janitors	0		2		5		0	
laborers	0		5		7		0	
pedlars	0		0		2		0	
porters	0		1		3		0	
waiters	0		6		3		0	
whitewashers	0		6		0		0	
Total	**61**	**100 %**	**109**	**100%**	**102**	**100%**	**156**	**100%**

Tables 14 through 16 include persons only if their names, occupations, and race have been identified. They include persons who led in desegregating educational institutions of all types, public and non-public, and on all levels from elementary through college. They include persons who tried to open white schools to blacks, to secure equal treatment for blacks in schools, to close separate black schools, and the like. If a person took more than one significant action, he is counted again for each action.

The numbers of persons listed as representing each occupation (editors, clergy, etc.), do not always add up to the total indicated for each occupational category (professionals, businessmen, etc.) because those occupations represented by very few persons have been omitted.

The occupation of housewife is not recorded because it does not serve to distinguish status. If a housewife is not known to have any occupation of her own other than housewife, and her husband's occupation is known, she is listed by his occupation on the assumption that it would help to indicate her status. Teachers in the black schools are generally excluded from the list under the assumption that their occupation inevitably involved them as leaders in school affairs. However, when teachers were active as leaders in group actions with non-teachers, as on a delegation, they are counted along with the others.

The figures are probably distorted by the greater availability of sources for some periods than others, and by the greater ease of identifying persons of some occupations than of others.

TABLE 15

Whites who Led in Desegregating Education, by Occupation

	1830s–50s		1860s–70s		1880s–90s		1900s–45	
	No.	%	No.	%	No.	%	No.	%
Professionals	**31**	**74%**	**24**	**75%**	**16**	**67%**	**136**	**94%**
artists-musicians	2		0		0		5	
author-lecturers	0		0		1		7	
clergy	4		3		4		8	
editor-journalists	1		3		1		20	
educational administrators	6		8		3		8	
executives of social agencies	0		0		0		18	
government officials	4		5		2		12	
labor union officials	0		0		0		4	
lawyers	5		3		5		31	
physician-dentists	0		0		0		5	
teachers	9		2		0		16	
Businessmen	**11**	**26%**	**7**	**22%**	**8**	**33%**	**8**	**6%**
agents (real est., ins., employment)	0		0		0		2	
bankers-brokers	0		1		1		3	
company officials	0		1		1		1	
landowners	3		0		0		0	
manufacturers	0		2		0		0	
merchants	8		3		6		2	
Skilled Workers	**0**	**0%**	**1**	**3%**	**0**	**0%**	**0**	**0%**
bookkeepers	0		1		0		0	
Unskilled Workers	**0**	**0%**	**0**	**0%**	**0**	**0%**	**0**	**0%**
Total	**42**	**100%**	**32**	**100%**	**24**	**100%**	**144**	**100%**

TABLE 16

Blacks and Whites who Led in Desegregating Education, by Periods

	Blacks Per Period Indicated	Whites Per Period Indicated	Blacks and Whites Combined Per Period Indicated	Blacks and Whites Combined Per Decade
1830s–1850s	61	42	103	34
1860s–1870s	109	32	141	71
1880s–1890s	102	24	126	63
1900s–1945	156	144	300	65
Total	428	242	670	233

NOTES

CHAPTER 1—Schools for Slaves

1. Hugh Hastings, *Ecclesiastical Records, State of New York* (Albany, 1901-16), p. 548.

2. Isaac N. P. Stokes, *Iconography of Manhattan Island,* 6 vols. (New York: Dodd, 1915-28), 4:84, 86.

3. John Sharpe, "Proposals," *New-York Historical Society Collections* (1880):357.

4. David Humphreys, *An Historical Account of the Incorporated Society for the Propagation of the Gospel in Foreign Parts* (London, 1730), p. 232.

5. H. P. Thompson, *Into All Lands: The History of the Society for the Propagation of the Gospel in Foreign Parts* (London: SPCK, 1951), p. 73.

6. Humphreys, *Historical Account,* p. 236.

7. Sheldon C. Cohen, "Elias Neau, Instructor to New York's Slaves," *New-York Historical Society Quarterly* (Jan. 1971): 8-12; Humphreys, *Historical Account,* p. 237.

8. Edgar L. Pennington, "Thomas Bray's Associates and Their Work Among the Negroes," *Proceedings of the American Antiquarian Society* (Oct. 1938):382.

9. Sharpe, "Proposals," pp. 348-50.

10. William W. Kemp, *Support of Schools in Colonial New York by the Society for the Propagation of the Gospel* (New York, 1913), pp. 257-60.

11. Humphreys, *Historical Account,* p. 219.

12. Frank J. Klingberg, *Anglican Humanitarianism in Colonial New York* (Philadelphia: Church Historical Society, 1940), pp. 164-65; Robert Bolton, *History . . . of the County of Westchester,* 2 vols. (New York, 1881), 2:184; Kemp, *Support of Schools,* p. 185.

13. Carter G. Woodson, *Education of the Negro Prior to 1861* (New

York: Arno, 1919; 1968), pp. 46–47; Bliss Forbush, *Elias Hicks* (New York: Columbia University Press, 1956), pp. 30–31; John Cox, *Quakerism in the City of New York* (New York: Privately printed, 1930), pp. 59–60.

14. Hastings, *Ecclesiastical Records,* pp. 2952–55.

15. Charles E. Corwin, "Efforts of the Dutch Colonial Pastors for the Conversion of the Negroes," *Journal of the Presbyterian Historical Society* (1927):433–34. Samuel R. Scottron (in *New York Age,* July 13, 1905) says that ca. 1750 the Dutch Reformed Churches of Bushwick and Flatbush, followed by the Sands Street Methodist Church of Brooklyn, as well as churches of other denominations, included Negroes in their parish schools. He says these parish schools were still open to Negroes even after the New York Manumission Society opened its school in New York City in 1787.

16. Edgar J. McManus, *History of Negro Slavery in New York* (Syracuse: Syracuse University Press, 1966), pp. 47–48, 57, 191; Samuel Miller, *Discourse Delivered April 12, 1797* (New York, 1797), p. 14.

17. Klingberg, *Anglican Humanitarianism,* p. 136; Anne Grant, *Memoirs of an American Lady,* 2 vols. (London, 1808), 1:52–54.

18. Stanley A. Ransom, *America's First Negro Poet: The Complete Works of Jupiter Hammon* (Port Washington: Kennikat Press, 1970), pp. 13, 69.

19. Charles A. Vertanes, "Jupiter Hammon," *Nassau County Historical Journal* (Winter 1957):5–6; Ransom, *America's First,* pp. 69, 75, 99, 108–109, 113–14.

20. Pennington, "Thomas Bray's Associates," p. 382; Klingberg, *Anglican Humanitarianism,* pp. 130–32.

21. Klingberg, *Anglican Humanitarianism,* pp. 46, 145, 159–60, 174, 179.

22. Humphreys, *Historical Account,* p. 260; Woodson, *Education,* pp. 33–34; Joseph Hooper, *History of St. Peter's Church in the City of Albany* (Albany, 1900), p. 79.

23. McManus, *History,* p. 77.

CHAPTER 2—White Benevolence

1. Leslie H. Fishel and Benjamin Quarles, *The Black American: A Documentary History* (Glenview, Ill.: Scott, Foresman, 1970), p. 53.

2. Henry B. Fearon, *Sketches of America* (London, 1818), p. 46.

3. New York State Colonization Society, *Proceedings* (1830):10.

4. *Ibid.* (1829):8.

5. Duke De La Rochefoucault Liancourt, *Travels Through the United States,* 2 vols. (London, 1799), 2:233; Sojourner Truth, *Narrative* (Boston, 1875), pp. 208–209; Thomas James, *Wonderful, Eventful Life* (Rochester, 1887), pp. 3–4; Austin Steward, *Twenty-Two Years a Slave* (Rochester, 1856), pp. 82–83.

6. Two schools were run by the Clarkson Association in New York City, one for females, the other for males: see Abigail Mott, *Biographical Sketches . . . of Persons of Color* (New York, 1839), pp. 111–12, 328; John Cox, *Quakerism in the City of New York* (New York: Privately printed, 1930), pp. 63–64. Black elementary schools were run by Quakers in Huntington, Hempstead, and Amityville, Long Island (*Brief History of the Charity Society of the Jericho and Westbury Monthly Meetings,* 1921, p. 10).

7. Charles C. Andrews, *History of the New York African Free Schools* (New York, 1830), p. 55.

8. Henry Highland Garnet, *Memorial Discourse* (Philadelphia, 1865), ✗ pp. 21–23.

9. New York Manumission Society, Records, vol. 8, pp. 67–68, 78, at New-York Historical Society; T. Robert Moseley, "History of the New York Manumission Society" (Ph.D. dissertation, New York University, 1963), pp. 217–18; recollection of Elizabeth Jennings Graham in *New York Age,* Sept. 20, 1890; Harry A. Williamson in Prince Hall Lodge of Masons, *Proceedings* (1921):97.

10. Thomas Hamilton, *Men and Manners in America,* 2 vols. (Edinburgh, 1833), 1:92–95; Garnet, *Memorial Discourse,* pp. 23–24.

11. *New York Colored American,* June 22, 1839.

12. *Albany Patriot,* Dec. 18, 1844.

13. *Brooklyn Long Island Star,* June 2, 1830.

14. Moseley, "History," pp. 247–49; Thomas Boese, *Public Education in the City of New York* (New York, 1869), p. 227; William O. Bourne, *History of the Public School Society of the City of New York* (New York, 1873), pp. 677–79; Public School Society, Minutes, May 13, 1836, New-York Historical Society.

15. *New York Colored American,* July 22, 1837, April 19, 1838.

16. New York State, *Laws,* 1812, chap. 242, section 18; Albany Lancaster School Society, Minutes, Feb. 2, 1829, at State Library, Albany. Similarly, the law creating the New York Free School Society (later called the Public School Society) described it as for indigent children and did not mention race, so that blacks were said to believe that they could insist on entering its schools. New York State, *Laws,* 1805, chap. 108; Samuel R. Scottron in *New York Age,* July 13, 1905.

17. Franklin Ellis, *History of Columbia County* (Philadelphia, 1878), p. 193.

18. *Poughkeepsie Telegraph,* Jan. 10, May 9, 1838; Oct. 5, 1837; March 16, 1842.

19. *Catskill Recorder,* in *Boston Liberator,* June 2, 1832.

20. *Schenectady Reflector,* March 7, 1851.

21. *Poughkeepsie Telegraph,* in *New York Colored American,* Oct. 28, 1837; *New York Colored American,* Nov. 11, 1837.

22. New York State Colonization Society, *Proceedings* (1829):18; William Jay, *Inquiry* (New York, 1835), pp. 24–26; Carter G. Woodson, *Negro Orators* (Washington: Associated Publishers, 1925), p. 81.

23. *New York Colored American,* March 28, 1840.

24. New York City Colonization Society, *Proceedings* (New York, 1835):18.

25. Albany Lancaster School Society, Minutes, Feb. 3, 1834.

CHAPTER 3—Sunday Blessing

1. *New York Freedom's Journal,* July 27, Nov. 23, 1827; African Methodist Episcopal Church, *Minutes of the Four Last Annual Conferences* (Philadelphia, 1834), p. 21.

2. *Sunday School Repository,* IV, 1820, p. 435, in Edwin W. Rice, *The Sunday School Movement* (Philadelphia, 1917), p. 65.

3. New York Female Union for . . . Sabbath Schools, *Tenth Report,* 1826, p. 8; Isaac Ferris, *Semi-Centennial Memorial Discourse of the New York Sunday School Union* (New York, 1866), p. 25; *Albany Daily Advertiser,* Dec. 3, 1822, in Joel Munsell, *Annals of Albany,* 10 vols. (Albany, 1850–59)7:185–89; Sunday School Teachers of the State of New York, *Doings of the Third Annual Convention* (New York, 1858), p. 22; James W. C. Pennington, *Fugitive Blacksmith* (London, 1849), p. 51.

4. *Sunday School Repository,* June 1818, p. 71; Christine M. Cantine to Caroline Ludlow Frey, Aug. 18, 1828, Frey family papers, New-York Historical Society; Austin Steward, *Twenty-Two Years a Slave* (Rochester, 1856), p. 132; *New York Freedom's Journal,* Nov. 23, 1827; *New York Colored American,* April 8, 1837.

5. Henry R. Stiles, *History of the City of Brooklyn,* 3 vols. (Brooklyn, 1867–70), 3:958; Warren H. Smith, *Hobart and William Smith: The History of Two Colleges* (Geneva, N.Y.: Hobart and William Smith Colleges, 1972), p. 22; Gertrude L. Vanderbilt, *Social History of Flatbush* (New York, 1899), pp. 313–15; *New York Weekly Anglo-African,* Nov. 5, 1859; Moses M. Bagg, *Pioneers of Utica* (Utica, 1877), pp. 414–15; Arch Merrill, *The Lakes Country* (Rochester: Printed by L. Heindl, 1944), pp. 93–94.

6. *New York Colored American,* Sept. 28, 1839; *Sunday School Facts* (New York, 1821), p. 12.

7. *A Visit of One Thousand Sabbath School Teachers of Massachusetts to New York* (Boston, 1855), pp. 16–17, 21, 23.

8. *Brooklyn Long Island Star,* May 11, 1826; *Rochester Observer,* Oct. 3, 1828; *Brooklyn Daily Eagle,* June 6, 1866; *New York Daily Tribune,* June 11, 1866.

9. *New York National Advocate,* in *Brooklyn Long Island Star,* Dec. 20, 1815.

10. *Albany Daily Advertiser,* Dec. 3, 1822; *Milestones* (Nov. 1906):5.

11. *Albany Daily Advertiser,* Dec. 3, 1822; Christine M. Cantine to

Caroline Ludlow Frey, Aug. 18, 1828; Carleton Mabee, *Black Freedom: The Nonviolent Abolitionists from 1830 through the Civil War* (New York: Macmillan, 1970), pp. 276–77; *Sunday School Repository* (April 1818):27–28.

12. Robert Lynn and Elliott Wright, *The Big Little School: Sunday Child of American Protestantism* (New York: Harper and Row, 1971), pp. 39–40; *New York Weekly Anglo-African,* Aug. 24, 1861.

13. James Milnor, *Plea for the American Colonization Society* (New York, 1826), pp. 13–15.

14. *New York Colored American,* Oct. 14, 1837; July 21, 1838.

15. *Rochester North Star,* Feb. 11, 1848; Lynn and Wright, *Big Little School,* pp. 36–38; Lewis Tappan, *Letters Respecting a Book Dropped from the Catalogue of the American Sunday School Union in Compliance with the Dictation of the Slave Power* (New York, 1848).

16. *Brooklyn Long Island Star,* Oct. 20, 1830.

17. Stephen H. Tyng, *Forty Years Experience in Sunday Schools* (New York, 1863), p. 139.

18. Amos Beman to Reverend P. D. Oakey, Aug. 4, 1865, Amos Beman scrapbooks, Beinecke Library, Yale University.

CHAPTER 4—Black Initiative

1. Benjamin J. Lossing, *Lives of Celebrated Americans* (Hartford, 1869), p. 405.

2. Act of incorporation, in New York State, *Laws,* 1816, chap. 87.

3. *Albany Daily Advertiser,* in Joel Munsell, *Collections on the History of Albany,* 4 vols. (Albany, 1865–71), 2:387; Albany Board of School Commissioners, *Report* (1852):8; New York State Superintendent of Common Schools, *Annual Report* (1824): Appendix, p. 28; Albany Lancaster School Society, Minutes, April 13, 26, 1826, State Library, Albany.

4. *Brooklyn Long Island Star,* Jan. 18, 1815; May 8, 1816. For a fuller account of black initiative in early Brooklyn, see Carleton Mabee, "Early Black Public School," *Long Island Forum* (Nov. 1973):214–16; (Dec. 1973):234–36.

5. *Brooklyn Long Island Star,* April 3, 1833.

6. Spooner's Brooklyn *Directory* for 1829, p. 76; for 1830, p. 83.

7. *Brooklyn Long Island Star,* July 19, 1827; Oct. 20, 1830; March 23, Nov. 23, 1831; April 18, 1832.

8. *Brooklyn Evening Star,* Feb. 3, 4, 1841; Feb. 8, 1842.

9. *Brooklyn Long Island Star,* Feb. 25, March 4, 1830; Jan. 22, 1835; July 10, 1834; May 2, 1836.

10. *Brooklyn Long Island Star,* April 3, 1833.

11. *Brooklyn Star,* letter dated Nov. 23, 1842, in *American and Foreign Antislavery Reporter,* Jan. 1, 1843, p. 115; Daniel A. Payne, *Semi-Centenary . . .*

of the African Methodist Episcopal Church (Baltimore, 1866), p. 44; *Brooklyn Daily Eagle,* July 8, 1863.

X   12. *Troy Daily Press,* Aug. 19, 1865; *New York Emancipator,* Dec. 1, 1836, pp. 122–23; *New York Colored American,* April 1, 1837.

13. *Rochester Daily Advertiser,* March 27, 1850.

14. New York State Assembly, *Documents,* 1832, vol. 2, Doc. No. 77, dated Feb. 2, 1832, presents the words quoted as the Assembly committee's words. Recent authors have mistakenly, I believe, attributed these same words to the petition itself or to a school board committee.

15. *Rochester Daily Advertiser,* Feb. 28, 1833; *Rochester Rights of Man,* April 26, 1834.

16. *Lockport Niagara Courier,* Sept. 9, 1835, in Arthur O. White, "The Black Movement Against Jim Crow Education in Lockport, New York, 1835–1876," *New York History* (1969):269–70.

17. Lewis Tappan, *Life of Arthur Tappan* (Westport, Conn.: Negro Universities Press, 1871; 1970), pp. 158–61; *Boston Liberator,* June 29, 1833; Colored National Convention, *Minutes* (1833):38–39 (sic.).

18. On Peter Williams' school, see the conflicting evidence in William J. Simmons, *Men of Mark* (Cleveland, 1887), pp. 530, 657; Henry Highland Garnet, *Memorial Discourse* (Philadelphia, 1865), p. 28; Alexander Crummel in *Washington Post,* Dec. 10, 1894; *College for Colored Youth: An Account of the New Haven City Meeting* (New York, 1831), pp. 5–6; B. F. De Costa, *Three Score and Ten: The Story of St. Philips' Church, New York City* (New York, 1889), pp. 33–34; *New York Colored American,* Oct. 24, 1840.

19. Garnet, *Memorial Discourse,* p. 28.

20. *New York Observer,* Dec. 21, 1833, p. 204.

21. *Boston Liberator,* June 29, 1833.

22. David Ruggles to Gerrit Smith, April 22, 1836, Gerrit Smith papers, Syracuse University.

23. *New York Colored American,* March 25, 1837.

24. *New York Colored American,* May 11, June 1, Aug. 31, Oct. 19, 1839.

25. New York State Colored Convention, *Minutes* (New York, 1840):5, 7, 28.

26. J. W. Loguen, *Reverend J. W. Loguen as a Slave and as a Freeman* (Syracuse, 1859), pp. 340–73.

27. Lewis Tappan to Gerrit Smith, Jan. 4, 1839, Gerrit Smith papers.

28. James McCune Smith to Gerrit Smith, May 12, July 7, 1848, Gerrit Smith papers.

29. *Rochester North Star,* Jan. 21, May 19, 1848.

30. New York State Superintendent of Common Schools, *Annual Report,* for 1849, pp. 134–35.

31. New York Public School Society, Minutes, July 7, 1848; Jan. 4, 1850, New-York Historical Society; New York Public School Society, *Annual Report* (1850):10.

32. *New York Freedom's Journal,* Feb. 15, 1828; James McCune Smith to Gerrit Smith, Dec. 28, 30, 1846, Gerrit Smith papers.

CHAPTER 5—Public Responsibility

1. New York State Superintendent of Common Schools, *Annual Report,* Jan. 15, 1845, p. 145.

2. New York State Assembly, *Journal* (1824):21; New York State, *Revised Statutes,* for 1827 and 1828, vol. 1, 1829, p. 478.

3. New York State, *Statutes . . . Relating to Common Schools* (1841), p. 28; *Rochester Daily Democrat,* Feb. 20, 1841; New York State Superintendent of Common Schools, *Statutes . . . Relating to Common Schools . . . with Forms and Regulations* (1847), p. 149.

4. Albany Board of Public Instruction, *Annual Report,* for 1872, p. 77.

5. New York State Assembly, *Documents,* 1832, vol. 2, Doc. no. 77; New York State Superintendent of Common Schools, *Annual Report,* Jan. 15, 1845, p. 145; *New York Globe* in *Auburn Cayuga Patriot,* April 15, 1846; *Kinderhook Rough Notes,* July 15, 1858.

6. New York State Superintendent of Public Instruction, *Eleventh Annual Report,* for 1864, p. 277; New York State Superintendent of Public Instruction, *Laws of New York Relating to Common Schools, with Comments,* (1868), pp. 304–305; Austin Steward, *Twenty-Two Years a Slave* (Rochester, 1856), p. 320.

7. Hosea Easton, *A Treatise* (Boston, 1837), p. 41; *Poughkeepsie Daily Eagle,* June 22, 1872.

8. New York State Assembly, *Journal* (1824):21; New York State, *Statutes . . . Relating to Common Schools* (1841), p. 33; S. S. Randall, *A Digest of the Common School System of the State of New York* (Albany, 1844), pp. 235–36.

9. New York State Superintendent of Common Schools, *Annual Report,* Jan. 13, 1847, pp. 20–21; New York State Superintendent of Common Schools, *Statutes . . . Relating to Common Schools . . . with Forms and Regulations* (1847), p. 148.

10. Buffalo Superintendent of Common Schools, *Seventh Annual Report,* for 1843, p. 8; *Jamaica Long Island Democrat,* Jan. 4, 1859; James McCune Smith to Gerrit Smith, Dec. 28, 30, 1846, Gerrit Smith papers, Syracuse University.

11. Clipping, marked *Catskill Enterprise,* Sept. 26, 1901, at Greene County Historical Society; *Newburgh Gazette,* Dec. 27, 1834; Samuel W. Eager, *Outline History of Orange County* (Newburgh, 1846–47), p. 221.

12. *Brief History of the Charity Society of Jericho and Westbury Monthly Meeetings* (1921), p. 10; John B. Shiel, "175 Years in One Book," *Long Island Forum* (March 1970):47; New York State Superintendent of Common

Schools, *Statutes . . . Relating to Common Schools . . . with Forms and Regulations* (1847), p. 149.

13. *Poughkeepsie Telegraph,* April 5, 1843; March 6, 1844.

14. *Schenectady Reflector,* March 7, 1851; George R. Howell and John H. Munsell, *History of the County of Schenectady* (New York, 1886), p. 125; Schenectady Board of Education, Minutes, July 1, Sept. 13, Oct. 11, 1854, at Schenectady Board of Education office.

15. New York State Superintendent of Public Instruction, *Second Annual Report,* for 1855, pp. 6, 133.

16. For example, in Albany in 1869 the cost per pupil in the black school was $32, in all schools $19 (Albany Board of Public Instruction, *Third Annual Report,* 1869, p. 38); in Buffalo in 1852, for the black school it was $15 per pupil, for all schools, $8 (Buffalo Superintendent of Public Schools, *Sixteenth Annual Report,* for 1852, p. 27).

17. *New York Weekly Anglo-African,* June 23, 1860.

18. *New York Weekly Anglo-African,* March 22, 1862.

19. New Rochelle Board of Education, Minutes, July 12, Oct. 11, 1870, at New Rochelle Board of Education office; *Kinderhook Rough Notes,* Jan. 13, 1859; *Hudson Daily Star,* Feb. 20, 1869.

20. New York State Superintendent of Public Instruction, *Code of Public Instruction* (1856), p. 344.

21. New York State, *Laws,* 1864, chap. 555, title 10.

22. *New York Times,* Jan. 18, 1911.

CHAPTER 6—Mobbing a Teacher

1. James W. C. Pennington, *Text Book of the Origin and History . . . of the Colored People* (Hartford, 1841), p. 79.

2. *Rochester North Star,* April 17, 1851; Brooklyn Board of Education, *Proceedings* (1869):191–92; (1873):55. In Rochester "about a dozen ragged white children" attended a black public school, their parents explaining that they did so "because it is convenient." *Rochester North Star,* Dec. 21, 1849.

3. *New York Weekly Anglo-African,* June 23, 1860.

4. Advertisements in *Newburgh Daily News,* Dec. 31, 1860, and *Newburgh Weekly Telegraph,* Feb. 12, 1863; interview with a white woman who attended the academy, by James Sanders, Newburgh, March 25, 1975; *Newburgh Evening News,* April 28, 1969, p. 13B.

5. *Rochester Frederick Douglass' Paper,* March 10, 1854.

6. John A. Dix, *Decisions of the Superintendent of Common Schools of the State of New York* (Albany, 1837), pp. 139–40.

7. William G. Allen, *American Prejudice Against Color* (London, 1853), pp. 4–87, 94.

8. *New York Globe,* May 5, Oct. 6, 1883, Jan. 26, 1884.

CHAPTER 7—Should Whites Teach Blacks?

1. American Convention for Promoting the Abolition of Slavery, *Minutes* (New York, 1969), convention of 1805, p. 34.

2. William J. Brown, *Life* (Providence, R.I., 1883), p. 88; Carleton Mabee, *Black Freedom: The Nonviolent Abolitionists from 1830 through the Civil War* (New York: Macmillan, 1970), p. 154; J. Reuben Sheeler, "The Struggle of the Negro in Ohio for Freedom," *Journal of Negro History* (April 1946): 217–18.

3. Frederika Bremer, *Homes of the New World,* 2 vols. (New York, 1853), 1:586; Brooklyn Board of Education, *Proceedings* (March 2, 1869):192; Frances Blascoer, *Colored School Children in New York* (New York, 1915), p. 87.

4. Lockport Board of Education, Minutes, Mar. 31, 1871, at Lockport Board of Education office; *Hudson Daily Republican,* Jan. 12, 20, 1877; *Flushing Journal,* March 7, 1891; Joseph Henry, *Papers,* I (Washington: Smithsonian, 1972), p. 285.

5. William Hamilton, *An Oration Delivered in the African Zion Church* (New York, 1827) in Dorothy Porter, *Early Negro Writing* (Boston: Beacon, 1971), p. 103.

6. *Boston Impartial Citizen,* June 28, 1851.

7. *Christian Recorder,* July 12, 1883; *Brooklyn Daily Eagle,* July 8, 1863.

8. *New York Weekly Anglo-African,* Aug. 12, 26, 1865.

9. *New York Emancipator,* Dec. 1, 1836, p. 122; *New York Freeman,* March 12, 1887.

10. Buffalo Superintendent of Public Schools, *18th Annual Report,* for 1854, p. 23.

11. Troy Board of Education, *Proceedings* (Aug. 7, 28, 1855); Troy *Northern Budget,* Sept. 5, 1855; Troy Board of Education, *Manual* (1855):4; Mabee, *Black Freedom,* ch. 11; *Troy Daily Whig,* Aug. 14, 1855.

12. Troy Board of Education, *Proceedings* (Oct. 2, Nov. 8, Dec. 4, 1855).

13. *New York Weekly Anglo-African,* Nov. 19, 1859; Feb. 25, June 2, 9, 1860; Albany Board of Education, *Annual Report,* for 1859–60, p. 11; for 1860–61, p. 38; for 1861–62, p. 14.

14. *Poughkeepsie Daily Eagle,* Jan. 4, Feb. 8, 1872; Oct. 23, Nov. 13, 1873.

15. Brooklyn Board of Education, *Minutes* (1869):189–91.

CHAPTER 8—Preparing Teachers

1. *New York Freedom's Journal,* June 1, 1827; *Rochester North Star,* May 19, 1848; *Boston Impartial Citizen,* June 28, 1851.

2. *Rochester Daily Democrat,* Aug. 11, 1849; New York City Board of Education, *Annual Report,* for 1874, p. 28.

✗ 3. Ada Boseman in Troy High School, and Emma Fox, M. Lena Smith, and Ada L. Townsend in Flushing High School.

4. A. Emerson Palmer, *New York Public School* (New York, 1905), p. 89. Other black schools which claimed to be normal schools included: (A.) the New York Conference High School which existed from about 1887 to 1890 in Jamaica. It was founded by Horace Talbert, an AME pastor who had studied at Wilberforce College and Boston University. (B.) The Binghamton Normal, Industrial, and Agricultural Institute which existed from about 1912 to 1914 on a farm outside of Binghamton. It was founded by Fred C. Hazel, a graduate of Hampton Institute.

5. New York City Board of Education, *Annual Report,* for 1854, appendix on normal schools, p. 6.

6. Alexander Crummell, "John Peterson, for Fifty Years School Teacher in African School No. 1," 1886, sermon no. 395, Crummel papers, Schomburg Center.

7. Anthony R. Mayo, *Charles Lewis Reason* (Jersey City, N.J., 1943), p. 11.

8. New York City Board of Education, *Annual Report,* for 1857, appendix, p. 138; for 1858, appendix, p. 202; for 1865, appendix, pp. 35, 71; Henry Kiddle, Thomas F. Harrison, N. A. Calkins, *How to Teach* (New York, 1874).

9. New York City Board of Education, *Documents,* for 1857, doc. 19, p. 4; New York City Board of Education, *Annual Report,* for 1864, appendix, p. 16.

10. Although Miss C. V. Usher is not in the published list of graduates of the Albany Normal School, an Albany correspondent in the New York *Weekly Anglo-African,* Feb. 18, 1860, claimed that she had just completed several years work at the school (see also *ibid.* March 24, 31, 1860). Martin R. Delany, *The Condition . . . of the Colored People* (Philadelphia, 1852), p. 132, claimed that Mary Elizabeth Miles, who taught at the Albany black public school in the mid-1840s, had graduated from the Albany Normal. However, she is not in the published list of graduates; she had already attended the state normal at Lexington, Mass.; and the archivist at the State University at Albany (formerly the Albany Normal) wrote me, Feb. 1, 1974, that he could not find any record of her as a student.

11. Sarah C. Bierce (later Mrs. W. S. Scarborough) graduated 1875. (Eileen Poucher, State University College, Oswego, to CM, May 16, 1974.)

12. Samuel W. Patterson, *Hunter College: Eighty-Five Years of Service* (New York: Lantern Press, 1955), p. 17; Thomas Hunter, *Autobiography* (New York: Knickerbocker, 1931), pp. 231–32; *Washington New National Era,* June 26, 1873; New York City Board of Education, *Annual Report,* for 1873, pp. 42, 355, 357; President of the Normal College, *Annual Report,* for 1873, pp. 9, 45; for 1874, pp. 61–63; for 1876, pp. 68–72; for 1877, p. 86.

13. Hunter, *Autobiography,* pp. 230–34; *New York Times,* June 6, 1897.

14. *New York Freeman,* Nov. 21, 1885; June 25, 1887; Brooklyn Superintendent of Public Instruction, *Annual Report,* for 1888, p. 34.

15. Brooklyn Superintendent of Public Instruction, *Annual Report,* for 1887, p. 34; *New York Freeman,* June 25, 1887.

16. Booker T. Washington, *Papers,* IV, Urbana, University of Illinois, 1975, pp. 131–32, 361–62, 364; William L. Bulkley, "The Industrial Condition of the Negro in New York City," *Annals of the American Academy of Political and Social Sciences* (1906), pp. 595–96; Nancy J. Weiss, *The National Urban League* (New York: Oxford University Press, 1974), pp. 24, 27.

17. Frances Blascoer, *Colored School Children in New York* (New York, 1915), pp. 13, 48; *Milestones* (April 1907):1–2, 8; (May 1910):8; U.S. Bureau of Education, *Negro Education* (1917)2:696; Carleton Mabee, "Charity in Travail: Two Orphan Asylums for Blacks," *New York History* (Jan., 1974):70–76.

18. Maritcha R. Lyons, "Memories of Yesterdays," Brooklyn, 1928, pp. 17–20, Lyons family papers, Schomburg Center.

19. *Brooklyn Daily Eagle,* March 7, 1901; *New York Age,* July 22, 1909.

CHAPTER 9—How Much Freedom for Black Teachers?

1. In counting protesters, the author excludes protest directly related to the teachers' own school or school system on the ground that such protest might be merely self-serving and thus not relevant to the present purpose. Of the comparable 252 white teachers who taught in the black schools in the state in the same period, only 4 percent were protesters.

2. *Rochester North Star,* July 14, 1848.

3. Of the 104 protesters, only 24 percent were women. If women teachers whose fathers, brothers, or husbands were protesters were themselves counted as protesters on the nineteenth century assumption that the men would be the natural spokesmen of the views of the women in the family, the percentage of protesters would rise sharply.

4. *New York Colored American,* March 13, 1841.

5. *New York Weekly Anglo-African,* Dec. 3, 1859 (text of letter in James Redpath, *Echoes of Harper's Ferry* [Boston, 1860], p. 419); Dec. 17, 31, 1859; Feb. 11, 1860.

6. William Levington, *An Address Delivered Before the Female Benezet Philanthropic Society of Albany,* Albany, 1822, p. 3.

7. Martin E. Dann, *The Black Press, 1827–1890* (New York: Putnam's, 1971), p. 28; *New York Age,* Dec. 14, 1889.

8. *New York Age,* April 7, 1888.

9. *Brooklyn Standard Union,* Sept. 17, 1894.

10. *Williamsburg Gazette,* March 9, 16, 23, 1842.

11. *Boston Liberator,* April 19, 1834; New York Manumission Society, Records, vol. 8, p. 124, New-York Historical Society.

12. *New York Weekly Anglo-African,* Aug. 20, 1859.

13. This black Staten Island teacher was Thomas W. Cardozo, later the corrupt Superintendent of Public Instruction for Mississippi.

14. Statement by Dr. James McCune Smith (evidently prepared to recommend Wilson for employment), June 2, 1864, American Missionary Association papers, Dillard University.

15. In the extensive coverage of the Wilson issue in the Brooklyn *Daily Times* and *Daily Eagle,* both of July 8, 1863, there is no suggestion of Wilson's protest activity being a factor.

16. John H. Franklin, *From Slavery to Freedom* (New York: Knopf, 1967), pp. 390–92; *Colored American Magazine* (Aug. 1907):91; Carter G. Woodson, *The Negro Professional Man and the Community* (New York: Negro Universities Press, 1934; 1969), p. 55; *New York Amsterdam News,* Jan. 29, 1938; Howard K. Beale, *Are American Teachers Free?* (New York: Scribner's, 1936), pp. 450–53.

17. George S. Counts, *The Social Composition of Boards of Education* (Chicago: University of Chicago Press, 1927), ch. 4.

18. *Albany Patriot,* Dec. 18, 1844. Compare with Howard K. Beale, *History of Freedom of Teaching in American Schools* (New York: Octagon, 1941; 1966), p. 155, which says that, in the period 1830 to 1861 in the North, teachers played little part in the slavery controversy; expressing strong opinions on it would have got them into trouble.

19. *Brooklyn Evening Star,* March 15, 1841; New York State Superintendent of Public Instruction, *Laws . . . Relating to Common Schools . . . and a Digest of Decisions* (1868), p. 410.

20. Thomas Hunter, *Autobiography* (New York: Knickerbocker, 1931), pp. 106–20, 154–55.

21. Austin Steward, *Twenty-Two Years a Slave* (New York, 1856; 1968), pp. 313–14; Benjamin Quarles, *Black Abolitionists* (New York, Oxford University Press, 1969), p. ix.

CHAPTER 10—Who Led on Black School Issues?

1. E. Franklin Frazier, *Black Bourgeoisie* (New York: Free Press, 1957; 1965), pp. 235–37.

2. *Boston Liberator,* Dec. 7, 1855, p. 196.

3. *Rochester Frederick Douglass' Paper,* Sept. 21, 1855.

4. *New York Age,* July 13, 1905.

5. Daniel C. Thompson, *The Negro Leadership Class* (Englewood Cliffs, N.J.: Prentice-Hall, 1963), p. 44.

6. Black journalists were perhaps the nearest occupational group in nineteenth century New York State to being what James Q. Wilson, *Negro Politics: The Search for Leadership* (New York: Free Press, 1965), p. 310, was to call "functional" leaders such as the professional staff of the NAACP rather than "personality" leaders such as black pastors.

7. United States Census, *Statistical View,* for 1850, p. 80; New York State *Census,* for 1855, p. 178; United States Census, *Population,* for 1880, part 2, p. 590.

8. Martin R. Delany, *The Condition . . . of the Colored People* (New York, Arno, 1855; 1969), p. 206; *Poughkeepsie Daily Eagle,* Aug. 2, 1872; *Troy Daily Press,* Aug. 19, 1865.

CHAPTER 11—How Much Black Control?

1. Carter G. Woodson, *Mis-Education of the Negro* (Washington: Associated Publishers, 1933), pp. 22–23. Recent books which describe black education in the North give considerable attention to black agitation to abolish segregated schools but not significantly otherwise to the issue of black control over public schools.

2. *New York Colored American,* Feb. 16, 1839.

3. *Anglo-African Magazine* (July, 1859):224; *Troy Daily Times,* May 9, 1872.

4. Troy Board of Education, *Proceedings* (Feb. 23, 1858); Albany Board of Public Instruction, *Proceedings* (July 3, 1866); (Oct. 21, 1867).

5. *Brooklyn Daily Eagle,* Feb. 3, 1869; *New York Globe,* Dec. 22, 1883.

6. Carleton Mabee, "Brooklyn's Black Public Schools: Why Did Blacks Have Unusual Control Over Them?" *Journal of Long Island History* (Spring, 1975):23–38.

7. John A. Dix, *Decisions of the Superintendent of Common Schools of the State of New York* (Albany, 1837), pp. 318–19; *Williamsburg Gazette,* March 9, 16, 1842 (sic.); *Douglass' Monthly* (March 1859):33.

8. Records of School District No. 6, Town of Babylon (Amityville), Aug. 26, 1884, at Amityville Union Free School District office; *Flushing Journal,* Oct. 17, 1891.

9. Troy Board of Education, *Proceedings* (May 28, 1861, Jan. 14, 1862); *New York Weekly Anglo-African,* March 22, 1862.

10. New Rochelle Board of Education, Minutes, 1857–1888, passim; Roslyn Board of Education, Minutes, 1900–1904, passim; *New York Daily Tribune,* March 5, 1900; *Brooklyn Daily Eagle,* March 7, 1900.

11. Noah Webster to Amos Beman, April 27, 1843, Beman papers, Beinecke Library, Yale University; *Rochester Frederick Douglass' Paper,* Nov. 17, 1854; *Albany Patriot,* Dec. 18, 1844; New York State Superintendent of Public Instruction, *Forty-third Annual Report,* for 1895–96, pp. 1280–84.

12. United States Bureau of Refugees, Freedmen, and Abandoned Lands, *Semi-Annual Report on Schools for Freedmen* (Jan. 1, 1869):54; *Brooklyn Freedman's Torchlight,* Dec., 1866.

13. *Rochester North Star,* April 13, 1849; *New York Freeman,* July 10, 1886; *New York Age,* July 6, 1889; *Flushing Journal,* May 3, 1890.

14. List of visitors from Colored Grammar School No. 6, New York City, "Visiting Book," 1854–1892, at Howard University.

15. *Anglo-African Magazine* (July, 1859):222–24.

16. *Geneva Gazette,* Jan. 5, 1872; *Newburgh Weekly Journal,* Feb. 18, 1863.

17. *Rochester Daily Democrat,* July 12, 1841; *Flushing Journal,* Feb. 1, 1890.

18. *New York Weekly Anglo-African,* Jan. 7, 1860.

19. New York City Board of Education, *Journal* (1878):818.

20. *New York Weekly Anglo-African,* July 30, 1859; Feb. 4, 1860; *Rochester Frederick Douglass' Paper,* July 22, 1859.

21. *New York Tribune,* Oct. 19, 1858.

CHAPTER 12—Did Blacks Need a Black College?

1. Alexander Crummell to Gerrit Smith, Dec. 23, 1839, Gerrit Smith papers, Syracuse University.

2. New York *Rights for All,* July 17, 1829.

3. *College for Colored Youth, An Account of the New Haven City Meeting* (New York, 1831); National Negro Conventions, *Minutes* (New York, 1969), convention of 1831, pp. 5–9; *Boston Liberator,* Sept. 24, 1831, Sept. 22, 1832.

4. New York *Journal of Commerce,* Sept. 15, 1831, in *College for Colored Youth,* p. 17.

5. National Negro Conventions, *Minutes,* convention of 1847, pp. 9–10; *Rochester North Star,* Dec. 3, 1847, Jan. 21, 1848.

6. National Negro Conventions, *Minutes,* convention of 1853, pp. 30–38; *Rochester Frederick Douglass' Paper,* March 4, 1853, Jan. 2, Sept. 8, 1854, Feb. 16, 1855.

7. I can identify by name and with reasonable certainty as black eleven students at Oneida Institute (from Oneida Institute, *Catalogue,* 1835, 1836, and miscellaneous sources), and twenty-nine at Central College (from Albert H. Wright, *Pre-Cornell and Early Cornell . . . Cornell's Three Precursors: I, New York Central College* (Ithaca: Cornell University Press, 1960), and the papers of

Central College at Cortland County Historical Society, Cortland, and the Public Library, McGraw (formerly McGrawville).

8. Beriah Green to Gerrit Smith, April 12, 1837, Gerrit Smith papers.

9. Cortland? *Impartial Citizen* in *McGrawville Express,* Dec. 6, 1849.

10. *Boston Impartial Citizen,* Feb. 1, 1851.

11. George B. Vashon to trustees of New York Central College, June 24, 1857, Cortland County Historical Society.

12. James McCune Smith to Gerrit Smith, Jan. 29, 1859, Gerrit Smith papers.

13. *New York Weekly Anglo-African,* Sept. 3, Nov. 18, 1865.

14. Trustees of New York Central College, circular, Feb. 1866, at Cortland County Historical Society.

15. Eastman College still excluded blacks in the 1880s. (*New York Times,* Feb. 10, 1881; *New York Freeman,* June 12, 1886.)

16. However, a Negro girl attended Vassar just before 1900, passing as a white until she graduated. See W. E. B. DuBois, *The College Bred Negro* (Atlanta, 1900), p. 34. Vassar announced that it was ready to accept blacks in 1934. (*New York Amsterdam News,* Dec. 22, 1934.) The Vassar Alumni Association reported (to CM, July 29, 1970) that it had no record of when Vassar openly admitted its first black student.

17. *Poughkeepsie Daily Press,* Jan. 16, 1871; *Washington New National Era,* Jan. 19, 1871.

18. *Poughkeepsie Daily Eagle,* Sept. 22, 23, 24, 1870; *New York Times,* Sept. 24, 1870.

19. *Poughkeepsie Daily Eagle,* Oct. 19, 1870.

20. William Wells Brown, *St. Domingo* (Boston, 1855), p. 37.

21. *Poughkeepsie Daily Press,* Feb. 20, 1871; May 28, 1872. I have not been able to discover anything further about Toussaint College in the meager papers of John M. Langston at Fisk University or of Hiram Revels at the Schomburg Center.

22. The text of the original bill is in New York State Assembly, *Legislative Bills,* 1871, no. 128. The text of the law as passed is in New York State, *Laws,* 1871, chapter 257.

23. *Poughkeepsie Daily Press,* March 15, 1871.

24. *Poughkeepsie Daily Eagle,* May 20, 1871.

25. *Poughkeepsie Daily Eagle,* April 27; *Troy Daily Times,* May 8, 9; *Troy Daily Press,* May 9; *Troy Daily Whig,* May 9, 10, 1872.

CHAPTER 13—Protest Upstate

1. *New York Colored American,* June 2, 1838; May 18, 1839; Association for the Benefit of Colored Orphans, Minutes, July 7, 1838, at New York Historical Society.

✗   2. Carleton Mabee, *Black Freedom: The Nonviolent Abolitionists from 1830 Through the Civil War* (New York: Macmillan, 1970), ch. 11.

3. *Buffalo Commercial Advertiser,* April 27, 1842; *Buffalo Democratic Economist,* April 27, 1842.

4. Petition of "Sundry Colored Citizens," March 31, 1846, Buffalo Common Council Minutes, at City Clerk's office, Buffalo; Arthur O. White, "The Black Movement Against Jim Crow Education in Buffalo, New York, 1800–1900," *Phylon* (Winter 1969):380–81.

5. *Buffalo Democratic Economist,* April 27, 1842; American Antislavery Society, *Annual Report,* 1837, pp. 130–34; Mabee, *Black Freedom,* p. 156.

6. Buffalo Superintendent of Public Schools, *19th Annual Report,* for 1855, p. 9; *21st Annual Report,* for 1857, p. 13.

7. *Rochester North Star,* Sept. 22, 1848; Nov. 2, 1849; Rochester Board of Education, Proceedings, Oct. 1, 1849, at Rochester Board of Education office.

8. *Rochester North Star,* Nov. 2, 9, Dec. 7, 21, 1849; *Rochester Daily Advertiser,* Jan. 17, 1850.

9. *Rochester Daily Democrat,* Aug. 11, 1849; *Rochester Daily Advertiser,* March 27, 1850.

10. Rochester Board of Education, Proceedings, Oct. 6, 1851; Rochester Superintendent of Public Schools, *9th Annual Report,* 1852, pp. 20–21; *Rochester Frederick Douglass' Paper,* Sept. 8, 1854.

11. Rochester Superintendent of Public Schools, *12th Annual Report,* 1855, p. 14; Lucy N. Colman, *Reminiscences* (Buffalo, 1891), p. 16; Rochester Board of Education, Proceedings, April 10, May 5, July 7, 1856; Judith Polgar Ruchkin, "The Abolition of 'Colored Schools' in Rochester, New York, 1832–1856," *New York History* (July 1970):378; Rochester Superintendent of Public Schools, *13th Annual Report,* 1856, p. 18.

12. *Kinderhook Rough Notes,* July 15, 1858; Jan. 13, 1859.

13. *Boston Impartial Citizen,* Feb. 8, 1851; *Rochester North Star,* July 18, 1850.

14. *Rochester Frederick Douglass' Paper,* June 26, 1851; State Convention of Colored People, *Proceedings* (Albany, 1851):3, 33.

15. *Anglo-African Magazine* (July 1859):222–24; New York City Board of Education, *Annual Report,* for 1859, Appendix, "Report of the City Superintendent," p. 19.

16. Brooklyn Board of Education, *Manual* (1873):lxix; Brooklyn Board of Education, *Proceedings* (1873):235.

17. *New York Weekly Anglo-African,* Feb. 25, 1860.

18. *Rochester Frederick Douglass' Paper,* Sept. 22, Oct. 6, 1854; Sept. 28, 1855.

19. *Rochester Frederick Douglass' Paper,* Aug. 25, 1854; National Negro Conventions, *Minutes* (New York, 1969), convention of 1855, pp. 28–29; *Boston Liberator,* Aug. 12, 1859, p. 128.

CHAPTER 14—Janitor Johnson's Law

1. Troy Board of Education, *Proceedings* (March 5, 18, 1862); (April 7, May 26, Sept. 15, 1863); (Jan. 2, 1866).
2. *Ibid.* (March 7, 9, 1864); *Troy Daily Whig,* March 7, 9, 25, 1864.
3. Troy Board of Education, *Proceedings* (April 5, March 7, 1864); New York State Senate, *Journal* (1864):255, 440.
4. Samuel J. May to Andrew D. White, March 11, 1864, in James Smith, "The Separate but Equal Doctrine," *Journal of Negro History* (1956): 138–47.
5. Lockport Board of Education, Minutes, 1867–1872, at Lockport Board of Education office; *Lockport Daily Journal,* Jan. 4, 6, 8, 1873, in Arthur O. White, "The Black Movement Against Jim Crow Education in Lockport, New York, 1835–1876," *New York History* (July 1969):279–81.
6. Nathan Howard, *Practice Reports in the Supreme Court and Court of Appeals of the State of New York,* vol. 40 (Albany, 1877), pp. 249–57; *Buffalo Courier,* May 12, 1868; *Buffalo Express,* May 15, 1868; Buffalo Common Council, *Proceedings* (1870):309; Buffalo Superintendent of Education, *34th Annual Report,* for 1871, pp. 131–33; Arthur O. White, "The Black Movement Against Jim Crow Education in Buffalo, New York, 1800–1900," *Phylon* (Winter 1969): 392–93.
7. *Albany Evening Journal,* in *Washington New National Era,* April 27, 1871.
8. Austin Abbott, *Reports of Practice Cases Determined in the Courts of the State of New York,* New Series, XIII (New York, 1873), pp. 159–66; William H. Johnson, *Autobiography* (Albany, 1900), pp. 182, 185, 187–88.
9. Troy Board of Education, *Proceedings* (May 4, 1869); School District No. 1, Town of Seneca (Village of Geneva), Minutes, Dec. 25, 1869, at Geneva Board of Education office.
10. *Troy Daily Press,* May 9, 1872.
11. *Poughkeepsie Daily Press,* Nov. 28, 1870; *Bath Steuben Farmers' Advocate,* March 21, 1873; New York State Assembly, *Journal* (1873):1:367, 372–73, 424, 449, 615–16; *Jamaica Long Island Democrat,* April 8, 1873; *New York Times,* March 20, 1873; New York State Senate, *Journal* (1873):507.
12. New York State, *Laws* (1873), chapter 186.
13. *New York Times,* May 16, 1873; *New York Daily Tribune,* May 16, 1873.
14. *Hudson Register,* in *Hudson Daily Star,* Sept. 9, 1873.
15. *Newburgh Daily Journal,* April 17, May 3, 1873.
16. *Middletown Mercury* in *Newburgh Daily Journal,* May 10, 1873; *Newburgh Daily Journal,* May 6, 8, 1873.
17. *Newburgh Daily Journal,* May 5, 10, Sept. 3, 1873.
18. *Bath Steuben Farmers' Advocate,* May 16, 1873; *Troy Daily Whig,*

April 17, June 4, 1873; *Troy Daily Times,* May 7, 15, June 4, 1873; Schenectady Board of Education, Minutes, June 2, 1873, at Schenectady Board of Education office; *Schenectady Weekly Union,* May 22, 1873.

19. *Poughkeepsie Daily Eagle,* in *Newburgh Daily Journal,* May 8, 1873.

20. *Poughkeepsie Daily Eagle,* Sept. 2, 3, 10, Oct. 9, 1873.

21. New York City Board of Education, *Annual Report,* for 1877, p. 32; for 1878, pp. 50–51.

22. New York City Board of Education, *Journal* (1878):545–46, 817–18; *New York Times,* May 23, 1878.

23. Brooklyn Board of Education, *Proceedings* (1873):92, 158, 201–204; *Washington New National Era,* Nov. 20, 1873.

24. Brooklyn Board of Education, *Proceedings* (1873):180, 190–91, 234–36; *Brooklyn Daily Eagle,* Sept. 14, 1875.

25. *Hempstead Inquirer,* Jan. 2, 1874; Hempstead Board of Education, Minutes, Oct. 12, 1880, at Hempstead Board of Education office.

26. New York City Board of Education, *Journal* (1879):258–60, 309–10; *New York Times,* March 25, 1879.

CHAPTER 15—Protection for Teachers Downstate

1. *New York Times,* June 18, 30, 1895.

2. *New York Globe,* Jan. 27, 1883.

3. *Ibid.* Jan. 20, 1883; New York City Board of Education, *Journal* (Jan. 17, 1883):79–81.

4. Seth M. Scheiner, *Negro Mecca: A History of the Negro in New York City, 1865–1920* (New York: New York University Press, 1965), p. 176; *New York Sun,* Feb. 13, 1883; *New York Globe,* Feb. 17, 1883.

5. The report of the case in H. E. Sickles, *Reports of Cases Decided in the Court of Appeals of the State of New York,* vol. 48 (Oct. 1883), p. 438–66, gives no first name for King. The *New York Times,* Sept. 16, 1964, quotes a Brooklyn principal as identifying the parent as William King, a laborer. I believe the parent is more likely Simon King. I do so especially for two reasons. (1). In Sickles, *Reports,* p. 438, the colored child, the appellant, is called "Theresa B. King"; and, p. 441, she is described as about twelve years old. The *Brooklyn Daily Eagle,* Oct. 9, 1883, in reporting the case, calls her "Theresa W. B. King." The manuscript U.S. Census, 1880, Brooklyn, Ward 11, reports that Simon King, mulatto, had living with him a step-daughter, also a mulatto, whose name was "Theresa Brookfield," aged 10, at school. (2). In the *New York Globe,* Dec. 22, 1883, Simon King was praised for being instrumental in opening all Brooklyn schools to black children.

6. *New York Globe,* Dec. 1, 1883, Jan. 19, 1884.

7. *New York Globe,* Jan. 5, June 21, 1884; Brooklyn Board of Education, *Proceedings* (1883):683–84.

8. *Brooklyn Daily Eagle,* March 8, 1893; *New York Globe,* July 5, 1884.

9. *New York Globe,* Dec. 1, 1883; *New York Freeman,* Dec. 13, 1884; Feb. 28, May 9, 1885; *New York Age,* March 1, 1890.

10. *New York Globe,* April 19, 26, 1884; New York State Assembly, *Journal* (1884):915, 1022, 1029; New York State Senate, *Journal* (1884):561, 590, 723; Lawrence Grossman, *The Democratic Party and the Negro: Northern and National Politics, 1868-92* (Urbana: University of Illinois Press, 1976), pp. 65-67.

11. *New York Globe,* April 7, 1883; May 3, 10, 1884.

12. *New York Tribune,* Sept. 10, 1884; *New York Sun,* Sept. 10, 1884; Anthony R. Mayo, *Charles Lewis Reason* (Jersey City, N.J., 1943), p. 10; *Christian Recorder,* Aug. 14, 1884; *New York Freeman,* Jan. 24, March 7, 1885; April 2, 1887; New York City Board of Education, *Journal* (1887):192-93, 198-202, 274-75.

13. *New York Daily Tribune,* Oct. 17, 30, 1895; Mary White Ovington, *Half a Man: the Status of the Negro in New York* (New York, 1911), p. 18.

14. *New York Age,* Oct, 25, Nov. 1, 15, 1890; Oct. 10, 1891; *Brooklyn Daily Eagle,* Dec. 2, 1892; Brooklyn Board of Education, *Proceedings* (1890):793, 873; (1892):340-41; *New York Times,* June 8, 1893.

15. *Brooklyn Daily Eagle,* Sept. 30, 1892; March 8, 1893; May 20, 1894.

16. *Ibid.* March 8, 1893; Brooklyn Board of Education, *Proceedings* (1893):183-87.

17. Maritcha R. Lyons, "Memories of Yesterdays," Brooklyn, 1928, pp. 20, 30-31, at Schomburg Center.

CHAPTER 16—Long Island's Black School War

1. A. Emerson Palmer, *New York Public School* (New York, 1905), p. 292; Seth M. Scheiner, *Negro Mecca: A History of the Negro in New York City, 1865-1920* (New York: New York University Press, 1965), p. 179; Charles Z. Lincoln, *Constitutional History of New York,* 5 vols. (Rochester, 1905-1906), 4:708; Diane Ravitch, *The Great School Wars: New York City, 1805-1973* (New York: Basic Books, 1974), pp. 25n-26n.

2. Palmer, *New York,* p. 292; Mary White Ovington, *Half a Man: The Status of the Negro in New York* (New York, 1911), pp. 18-19; Eve Thurston, "Ethiopia Unshackled: A Brief History of the Education of Negro Children in New York City," *Bulletin of the New York Public Library* (April, 1965):223; Gilbert Osofsky, *Harlem: The Making of a Ghetto* (New York, Harper & Row, 1968), p. 36.

3. *Jamaica Long Island Democrat,* April 26, 1853; Feb. 21, 1860.

4. *New York Freeman,* July 2, 30, Aug. 20, 1887; *New York Age,* Oct. 29, 1887; April 14, 1888.

5. *Brooklyn Daily Eagle,* Feb. 27, Aug. 7, 11, 14, Sept. 7, Oct. 12, 25, 1895; School District No. 6, Town of Babylon (Amityville), Records, Aug. 6,

Sept. 6, 1895; Aug. 4, 1896, at Amityville Union Free School District office; *Babylon South Side Signal,* March 2, 9, Sept. 7, 21, Oct. 12, 26, Nov. 2, 1895.

6. *Brooklyn Daily Eagle,* March 28, 1896.

7. *Jamaica Long Island Democrat,* Sept. 10, 24, Oct. 29, 1895.

8. *Brooklyn Daily Eagle,* March 26, 1896; *New York Times,* April 5, 1896; *Jamaica Long Island Democrat,* March 31, 1896.

9. New York State Superintendent of Public Instruction, *42nd Annual Report,* for 1894–95, p. 691.

10. Queens Borough Superintendent of Schools, *First Annual Report,* for 1898–99, p. 45; *Brooklyn Daily Eagle,* March 5, 1900; *Jamaica Long Island Farmer,* March 6, 1900.

11. *Brooklyn Daily Eagle,* May 8, 1896; *Jamaica Long Island Farmer,* May 15, 1896.

12. *Newtown Register,* Oct. 11, 1883; Aug. 28, 1884; *Jamaica Long Island Democrat,* July 7, 1896; March 23, 1897; Oct. 25, 1898.

13. *Jamaica Long Island Democrat,* April 28, Nov. 3, 10, 1896; Feb. 15, 1898; *Jamaica Long Island Farmer,* May 1, 29, 1896.

14. *Brooklyn Times,* in *Jamaica Long Island Democrat,* Dec. 5, 1899; *New York Times,* April 5, 15, 1896; *Brooklyn Daily Eagle,* Sept. 25, 1899.

15. *Jamaica Standard,* in *Jamaica Long Island Farmer,* May 1, 1896 (the *Standard* for the years of the Jamaica school war is not known to be extant); *Jamaica Long Island Farmer,* Sept. 27, 1895; April 24, May 29, 1896; *Jamaica Long Island Democrat,* April 28, July 7, Nov. 3, 1896.

16. *St. George Staten Islander,* May 23, 27, 1891; Evelyn M. King and Joseph N. Marone, "The Black Man in American History," (School District 30, Richmond, New York City Board of Education), 1970, p. 99; interview with Mrs. Catherine Johannes Browne, by Gail Schneider of the Staten Island Institute of Arts and Sciences, June 28, 1972; Arthur S. Tompkins, *Historical Record of Rockland County* (Nyack, 1902), p. 317.

17. *New York Times,* Dec. 13, 1897; Roslyn Board of Education, Minutes, Oct. 12, 18, 21, Nov. 1, 1897, at Roslyn Board of Education office; Hempstead Board of Education, Minutes, Aug. 2, 1898, at Hempstead Board of Education office.

18. G. Henry Mandeville, *Flushing* (Flushing, 1860), pp. 127–28; *History of Queens County* (New York, 1882), pp. 104–105; *Flushing Journal,* March 30, 1889; Jan. 25, June 28, 1890; Jan. 3, 1891; *Jamaica Long Island Farmer,* May 29, 1896.

19. *New York Age,* Nov. 7, 1891.

CHAPTER 17—Elizabeth Cisco Wins

1. *Jamaica Long Island Democrat,* March 23, 1897; the Greater New York City charter, which was New York State, *Laws* (1897), chapter 378.

2. Seth Low to "Prof. Sanford," Feb. 26, 1914, Seth Low papers, Co-

lumbia University; *Reports of the New York City Charter Commissions of 1896 and 1900* (New York, 1907):57; *Flushing Evening Journal,* Sept. 11, 1897. In an early draft of the charter, colored schools were mandatory; in later drafts they were permitted. The question of colored schools received little attention from the commission according to its records and Low's correspondence, both in the Seth Low papers.

3. Queens Borough School Board, *Journal* (Sept. 6, Nov. 1, 1898): *Jamaica Long Island Democrat,* Nov. 6, 15, 1898; April 18, Sept. 12, 1899.

4. People ex rel. Cisco vs. School Board, 161 *New York* (1900); *New York Daily Tribune,* Aug. 23, Sept. 26, 1899; *Jamaica Long Island Farmer,* Jan. 12, 1900; *Flushing Daily Times,* Jan. 18, 1911.

5. *Brooklyn Daily Eagle,* April 2, 20, 1900; *Rockville Center South Side Observer,* April 6, 1900 (this paper was edited by George Wallace's brother Charles); William Henry Johnson, *Autobiography* (Albany, 1900), p. 78.

6. *New York Times,* Jan. 18, 1911; *Jamaica Long Island Farmer,* March 13, 20, April 3, 1900. Unfortunately no runs of Flushing papers are known to be extant from February to April, 1900.

7. Johnson, *Autobiography,* p. 79; New York State Senate, *Journal* (1900):1306–1307, 1464; *Brooklyn Daily Eagle,* March 30, 1900.

8. George Sinkler, *The Racial Attitudes of American Presidents: From Abraham Lincoln to Theodore Roosevelt* (Garden City: Doubleday, 1972), p. 428; Theodore Roosevelt, *Letters,* 8 vols. (Cambridge: Harvard University Press, 1951–1954)2:1306.

9. New York State Assembly, *Journal* (1900):3023–24, 3195; New York State Senate, *Journal* (1900):1465; *Brooklyn Daily Eagle,* March 30, 1900; New York State, *Laws* (1900), chapter 492.

10. Johnson, *Autobiography,* pp. 91–93.

11. New York City Board of Education, *Annual Report,* for 1899–1900, p. 85; Hempstead Board of Education, Minutes, Aug. 7, 1900, at Hempstead Board of Education office; A. Emerson Palmer, *New York Public School* (New York, 1905), p. 292; Mary White Ovington, *Half a Man: The Status of the Negro in New York* (New York, 1911), p. 19; Seth M. Scheiner, *Negro Mecca: A History of the Negro in New York City, 1865–1920* (New York: New York University Press, 1965), p. 179; John Hope Franklin, *From Slavery to Freedom: A History of Negro Americans* (third edition) (New York: Knopf, 1967), p. 549.

12. Borough of Richmond School Board, *Minutes* (1899):47, 213, 412; (1900):143–44.

13. *AME Church Review* (April 1900):420.

CHAPTER 18—Black Schools Revive

1. Adam Clayton Powell, Jr., *Marching Blacks* (New York: Dial Press, 1945; 1973), p. 47; Emmett Coleman, *The Rise . . . of Adam Clayton Powell* (Bee-Line Books, 1967), p. 18.

2. *Crisis,* (Aug. 1923):171; (April 1934):116.

3. Mary White Ovington, *Half a Man: The Status of the Negro in New York* (New York, 1911), pp. 197–98.

4. Owen R. Lovejoy, *Negro Children of New York* (New York, 1932), pp. 5, 11–12; *Complete Report of Mayor La Guardia's Commission on the Harlem Riot of March 19, 1935* (New York: Arno, 1969):78–81, 85.

5. Provisional Committee for Better Schools in Harlem, "Call to a Conference," to be held March 19, 1936, NAACP papers, Library of Congress; *New York Amsterdam News,* Dec. 22, 1934; *Pittsburgh Courier,* Nov. 3, 1934; *Crisis* (July 1937):202; *New York Teacher* (May 1937):6; New York State Temporary Commission on the Condition of the Colored Urban Population, *Second Report* (1939):100–107.

6. Floyd Patterson, *Victory Over Myself* (New York: Random House, 1962), pp. 6–28.

7. Fern M. Eckman, *The Furious Passage of James Baldwin* (New York: M. Evans, 1966), pp. 11–89; Gerturde Elise Ayer, "Notes on My Native Sons," in John H. Clarke, ed., *Harlem: A Community in Transition* (New York: Citadel, 1964), pp. 143–44.

8. Lawrence Lucas, *Black Priest/White Church* (New York: Random House, 1970), pp. 16–24, 66–67; George K. Hunton, *All of Which I Saw* (Garden City: Doubleday, 1967), p. 15.

9. *Brooklyn Standard Union,* Jan. 29, 1895; McDonough Memorial Hospital, *Annual Report,* for 1898–99, and 1899–1900; Colored Home and Hospital, *Annual Report,* for 1900–1901, p. 8; Lincoln Hospital and Home, *Annual Report,* 1922, p. 18; 1923–1925, p. 54; Ada B. Thoms, *Pathfinders: A History of the Progress of Colored Graduate Nurses* (New York, 1929), pp. 13, 68–118.

10. Gerald A. Spencer, *Medical Symphony: A Study of the Contributions of the Negro to Medical Progress in New York* (New York, 1947), pp. 34–39; *New York Amsterdam News,* April 18, May 30, 1923; *New York Age,* March 31, 1923; *New York Times,* June 8, 1973; Edward H. L. Corwin, *Opportunities for the Medical Education of Negroes* (New York: Scribner's, 1936), pp. 12, 202–203, 213–14.

11. *Crisis* (Jan. 1938):10–11; (Jan. 1939):78–80; Gwendolyn Bennett, "The Harlem Community Art Center," in Francis V. O'Connor, ed., *Art for the Millions: . . . the WPA Federal Art Project* (Greenwich, Conn.: New York Graphic Society, 1973), pp. 213–15; Melvin R. Maskin, "Black Education and the New Deal: The Urban Experience," (Ph.D. dissertation, New York University, 1973), pp. 197–99, 331–37.

12. Civilian Conservation Corps Educational Advisers Conference, Proceedings, Governors Island, New York, June 1938, p. 210; Civilian Conservation Corps, Second Corps Area, Office of the Education Adviser, *Monthly Bulletin* (later called *Adviser*), 1935–1938; Barret G. Potter, "The Civilian Conservation Corps and New York's Negro Question," *Afro-Americans in New York Life and History* (July 1977):183–99.

13. *New York Times,* Jan. 17, 18, 19, 1911; Frances Blascoer, *Colored School Children in New York* (New York, Negro University Press, 1915; 1970), p. 140.

14. *New York Herald-Tribune,* Jan. 25, 1930; Superintendent of Rockville Center Public Schools to NAACP, Feb. 15, 1930, NAACP papers; *New York Times,* Sept. 10, 1930; *Crisis* (April 1941):139; (Feb. 1961):98.

CHAPTER 19—Resistance Persists

1. George S. Schuyler, *Black and Conservative* (New Rochelle: Arlington House, 1966), pp. 17–28.

2. Roslyn Board of Education, Minutes, May 6, Sept. 3, 1913, at Roslyn Board of Education office; "Colored School Notes," and notes on an interview with Mrs. Schula Alson, ca. 1963, both at Bryant Library, Roslyn; *Brooklyn Daily Eagle,* Sept. 8, 1913; *New York Age,* Sept. 18, 1913; *Crisis* (Nov. 1913):322; Roy W. Moger, *Roslyn Then and Now* (Roslyn: Board of Education, 1964), p. 66.

3. Interview with Emma De Witt and Mr. and Mrs. John Bruen, Sr., former pupils at the school, by the author and Robert Moson, Goshen, Jan. 28, 1975; interview with Charles J. Hooker, former Goshen supervising principal, by Moson, Feb. 27, 1975; Goshen School District, Minutes, Feb. 28, 1933; *Goshen Democrat,* March 3, 1933.

4. *Milestones* (April 1907):7; *Roslyn News,* May 9, 1913, in "Colored School Notes"; *Brooklyn Eagle,* April 16, 1923; *New York Herald-Tribune,* Jan. 25, 1930; letters, press releases, clippings, 1930–32, in Hillburn school controversy folders, NAACP papers, Library of Congress.

5. *New York Amsterdam News,* Feb. 19, March 12, 1938; "Bill Jacket Collection," 1938, chapter 134, New York State Library; New York State Assembly, *Journal,* pp. 70, 1010–11; New York State Senate, *Journal* (1938):369; *New York Times,* Feb. 27, 1938; New York State, *Laws* (1938), chapter 134.

6. Letters, etc., 1943, Hillburn school controversy folders, NAACP papers; *New York PM,* Sept. 9, 1943; *New York Herald-Tribune,* Sept. 30, 1943; *New York Times,* Oct. 12, 1943.

7. Carleton Mabee, "Charity in Travail: Two Orphan Asylums for Blacks," *New York History* (Jan. 1974):55–77; Riverdale Children's Association, *One Hundred Twentieth Anniversary, 1836–1956* (New York: Riverdale Children's Association, 1956); City-Wide Citizens Committee on Harlem, *The Story* (New York, 1943), p. 8.

8. *Crisis* (Aug. 1939):234; *Interracial Review* (May 1941):75.

9. W. E. B. DuBois, *Correspondence* (Amherst, University of Massachusetts Press, 1973), 1:328, 415.

10. *Crisis* (March 1923):205–206; (Aug. 1923):170; Howard K. Beale, *Are American Teachers Free?* (New York: Scribner's, 1936), pp. 507–508.

11. *Buffalo Courier Express,* Nov. 20, 1946, Feb. 16, 1973; Herold C. Hunt, "A Program of Public School Education for . . . New Rochelle" (Ph.D. dissertation, Teachers College, 1940), p. 184; *Interracial Review* (March 1939):37; New York State Temporary Commission on the Condition of the Colored Urban Population, *Second Report* (1939):100, 109; *New York Amsterdam News,* June 2, 16, July 7, 1945.

12. Leslie H. Fishel and Benjamin Quarles, *The Black American: A Documentary History* (Glenview, Ill.: Scott, Foresman, 1970), p. 525.

13. *New York Age,* May 31, 1917.

14. *New York Teacher,* March, 1939, p. 14.

15. *New York Age,* Dec. 15, 1945; Celia L. Zitron, *New York City Teachers Union, 1916–1964* (New York: Humanities Press, 1968), pp. 95–96.

16. *New York Herald-Tribune,* Oct. 2, 1945; Leonard Covello, *The Heart is the Teacher* (New York: McGraw Hill, 1958), pp. 237–43; *New York Age,* Oct. 20, Nov. 24, Dec. 15, 1945; *New York Amsterdam News,* Feb. 17, 1945; New York State Commission Against Discrimination, *Public Hearings* (1944)1:52–53; New York State Temporary Commission Against Discrimination, *Report* (1945):44, 47.

Perspective

1. New York State Superintendent of Common Schools, *Annual Report,* for 1846, p. 20; United States Census, *Population,* for 1940, 2, part 5:27.

2. United States Commissioner of Education, *Report,* for 1870, p. 477; United States Census, *Compendium,* for 1880, p. 1650; United States Census, *Abstract,* for 1930, p. 279.

3. Herman D. Bloch, *Circle of Discrimination: An Economic and Social Study of the Black Man in New York* (New York: New York University Press, 1969), chapters 2–3.

4. Frank J. Klingberg, *Anglican Humanitarianism in Colonial New York* (Philadelphia: Church Historical Society, 1940), p. 151; Charles C. Andrews, *History of the New York African Free Schools* (New York, 1830), pp. 46–47; New York State Superintendent of Public Instruction, *Annual Report,* for 1855, p. 138; interview with John Bruen, Sr., et al., by author and Robert Moson, Goshen, Jan. 28, 1975.

5. Andrews, *History,* p. 132; William L. Bulkley, "The School as a Social Center," *Charities* (Oct. 7, 1905):76.

INDEX

BLACK EDUCATION IN NEW YORK STATE

was composed in 10-point Compugraphic Times Roman and leaded two points
by Metricomp Studios, Inc.;
with display type in Times Roman Heavyweight Open
by Dix Typesetting Co., Inc.;
printed on 50-pound Warren acid-free Eggshell Smooth paper stock,
Smyth-sewn, bound with 80-point Binder's boards, and covered in Columbia Bayside Vellum,
by Maple-Vail Book Manufacturing Group, Inc.;
and published by

SYRACUSE UNIVERSITY PRESS
SYRACUSE, NEW YORK 13210